THE WAY OF SAINT JAMES
GR65: THE CHEMIN DE SAINT-JACQUES
LE PUY-EN-VELAY TO THE PYRENEES

About the Author

A chance viewing of a television programme in the early 1970s led to Alison's interest in the Pilgrim Road to Santiago, at that time barely known in Britain. A walker most of her life, she had the opportunity to walk the 1000-mile camino from Le Puy-en-Velay to Santiago all in one go in 1990, a time which coincided, fortuitously, with Cicerone looking for an author to write an original guide in English to the Spanish section of the route. Since then Alison has walked and explored many of the pilgrim roads through Europe (France, Germany, Switzerland, Norway and Portugal) as well as those she has written about. She is also the author of the two-volume Cicerone guide to the *Via Francigena*, the historic pilgrim route from Canterbury to Rome.

Alison is a former teacher of French, German and Spanish to adults and her other interests include playing the French horn.

Other Cicerone guides by the author
The Way of St James: Pyrenees–Santiago–Finisterre
The Via Francigena: Part 1 – Canterbury to the Great Saint Bernard Pass
The Via Francigena: Part 2 – Great Saint-Bernard Pass to Rome

Updates to this Guide

While every effort is made by our authors to ensure the accuracy of guidebooks as they go to print, changes can occur during the lifetime of an edition. Any updates that we know of for this guide will be on the Cicerone website (www.cicerone.co.uk/876/updates), so please check before planning your trip. We also advise that you check information about such things as transport, accommodation and shops locally. Even rights of way can be altered over time. We are always grateful for information about any discrepancies between a guidebook and the facts on the ground, sent by email to updates@cicerone.co.uk or by post to Cicerone, Juniper House, Murley Moss, Oxenholme Road, Kendal, Cumbria LA9 7RL, United Kingdom.

Register your book: To sign up to receive free updates, special offers and files where available, register your book at www.cicerone.co.uk.

THE WAY OF SAINT JAMES
GR65: THE CHEMIN DE SAINT-JACQUES
LE PUY-EN-VELAY TO THE PYRENEES

by
Alison Raju

JUNIPER HOUSE, MURLEY MOSS,
OXENHOLME ROAD, KENDAL, CUMBRIA LA9 7RL
www.cicerone.co.uk

Printed in China on behalf of Latitude Press Ltd
A catalogue record for this book is available from the British Library.
All photographs are by the author unless otherwise stated.

 The routes of the GR®, PR® and GRP® paths in this guide have been reproduced with the permission of the Fédération Française de la Randonnée Pédestre holder of the exclusive rights of the routes. The names GR®, PR® and GRP® are registered trademarks. © FFRP 2018 for all GR®, PR® and GRP® paths appearing in this work.

For all those who begin their journey as a
long-distance walker and end it as a pilgrim.

Acknowledgements

I would like to thank Marigold Fox for her assistance in compiling Appendix D and all those, too numerous to mention individually, who sent in comments and amendments following their pilgrimages.

Abbreviations used in the text

L indicates that you should turn/fork left; R that you should turn/fork R. (L) and (R) mean that something you pass is to your left or right. KSO = keep straight on. KSO(L) or KSO(R) = keep straight on L or R. FB = footbridge, FP = footpath, > = becomes, // = parallel. Km = kilometre. N followed by a number (such as N135) refers to the number of a main road, D to that of a local road. AP = *accueil pèlerin*, CH = *chambre d'hôte*, K = kitchen/cooking facilities. OT = tourist office, PTT = post office. RE = reservation essential. X = closed/except, ♦ = drinking water available. ATM = cash dispenser. SNCF is the abbreviation for the French national railway network. HT = high tension (cables).

Front cover: Detail of tympanum at Conques cathedral (Section 1) (Photo: Marigold Fox)

CONTENTS

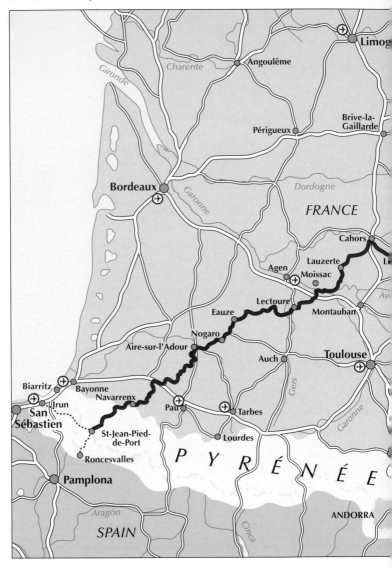

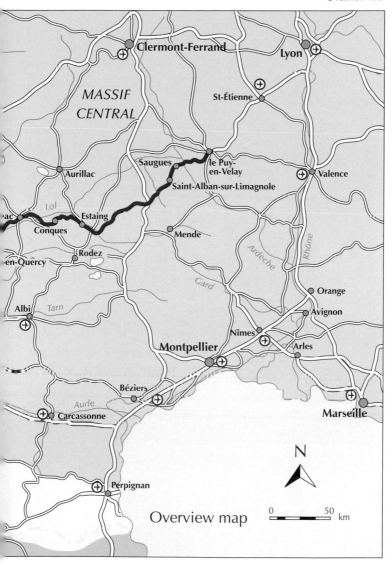

Overview map

N

0   50 km

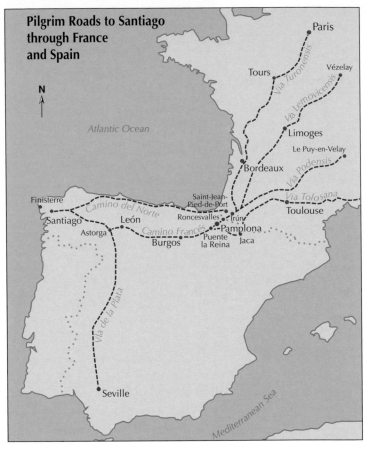

Pilgrim Roads to Santiago through France and Spain

N

Atlantic Ocean

Paris

Tours

Vézelay

Via Turonensis

Via Lemovicensis

Limoges

Le Puy-en-Velay

Bordeaux

Via Podensis

Via Tolosana

Finisterre

Camino del Norte

Saint-Jean-Pied-de-Port

Toulouse

Santiago

León

Roncesvalles

Irún

Astorga

Camino Francés

Pamplona

Burgos

Puente la Reina

Jaca

Vía de la Plata

Seville

Mediterranean Sea

Key to Route Maps

Pilgrim route on a road	══════	County boundary · · · · · · ·
Pilgrim route on a track	− − − −	Water
Road	────────	River
Railway	┼┼┼┼┼	Church ✝
Track	− − − − −	Settlement ●

INTRODUCTION

PILGRIM ROADS TO SANTIAGO THROUGH FRANCE AND SPAIN

The Way of St James as described in this book and its sequel covering the section through Spain is a long-distance footpath with a difference.

People have been walking it – as a pilgrimage route – for over a thousand years, and in 1987 the section from the Spanish monastery at Roncesvalles in the foothills of the Pyrenees to Santiago de Compostela became the first European Cultural Itinerary. The 1500km route, from Le Puy-en-Velay in the Haute Loire to the City of the Apostle in the western reaches of Galicia, has changed little in all that time. For although parts of it have now become modern tarred roads, and many of its 'hospitals' and other accommodation set up by religious orders along the way to minister to the needs of pilgrims have long since disappeared, the route through France – and the *camino* as it is known in Spain – still pass through most of the same villages, climb the same hills, cross the same rivers and visit the same chapels, churches, cathedrals and other monuments as did the path taken by our predecessors in centuries gone by.

The Way of St James is also a long-distance footpath with a difference in that many of those who walk the route through France and the vast majority of those who start on the Spanish side of the Pyrenees are not experienced walkers at all. Many have never done any serious walking in their lives and many will never do any again; for here, as in the past, walking is a means of transport, a means to an end, rather than an activity for its own sake.

Most long-distance footpaths in Britain, for example, avoid not only large towns but also even quite small villages; the Way of St James, on the other hand, because of its historic origins and the need for shelter, deliberately seeks them out. Several hundred thousand people now walk the Way every year, whether from points on the *camino* in Spain, from the Pyrenees, from different parts of France, or from even further afield. It is not uncommon, even nowadays, to meet Swiss, German, Belgian or Dutch pilgrims, for example, who have set out from home to make the entire journey on foot in one go.

The modern pilgrim

However, one of the differences between the modern pilgrim and his historical counterpart, whether he walks, goes by bicycle or on horseback, is that very few return home by the same means of transport.

View back over Conques (Section 1)

The modern pilgrim route has thus become a 'one-way street' and it is unusual, today, to encounter anyone with either enough time or the inclination to return to their point of departure by the same means as they used on their outward journey.

People make the journey from Le Puy-en-Velay to the Pyrenees and then on to Santiago for a variety of reasons. For some it is just another long-distance walk. For others the motives may be historical, cultural or religious, while for many it may also be a significant action or event in their lives: to mark their retirement, perhaps, to fill the gap between studying and taking a first job or to take time out to decide which way to go next after a turning point of some sort. In the 21st century, pilgrims are people of all ages and from all walks of life. The majority of those on the Le Puy route are from France, Switzerland, Belgium, Holland and Germany, but pilgrims come from all over the world, including a relatively small number from Britain.

Some travel alone, some in twos and threes, some in large groups (particularly those on foot). Many complete the entire journey in one stretch, which helps to maintain the feel of a genuine pilgrimage, rather than just a series of walking holidays. Other walkers, with more limited time, cover a section at a time over several years. But almost everyone who has walked the Way of St James, and especially those who did the whole route in one go, would probably agree that it has changed their lives in some way, even though that may not have been their original intention.

HISTORY

Pilgrims have been travelling to Santiago de Compostela on foot or on horseback (and, more recently, by bicycle) for over a thousand years. Godescalc, Bishop of Le Puy, who went there in AD951, was one of the first. At the height of its popularity in the 11th and 12th centuries, over half a million people are said to have made the pilgrimage from different parts of Europe each year, the majority of them from France.

Pilgrimages had been popular with Christians ever since Constantine the Great had the Church of the Holy Sepulchre built over the site of Christ's burial in Jerusalem in AD326, and the discovery, shortly afterwards, of the Holy Cross itself. Those journeying to this shrine were known as *palmeros* (palmers). *Romeros* went to Rome, the burial place of Saint Peter and the other great centre of Christian pilgrimage in the Middle Ages, along with Santiago de Compostela after the finding of the remains there of Saint James the Great (son of Zebedee, brother of John and Christ's cousin).

The high point of this third pilgrimage occurred between the years 1000 and 1500. However, although numbers dwindled after that due to the Reformation and other, political, factors, the stream of pilgrims trudging westwards from different parts of Europe to the far reaches of Galicia in north-west Spain never completely dried up, and since the late 20th century has been experienceing something of a resurgence.

The numbers of pilgrims on the Spanish section of the route has increased astronomically in recent decades, rising from some 4000–5000 per year in 1990 (based on the numbers of those who received their *Compostela* – certificate of pilgrimage – from the pilgrim office in Santiago) to a total of 278,232 (all routes) in 2016. Of these, 176,332 made their pilgrimages along the Camino Francés, the route from Roncesvalles at the foot of the Pyrenees on the Spanish side all the way to Santiago, while 3401 pilgrims are recorded as having walked all the way from Le Puy to Santiago in one go in 2016. A great many more, however, made the journey in several stages.

Legend

After the death of Christ, the disciples dispersed to different parts of the then known world, to spread the Gospel as they had been bidden. Little is known about the life of St James, but he went to Spain, where he spent a couple of years evangelising, apparently without a great deal of success. He returned to Jerusalem but was beheaded by Herod shortly afterwards, in AD44.

Immediately following his martyrdom his followers are said to have taken his body to Jaffa, on the coast,

Typical metal wayside cross

9

where a ship was miraculously waiting for them, and they set off back to Spain. They landed in Iria Flavia on the coast of Galicia, present-day Padrón, some 20km from what is now Santiago de Compostela, after a journey (in a stone boat!) which is purported to have taken only a week, thereby providing proof of angelic assistance. The body was buried in a tomb on a hillside, along with two of his disciples and forgotten for the next 750 years.

Early in the ninth century Pelagius, a hermit living in that part of Spain, had a vision (which he subsequently reported to Theodomir, bishop of Iria Flavia) in which he saw a very large bright star, surrounded by a ring of smaller ones, shining over a deserted spot in the hills. The matter was investigated and a tomb containing three bodies was found there, immediately identified as those of St James and two of his followers.

When Alfonso II, King of the Asturias (791–824), went there he declared St James the patron saint of Spain. He built a church and a small monastery over the tomb in the saint's honour, around which a town grew up. It was known as *campus de la stella* or *campus stellae*, later shortened to *compostela* – one explanation of the origin of the name. Another is that it derives from the Latin *componere* (to bury), as a Roman cemetery or early Christian necropolis is known to have existed under the site of the present-day cathedral in Santiago

– where the remains of St James are still believed to be housed today.

Establishing the pilgrimage

News of the discovery soon spread. It was encouraged to do so, both by Archbishop Gelmírez and the cathedral authorities (anxious to promote the town as a pilgrimage centre, thus attracting money to the area), and by the monks of Cluny (who saw in it the opportunity to assist the Spanish church in their long struggle against the Moors). Both factions were also helped by the fact that the Turks had seized the Holy Sepulchre in 1078, thus putting a stop to pilgrimages to Jerusalem.

However, Santiago was attractive as a potential pilgrim 'venue' in other respects too, as it fulfilled the various criteria necessary to make a pilgrimage there worthy of merit. It was far away (from most parts of France, for example) and difficult to reach, thus requiring a good deal of hardship and endurance to get there (and back again). It was sufficiently dangerous (wolves, bandits, fever, rivers that were difficult to cross, unscrupulous ferrymen) as well as being in Spain, then locked tight in a struggle with the Moors, and for this reason many pilgrims travelled in quite large groups. (A considerable corpus of pilgrim songs from previous centuries still exists, sung by the pilgrims as they walked.)

The road itself, both through France and in Spain, was also well supplied with shrines, relics and other sights worth seeing. As pilgrim numbers increased, roads, bridges and hospices were built. The pilgrimage churches were characterised by their ambulatories round the inside of the building to facilitate viewing of the relics exposed behind the high altar and were endowed with a growing number of relics, ensuring that pilgrims would pass that way to see them. Many churches in Spain are dedicated to St James, although there are very few today along the Le Puy route through France. Many others contain his statue, whether as apostle (*Saint Jacques apôtre*) or pilgrim (*Saint-Jacques pèlerin*). In Spain there is a third, important representation: St James the Moor-slayer, or *Santiago matamoros*, although there are only very few examples of this category in France. He is featured in paintings and stained glass too, with a halo as St James the Apostle but without when he is portrayed as a pilgrim.

Modern medallion of St James as a pilgrim, Le Puy (Section 1)

There are also a considerable number of very tiny chapels along the way that are dedicated to St Roch, the pilgrim saint from Montpellier. After a pilgrimage to Rome he devoted his life to caring for plague victims, but withdrew to live in a forest when he contracted a disease that left him with an unsightly sore on his left thigh. (For this reason St Roch is depicted in art with the front flap of his coat turned back to warn people to keep away from him, and is accompanied by the faithful dog who brought the saint his daily rations, often with a loaf of bread in its mouth.)

Legend has confused him with *Saint-Jacques pèlerin* at times, however, and he appears not infrequently in a 'pilgrim version' as well, with added hat, staff and scallop shells on his clothing, and there are many such representations of him along the Le Puy route. Many churches and chapels of St James changed their dedication in the 16th and 17th centuries in recognition of Saint Roch's role in curing plague victims. This explains the apparent scarcity of churches and chapels of St James along the route from Le Puy to the Pyrenees today, in contrast to the pilgrim road through Spain.

Why make a pilgrimage?

People went on pilgrimages for a variety of reasons: as a profession of faith, for instance; as a form of punishment (a system of fixed penalties for certain sins was in operation during the

Pilgrim information board in the Lozère (Section 1)

Middle Ages); as a means of atonement; as a way of acquiring 'merit' (and thus, for example, reducing or, in certain cases, cutting in half, the amount of time spent in Purgatory); or as an opportunity to venerate the relics of the many saints available along the principal routes to Santiago. (Indulgences were available to those who visited shrines.) No doubt, too, there were some who were just glad of the opportunity to escape their surroundings.

Later there were professional pilgrims who would (for a fee) undertake to do the pilgrimage on behalf of someone else who could afford the money but not the time to do it him

or herself. Those with the means to do so went on horseback, and some wealthy people made the pilgrimage along with a considerable retinue. The majority of pilgrims went on foot, however, and even among the rich there were some who preferred to walk rather than ride, because of the greater 'merit' they would attain.

The mediaeval experience

The pilgrim in former times was not at all sure that he would reach his destination, let alone return home in one piece, so before setting out he took leave of his family and employer, made his will and generally put his affairs in order. He (or she) obtained his credentials (pilgrim passport) from his bishop or church, which he could then present in order to obtain food and lodging in the many pilgrim 'hospitals' and other establishments along the way. This was both a precaution against the growing number of *coquillards* or pseudo-pilgrims and a means of providing proof of his journey. He had his papers stamped at different stages along the way so that once he arrived in Santiago he could obtain his *Compostela* or certificate of pilgrimage from the Cathedral authorities there. This in turn entitled him to stay in the pilgrim shelters on his return journey as well as furnishing evidence, if needed, that he had actually made the pilgrimage successfully.

The pilgrim had his staff and scrip (knapsack) blessed in church before setting out and travelled light, carrying little else but a gourd for water.

Brick dovecote in the Quercy (Section 2)

The scallop shell – the *coquille Saint-Jacques* – which has for many people become an essential ingredient of 'pilgrim uniform' nowadays was, in former times, something that was carried **back** from Santiago by the returning pilgrim; scallops were only to be found on the Galician coast and thus served as additional proof that the pilgrim had actually reached his or her destination.

The scallop shell was also the symbol embedded above doorways and elsewhere on the many and varied buildings that accommodated pilgrims along the different roads to Santiago. Pilgrims with money could stay in inns and other publicly available lodgings, but the vast majority probably stayed in the various hospices and other facilities provided for them.

Some of these were in towns (either in the centre, or outside the walls to cater both for latecomers and possibly contagious pilgrims). Others were in the countryside, often by bridges or at the crossings of important pilgrim route feeder roads: examples are the former hospital by the Pont d'Artigues near Saint Antoine, run by the Order of the Knights of Santiago, the Chapelle d'Abrin, shortly before La Romieu, and the surviving part of the Commandery of St John of Jerusalem at the junction of the route from Le Puy and the road from Moissac to Aire-sur-l'Adour via Agen.

Much of the pilgrim accommodation was provided by religious orders, such as the Benedictines and the

Antonins, and by churches and civic authorities as well as by benevolent individuals. The facilities offered varied considerably from one establishment to another, and surviving records from many of them indicate exactly what was provided for the pilgrim.

There are different explanations as to the origin of the *coquille Saint-Jacques*, but one is that when the followers of St James arrived in the port of Iria Flavia with the apostle's body they saw a man riding along the beach (a bridegroom in some versions). His horse took fright and plunged into the sea. When the pair re-emerged, both horse and rider were covered from head to foot in scallop shells (even today the beaches in this part of Galicia are strewn with them).

It was customary to set out in the springtime in order to reach Santiago for the feast of St James on 25 July and return home for the winter. This was especially true in Holy Years, when 25 July falls on a Sunday (the next ones are in 2021, 2027 and 2032 – a pattern of 6–11–6–5 years), the only time the *Puerta Santa* or Holy Door of the Cathedral of Santiago is open. The door is sealed up at the end of each Holy Year and then symbolically broken down again by the Archbishop in a special ceremony in the evening of 31 December preceding the new Holy Year. The Holy Year has also always been a year in which which special concessions and indulgences were, and still are, available to pilgrims.

13th-century tympanum frieze

The first guidebook

On returning home, many joined confraternities of former pilgrims in their own countries, the forerunners of the modern-day associations of 'Friends of St James' that now exist in many countries to support, promote and encourage the different routes to Santiago.

Many pilgrims then wrote accounts of their experiences, but as early as the 12th century the first real 'travel guide' was produced, probably between 1140 and 1150. Its author was for a long time believed to be one Aimery Picaud, a cleric from Parthenay-le-Vieux in the Poitou region of France, and it formed part of a Latin manuscript known as the *Codex Calixtinus*. Rather than a description of the journey of one particular individual, it was the first pilgrimage book intended to be used as a guide by prospective (especially French) pilgrims.

This book describes the four most important roads through France (see below) and divides the route from the Pyrenees to Santiago into 13 somewhat unequal stages. It lists, with comments, the places through which the route passes in Spain, indicates some of the hazards pilgrims may encounter and contains advice on the rivers along the way, indicating which are safe to drink from and which should be avoided.

The author also describes in some detail the inhabitants of the different regions through which the prospective pilgrim will pass, their language (including one of the earliest lists of Basque words), customs and characteristics, none of which compare at all favourably, in his opinion, with those of the people of his native Poitou. He includes a list of shrines to be visited along the different roads through France, a description of the city of Santiago and its churches and a detailed account of the Cathedral's history, architecture and canons.

It is now thought that this guide was not written by one person but was a compilation, designed (under the influence of the energetic Archbishop Diego Gelmírez) to promote Santiago de Compostela as a pilgrimage centre. Regardless of its authorship, this guide was certainly instrumental in popularising the itineraries of the four main pilgrim roads through France and the *Camino Francés* (or 'French road') in Spain. It has now been translated into English (see Appendix E).

Sunflower fields in the Gers (Section 3)

Routes to Santiago
The route described in this book is by no means the one and only 'Way of St James'. In former times, when pilgrims set out from their own front doors and made their way to Santiago from many different places, several well-established routes grew up (see map on page 6).

In France, for example, there were four main departure points, each with several 'feeder roads' (such as the one from Rocamadour to Moissac) joining them at different points along the way. The route from Paris, the *Via Turonensis*, passed through Orléans, Tours, Poitiers, Bordeaux and Dax. From Vézelay pilgrims took the *Via Lemovicensis* through Limoges, Périgeux, Bazas and Mont-de-Marsan, while those from Le Puy took the *Via Podensis* and passed through Conques, Cahors, Moissac, Aire-sur-l'Adour and Navarrenx.

All three routes joined up near Ostabat on the French side of the Pyrenees, to continue over the mountains to Roncesvalles and on across the north of Spain as the *Camino Francés* or 'French Way'. The fourth route, from Arles, and known as the *Via Tolosana*, visited Saint-Gilles du Gard, Toulouse, Auch and Oloron but crossed the Pyrenees further east at the Col du Somport, from where it is known as the *Camino Aragonés*, before merging with the other three routes at Puenta la Reina.

Although the name *Camino de Santiago* has nowadays become more or less synonomous with the *Camino Francés* in Spain, there were other important routes there too. These included the northern one along the Costa Cantabrica, the one taken by those English pilgrims who went by ship as far as Bordeaux and then continued on foot, while others sailed to La Coruña and then walked the rest of the way along one of the *Rutas del Mar*, one of which was known as the *Camino Inglés*. The *Vía de la Plata* or *Camino Mozárabe*, on the other hand, was the road taken by pilgrims from the south of Spain and others joining it by sea in Seville, passing through Mérida, Cáceres, Salamanca and Zamora before joining the *Camino Francés* at Astorga.

There were also routes from the east coast of Spain and two *caminos*, south to north, through Portugal – one inland, the other along the coast – as well as a whole network of routes reaching France from Austria, Switzerland, Italy, Germany, the Netherlands and countries much further afield.

What this guide covers
The 'Way of St James' described here corresponds to only a very small part of this complex web, to the section known as the *Via Podensis*, waymarked since the 1970s as the GR65. One of the most widely used nowadays and best-documented of the many pilgrim roads through France, it begins in Le Puy-en-Velay and passes through Conques, Figeac,

Cahors, Moissac, Aire-sur-l'Adour and Saint-Jean-Pied-de-Port.

The route description in this guide therefore begins in Le Puy-en-Velay, following the GR65 and continues through southern and south-western France to Saint-Jean-Pied-de-Port. The Spanish section of the route is covered in Cicerone's companion volume: *The Way of St James: Pyrenees–Santiago–Finisterre*.

If you wish to break your pilgrimage into two parts, and would prefer to cross the Pyrenees at the end of your French walk (when you are fittest) rather than at the start of your Spanish journey, this guide also includes (as Appendix A) details of the route from Saint-Jean-Pied-de-Port to Roncevalles (and Pamplona), two to three days more, and well served by public transport.

This is followed by an outline of the three- to four-day route from Saint-Palais direct to Irún (Appendix B), an option not yet covered in any other English-language guidebook. This option allows the pilgrim who prefers to continue on the *Camino del Norte* in Spain to do so, following the coastal route instead of the frequently over-saturated *Camino Francés*, and is becoming increasingly popular. Instead of continuing directly south to Saint-Jean-Pied-de-Port and over the Pyrenees to Roncesvalles, the pilgrim turns south-west and picks up the *Camino del Norte* at its starting point by the international bridge over the Río Bidasoa in Irún, the border

between France and Spain. (There is a separate Cicerone guide book to this route – see Appendix B.)

Appendix C contains a suggestion for yet another option, the *variante* along the valley of the Célé. Appendix D gives a listing of St James's and other pilgrim references along the way, a feature not found in any other guides to this route. Also included are suggestions for further reading (Appendix E), a list of useful addresses and websites (Appendix F) and a glossary of geographical and other frequently encountered terms (Appendix G). Appendices H, I and J contain, respectively, an index of principal place names, an index of maps and a summary of the route with distances.

Anyone in Britain who is thinking of walking, cycling or riding any part of the route should contact the Confraternity of Saint James for advice and membership (see Appendix F for contact details). Note, however, that the walker's route described in this book is **not** suitable for cyclists: anyone wishing to tackle this route by road bike should obtain John Higginson's *The Way of Saint James Cyclist Guide: A Cyclists' Guide from Le Puy-en-Velay to Santiago de Compostela* (or replacements or new editions), also published by Cicerone.

TOPOGRAPHY, ECONOMY AND LANGUAGE

The *Via Podensis* begins in Le Puy-en-Velay in the *département* of the

Haute-Loire and on the south-eastern edge of the Auvergne, a town famous for its bobbin-lace industry, its brown lentils and for being a pilgrimage centre in its own right (see page 43). The Velay is a volcanic region, its often barren landscape punctuated by innumerable *puys* (tall conical hills, derived from Latin *podium*) and latticed with ancient tracks and lanes frequently marked with old wayside crosses. From here the route makes its way across the Margeride plateau and through the Gévaudan, an area best known for the mysterious wild beast (*la bête du Gévaudan*) that claimed so many lives towards the end of the 18th century.

After that, continuing to climb, the *Via Podensis* eases its way up onto the even higher open plateau land of the Aubrac, with its *drailles* (wide drove roads), its *burons* (shepherds' bothies) and its lush green meadows rising to nearly 4000ft. Flocks were driven up from the valleys below every year to spend the summer months grazing there, an activity known as transhumance. Pastors, each with several hundred animals, would make their way there on foot, a journey often lasting several days. Today this task is normally carried out in motorised vehicles, although an attempt has been made to revive the tradition; the tall wooden statue of a pastor in the village of Aubrac marks the first such expedition in 1990. This area is also famous for its *aligot*, a very substantial dish made of cheese and mashed potatoes.

Wayside cross after emerging from Saint-Christophe (Section 1)

After the Aubrac the landscape changes dramatically. The route continues down through the deep wooded gorges of the Lot valley and along the river itself to Estaing, before climbing up again and then plunging down into Conques (the name itself means 'small valley'), deep in the recesses of the hills. By this time the GR65 has reached the old region of the Rouergue. After emerging from here the countryside begins to open out again, before continuing through the chalky wooded area of the Quercy with its traditonal dovecotes (*pigeonniers*), its half-timbered houses, its *caselles* and *gaviotes* (small round hut-like buildings of drystone wall construction) and its not infrequent dolmens. After that the

Via Podensis makes its way to Cahors through the *causse*, a term denoting an undulating limestone plateau covered with scrubby vegetation, little water and few distinguishing features.

By now the observant pilgrim will have noted the many Occitan terms used in place names along the way: *mas*, *borie*, *couderc*, for example (see glossary in Appendix G), a language (not a dialect) of Latin origin. Historically France was divided into two main sections linguistically, the northern half with its *langue d'oïl*, the south with its *langue d'oc*, each quite separate languages and so-named because of their respective terms for the word 'yes'.

Occitan (often referred to as 'Provençal' as well) has an extensive literature from the Middle Ages and later, and was once the only language spoken throughout the whole of the south of what we now know as France. But because the northern *langue d'oïl* was the one used in the royal court and because administrative power was increasingly centred in Paris, this became the official 'French' language spoken today. Occitan is still used by older people in country districts, but there are probably few speakers left in the 21st century for whom it is their mother tongue. In recent decades there has been a revival of interest in the language, and as well as the emergence of modern authors writing in Occitan it can now be taught in schools and taken as a subsidiary subject both in the *baccalauréat* and at university level, as can Basque and Breton in other areas of France. Occitan also has several dialects, Béarnais and Gascon being those that the pilgrim will encounter in toponomy along the Way of St James (*luy*, *gave*, for example – see Appendix G).

After Cahors the countryside gradually flattens out, beginning with the rolling landscapes of the *département* of the Tarn et Garonne and then, after crossing the Garonne itself near Moissac, on through the Gers (the least wooded *département* in France), with its rural bullrings, castles and *bastides* (small fortified towns) perched on hilltops, punctuating the vast undulating fields of corn, sunflowers and other crops. This is the old Armagnac region, famous for its brandy, after which the pilgrim goes on into the *département* of the Landes near Aire-sur-l'Adour.

Here the landscape is almost completely flat arable land and the scenery is unremarkable. Its large-scale agriculture is the consequence of the *remembrement* of recent decades, the regrouping of small, uneconomic portions of land into larger, more viable units resulting in huge geometrically laid-out fields with irrigation channels and few hedge boundaries. Then, slowly, the terrain becomes hillier again as the pilgrim passes through the Béarn, once a separate kingdom, before the route makes its way towards the foothills of the Pyrenees and the Basque country.

The Basque country as a geographical entity (as opposed to the present-day Spanish autonomous *región* of the País Vasco) flanks both sides of the Pyrenees, three of its provinces lying in France (Laborde, Soule and Basse-Navarre), the other four in Spain (Alava, Guipúzcoa, Navarra and Viscaya). As you approach Saint-Jean-le-Vieux and Saint-Jean-Pied-de-Port you will begin to notice features that you will also encounter well into Spain, such as a changing local architecture; the large Basque houses with their overhanging eaves, often ornately decorated, and outside staircases and balconies running the whole length of one or more sides of the building are common, as is also the *frontón* or pelota court, to be found in almost every village of any size.

The Basque language (*Euskerra* in Basque) is unrelated to any of the Romance languages and its origins are still the subject of scholarly debate. It was formerly much more in evidence in the Basque provinces in Spain – whether in ordinary conversation, on television or on signs and notices – than it was on the French side, but since the late 1990s Basque has been used on bilingual road signs there too. With your arrival in this part of France in the foothills of the Pyrenees begins the transition to the Way of St James in Spain.

Vernacular architecture

Along the way you will see not only many interesting cathedrals, churches and other monuments of outstanding scale, character and significance but also examples of what is best described as 'vernacular architecture': wayside crosses, old bridges, *lavoirs* (communal laundry facilities), water mills, *métiers à ferrer les boeufs* (a device for immobilising oxen while they were being shod for work in the fields), *caselles*, *gaviotes* (different types of small, circular drystone buildings to protect shepherds and other workers from the elements), dovecotes and so on. Such features are indicated in the guide as you go along.

BEFORE YOU GO

Preparation

* Read up as much as you can about the Way – its history, art, architecture and geography – as well as other people's accounts of their journeys. Suggestions for further reading are given in Appendix E.

Training

* If you are not already used to walking or used to carrying a rucksack day in, day out, get in plenty of practice before you go. Consider joining your local rambling club at least six months in advance and go out with them as often as you can. Most clubs have walks of different lengths and speeds so you can start with a shorter, slower one if you need to and gradually build up your speed

and stamina. In this way you can benefit from walking with other people (usually friendly), walk in the countryside, have someone to lead who knows the way and suitable places to go (which you may not) and you can also practise walking in hilly places (which you will need).

• Then start increasing the amount of weight and luggage you take out with you until you can carry everything you need. After that, go out walking on at least two consecutive days on several occasions, in hilly places, carrying all your proposed gear with you: walking 25km on a 'one-off' basis is a very different matter from getting up again the following morning, probably stiff and possibly footsore, and starting out all over again. In this way you should have an enjoyable journey, with trouble-free feet and back.

• Decide what type of footwear you will be taking – walking shoes, lightweight boots, heavy (thick-soled) trainers and so on – and break them in well before you go.

Language

• Don't expect anybody – anybody at all – to speak English! Assume you will have to speak French all the time for everything you need, however complicated. So if you are not already fairly fluent, consider a year's evening classes or home study with tapes/CDs in your preparations; you will find yourself extremely isolated if you are unable not only to carry out practical transactions but also to converse with the many French-speaking pilgrims and other people you meet along the Way.

Two-legged

Unless you plan to go with someone you already know well and have walked with before (family member or long-standing friend), think very carefully indeed about your choice of companion, especially if you feel that you must go with someone else and better anybody at all than nobody. This area can be an absolute minefield and the following, in no particular order, are a few things to think about beforehand, rather than discover too late that they will cause problems. Some aspects are obvious: does the other person walk at the same speed as you, for example, or do the same sort of daily distances? Others are less so, however.

• If you do both walk at the same speed, does the other person like to continue non-stop until reaching a destination, only pausing for a quick drink or snack or, instead, like to sit down for a while and admire the view as and when a suitable place appears?

• Do you (or your potential companion) like to:
– get up at dawn and start immediately while the other finds it difficult

to get going in the morning? (Ditto early/late nights.)
– stay in hotels while the other person prefers to stay in gîtes d'étape or other economical accommodation?
– eat out in restaurants all the time while the other person wants to do his/her own cooking in gîtes/campsites?

• Does one of you speak fluent French while the other one is monolingual English? While it may seem convenient for the non-French speaker to have a companion who can cope with all things practical, linguistically it can be frustrating for both of you when, for example, you get talking to other pilgrims or people who live along the way as either the French-speaker has to translate constantly (something which is completely exhausting on a regular basis) or the other person is excluded from the conversation.

• Does one or the other of you talk non-stop all the time while the other prefers to walk mainly in silence?

• Does one of you (but not the other) like to pause and visit churches and other monuments along the way?

• Do you both – something that is often overlooked until it is too late – have the same level of funds available?

If walking speed, rhythm and rests are the only problem, you can often resolve these by walking separately during the day and meeting up again in the evening (with plenty to talk about). Other issues are more difficult to resolve but they can make or completely mar a pilgrim journey in the constant company of another person.

It should be obvious, of course, that if you have not already undertaken a long journey on foot with your proposed companion you will need to do several 'test walks' first to enable (both of) you to make a decision on this matter.

Finally, however, there is one more thing to take into consideration but which is not often thought through beforehand: what sort of moral obligation do you both have (or not) to the other person to 'stick with them through thick and thin' in the event that something crops up that prevents one of you (but not both) from continuing? A serious injury, for example, or some family matter that could not have been foreseen? This problem is particularly acute if you are making a very long pilgrimage together. Should something like this occur unexpectedly it will be a lot easier to resolve if you have thought – and talked – about it before you set off together.

Four-legged
Do **not** – ever – be tempted to take your dog with you!

• You will meet other, local dogs along the way who are on their own territory and do not take kindly to strange ones.

• Hardly any accommodation of any type, except campsites,

accepts them. On accommodation lists places routinely say 'chiens refusés'.

- You may well have transport problems returning home, especially in Spain.
- Most dogs, although used to going out all day long, are not accustomed to continuous long-distance walking and they, like their two-legged companions, are prone to problems with their feet.
- Dogs, on average, it seems, need to sleep about 15 hours a day, which would obviously limit the amount of time/distances you would be able to walk on a daily basis.

EQUIPMENT

Rucksack At least 50 litres in capacity if carrying a sleeping bag

Footwear Both to walk in and a spare pair of lightweight trainers/sandals that you can walk in if need be

Waterproofs Even in summer it may rain, especially in the Basque country. A poncho (a cape with a hood and space inside for a rucksack) is far more useful (and far less hot) than a cagoule or anorak (although it can cause problems in high winds)

Pullover or fleece jacket Parts of the route are high up and it can get cold at night, even in summer

First aid kit Include a needle for draining blisters, and scissors. The type of plaster sold by the metre is more useful than individual dressings. Also high-factor sunscreen if you burn easily. Insect repellant in July and August

Torch/head torch

Large water bottle At least 2 litres in capacity if walking in July and August

Sleeping bag Essential if you are either camping or continuing into Spain and will be staying in *refugios* there, but if you are only doing the French section and are staying in gîtes d'étape a sheet sleeping bag will normally be sufficient as blankets are usually provided

Thin pillowcase Useful in gîtes (or tent) to hold clothes together when pillows are not provided

Sleeping mat If camping

Stick Useful for fending off/frightening dogs and testing boggy terrain

Guidebook and maps

Compass (if you know how to use it)

Sun hat Preferably with wide brim

Small dictionary

Mug, spoon, plate and knife

A **tent** is useful if you intend to camp a lot (although you can walk the entire route from Le Puy to the Pyrenees staying in gîtes); in this case you will also need a 'camping gaz'-type stove or similar

Passport

EHIC card

Pilgrim passport (see below)

Money

In general, travel as light as you can, not just for the weight but because of the constant hills and, depending on the season, the heat. However, if you are operating on an extremely tight (eg student-level) budget, where you can't afford any unpleasant financial surprises, you will inevitably have to carry more weight – food and drink, for example – than someone who can afford to eat out all the time.

CRÉANCIALE (PILGRIM PASSPORT)

Modern pilgrims who seek proof of their pilgrimage also carry a 'pilgrim passport' (*créanciale* in French) which they have stamped at regular intervals along the Way (in churches, tourist offices, town halls, *accueils pèlerins/ accueils paroissiaux* and many gîtes d'étape) and which they then present

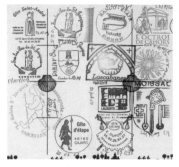

Stamps in a pilgrim passport

to the Cathedral authorities in Santiago to help them obtain their *Compostela* (certificate of completion of pilgrimage) (see page 13). More information about 'pilgrim passports' is available from the Confraternity of St James (see Appendix F for contact details) but the *Créanciale* itself, issued by the Eglise de France, is available (in person only) from the Cathedral in Le Puy when you arrive there.

This serves not only as a souvenir of all the places you stayed on your long journey to Santiago and as evidence that you have completed at least the last 100km of the Way of St James (if you're making the pilgrimage on foot – 200km for cyclists), but a pilgrim passport is also required if you wish to sleep in the increasing number of strictly pilgrim-only places of accommodation along the Le Puy route, as well as on the *Camino* in Spain.

Créanciale

du pèlerin de Saint-Jacques de-Compostelle

"Viens et suis-moi"
Luc 18,22

Créanciale (pilgrim passport)

GETTING THERE AND BACK

Depending on where you live or are coming from, you can travel from London to Lyon Part-Dieu via Lille Flandres on Eurostar (although there are now an increasing number of direct London–Lyon services on this route; check www.sncf.com for details, available in English). From there a local train takes you to St-Etienne-Châteaucreux, from where an SNCF coach continues to **Le Puy**. If, on the other hand you are travelling from elsewhere via Paris, you would take the TGV to Lyon from the Gare de Lyon and then continue as described above.

If you are not walking all the way to Santiago in one go, there are several places where it is relatively easy to break your journey and then return later to continue. **Figeac** can be reached from Paris Austerlitz (by TGV), changing to a local train in Brive-la-Gaillarde. **Cahors** is on the Paris Austerlitz–Toulouse line and is accessible directly by TGV. **Moissac** can be reached by TGV from Paris Montparnasse 1, then changing to a local train in Agen. To break/restart your journey in **Aire-sur-l'Adour** take the TGV from Paris Montparnasse 1 or 2 to Pau, from/to where there is an SNCF coach service.

For other possible places to break your journey see www.sncf.com, and to check the availability of long-haul coach services during the summer months (London–Lyon, for example) see www.eurolines.co.uk/en

Saint-Jean-Pied-de-Port can be reached/left by local train to Bayonne (three to four services a day) and then to/from Paris Austerlitz by TGV. Note, too, that as this service also stops in Bordeaux, to which several regional aiports in Britain operate direct flights, this could be another option to consider if you are not walking all the way to Santiago in one go. Alternatively, both EasyJet and Ryanair operate flights from London Stansted to Biarritz, only a short local bus ride to Bayonne railway station. However, as budget airline services are particularly subject to change it is advisable to check this information well before planning your journey. There is also a daily bus service from Pamplona to Saint-Jean-Pied-de-Port from March to the beginning of November – see page 168 for details.

If you are crossing the Pyrenees to finish the French section of your journey there, you can continue/return by train or coach from Madrid or Bilbao to **Pamplona** and then by local bus to/from **Roncesvalles**.

PLANNING YOUR SCHEDULE

The walk from Le Puy to Saint-Jean-Pied-de-Port can be completed in four to five weeks by anyone who is fairly fit and who also likes to visit places of interest along the way. It can be undertaken in sections, too, by those who lack the time to do it all in one go or who would just like to cover certain stretches, and indications are given in the text as to how to reach (or leave) the main towns along the Way.

Allow plenty of time when planning your itinerary, especially if you are not an experienced walker. Start with fairly short stages and always stop before you are tired. You can then increase the distances as you get fitter and into the swing of things. Try not to plan too tight a schedule either, but allow plenty of time and flexibility to account for unforeseen circumstances (pleasant or otherwise).

Where and how many rest days you take is up to you (although Conques, Cahors and Moissac are 'musts'), as is whether you include several short days' walking in your programme, arriving at your destination during the late morning so as to have the remainder of the day completely free. If you are extremely tired, however, or having trouble with your feet, a complete day off works wonders (particularly in a small place with no 'sights' to be visited) and is well worth the disruption to your schedule that it might initially seem to be.

If you are walking all the way to Santiago in one go, consider taking a day off in Saint-Jean-Pied-de-Port as you leave the French section of the route behind you and set out on the next (much easier physically, once you have crossed the Pyrenees) part of the route through Spain.

Métier à ferrer les boeufs,
Rieutort d'Aubrac (Section 1)

ACCOMMODATION

There are four broad types of accommodation available along the route: campsites, gîtes d'étape, *chambres d'hôte* and hotels, alongside the slowly developing network of *accueils chrétiens* (see below). Do not confuse these with *accueils pèlerins* or *accueils paroissiaux*, however, which is a service provided by volunteers (eg from a church) and where passing pilgrims are offered a hot or cold drink, can have their pilgrm passports stamped, can ask for information or just sit down for a rest. (Note, too, that these do not offer sleeping accommodation.)

Most towns, even small, and especially those on a river, have a campsite, and many farms along the way also offer *camping à la ferme*. Campsites vary in price according to the facilities they offer, but as more and more sites are being upgraded it may now be very little cheaper to camp than to stay in a gîte d'étape (see below). The only real advantage in carrying a tent is the freedom to stop when and where you want as campsites are so numerous. Most are closed in winter (from *Toussaint* – All Saints Day, a public holiday on 1 November – to Easter) but opening times, where known, are indicated in the text. Note, however, that several of the larger campsites also have caravans or mobile homes that they rent out to pilgrims per person per night, normally with cooking facilities too (Livinhac le Haut, Aire-sur-l'Adour,

for example) so if you are having difficulty finding somewhere to sleep this is an option worth checking out.

It is also possible to walk the entire route from Le Puy to the Pyrenees staying in gîtes d'étape, and without having to cover enormous distances between stops either. These contain simple, dormitory-type accommodation and a minimum of one hot shower, and the municipally run ones, at least, offer cooking facilities (these are indicated with a 'K' in the text). In 2016 they cost between €10 and €18 per person per night. Blankets are usually provided so normally only a sheet sleeping bag is needed. Most include special clothes-washing sinks and, increasingly, for a small fee, the use of a washing machine.

The gîtes d'étape (as opposed to other types of gîte) are for walkers, cyclists and riders only. There are now plenty within easy walking distance of each other (every 15km or so) as far as Conques, but after that they are often further apart (around 20–25km). Many are municipally run (*gîte communal*) and will contain all the above facilities.

In some places, however, establishments that describe themselves as gîtes d'étape provide no cooking facilities at all and few opportunities, for example, to wash clothes. These are often run by restaurants, hotels, riding schools or bed and breakfast establishments that attach a dormitory and showers and provide meals, usually with a *soirée étape* or *forfait pèlerin*

Looking back at Lauzerte (Section 2)

(ie a special rate for dinner, bed and breakfast) but which, pilgrims report increasingly, may be a pre-condition of staying there. So be on your guard and check carefully before making a reservation, especially if you are on a tight budget. This type of gîte is also, usually, more expensive than the municipally run ones.

In popular areas it is advisable to phone the day before (or, if you have already made a reservation, phone the preceding day to confirm it), especially at holiday times or on weekends with a *pont* (a public holiday on a Thursday or a Tuesday when people take Friday or Monday off as well) as, at these times in particular, walking clubs and other groups sometimes book (and pay for) the whole gîte, even if they do not always fill all the beds. In such cases it is usually possible to sleep there once you are actually on the spot, but a good level of French will be needed to negotiate.

Gîtes d'étape may seem too spartan for some people's tastes, but they are a very good way to meet and get to know other pilgrims, as are the *refugios* in Spain, especially if you are walking or cycling the entire route. Many, like the campsites, are only open from Easter to October, but information regarding their availability is given where known. Note, too, that although accommodation may be indicated as being available 'all year', you will normally need to phone in advance to make a reservation out of season (eg late October to March). Conversely too, however, establishments that indicate that they are only open (for example) from April to the end of September are often prepared to take bookings at other times – although, once again, a good level of French will be needed to negotiate.

Those who prefer to stay in *chambres d'hôte* (abbreviated to 'CH' here) – the French equivalent of bed and breakfast in country areas and usually offering the option of a *soirée étape* (an evening meal as well) – will also have no trouble as these establishments are becoming increasingly numerous. It is usually enough to phone a day or so ahead, but given the proliferation of these facilities and the fact that many of them only offer one or two rooms, contact details have only been given in this text when there are only one or two such offerings in the place concerned; where the supply is plentiful you can either contact the tourist office (OT) in question or consult the *Miam Miam Dodo* guide (see below),

The word *hôtel* in France covers everything from luxurious four-star accommodation (France does not have hotels classified with five stars) to a very basic *pension* and their prices normally reflect the facilities available. French hotels have now been reclassified, however, and they usually have 'NN' (*nouveaux normes*) after their star rating. If you prefer to stay in hotels you will find the many tourist offices (*office de tourisme*,

referred to as 'OT' in this guide, telephone numbers included) a useful source of information, although the entries in the *Miam Miam Dodo* guide referred to above are very comprehensive. A hotel offering a *forfait pèlerin* (or *soirée étape*) has, like other establishments, a special rate for dinner, bed and breakfast.

Gradually, however, a fifth category of accommodation, strictly for pilgrims only (a *créanciale* – pilgrim passport, see below – is essential to be able to access them), has begun to establish itself on the Le Puy route, often described as *accueils chrétiens*. These provide dormitory-type accommodation, frequently offer a shared meal in the evening, breakfast the following morning, sometimes the opportunity for evening prayers and, like the *refugio* system in Spain, usually operate on a donation (*libre participation*) basis. They are often run by former pilgrims or some churches and their availability is also indicated in the relevant sections of this guide. Do not confuse these, however, as indicated above, with the *accueils pèlerins* – a service offered (usually from Easter to October) by volunteers, often former pilgrims, from an increasing number of churches and local pilgrim associations. (These are abbreviated in the text as 'AP'.)

Miam Miam Dodo

As well as the information given in this guide, another source of very up-to-date information on where to sleep and eat along the Way, highly recommended to accompany this book, is the somewhat curiously entitled *Miam Miam Dodo* already alluded to. (Its title translates as something like 'Yum-Yum-Bye-Byes'…) This covers all types of accommodation (including hotels) and services (shops, restaurants, banks, internet facilities and so on), is extremely detailed and is checked, revised and reprinted annually (make sure you get the GR65 Le Puy latest edition), and although it is in French its schematic presentation makes it very easy to use, even for those with only a limited knowledge of the language. It also lists facilities within a 5km radius of places on the route. It is available direct from its authors (see Appendix F), from the Confraternity of St James's online bookshop, from the cathedral and other bookshops in Le Puy and in places along the route as well as in some gîtes d'étape.

Booking ahead

While it might appear an attractive option to book all your accommodation for your entire journey before you leave home (particularly if you are not a confident French speaker), this can have drawbacks in terms of flexibility. You will be tied down to a timetable that will prevent you from taking a day off when you are very tired, for example, or staying an extra day somewhere you find particularly interesting, or, conversely, continuing ahead when you find you are fitter

than you expected and so have miscalculated the sort of daily distances you can cope with on a regular basis. It is therefore suggested that you reserve ahead for no more than three nights at a time – and many pilgrim-only places of accommodation on this route do not accept bookings for more than one or two days in advance anyway. Here, as with the question of whether or not to use baggage transfer services (see below), you will probably find that your journey is a more 'pilgrim' (as opposed to a purely holiday) experience if you give yourself the freedom and flexibility to take each day of your journey as it comes.

(If your concerns are purely linguistic and you sleep mainly in hotels or *chambres d'hôtes*, you will almost always find that the proprietor is more than willing to phone ahead for you on your behalf – they all tend to know each other anyway! Similarly, if you stay mainly in gîtes d'étape, you can very often find another person willing to phone for you, although be sure to hand them your own phone to use, so that you – and not the helpful person – pays for the call.)

BAGGAGE TRANSFER (SHERPA) SERVICES

A considerable number of taxi and transport firms now provide a baggage transfer service, collecting your rucksack from one overnight stop (hotel, *chambre d'hôte*, gîte d'étape) and delivering it to the next, for a fee of about €8 per item per person. These are far too numerous to include here, but if you are interested you can find a complete listing of such services in the current edition of *Miam Miam Dodo*. Some of them also offer the option of returning you to your starting point eastwards (if you are only doing a section of the route) when they return empty after delivering the day's bags.

However, while this might initially appear to be an attractive option, think about it very carefully before you decide (unless, of course, you are considering it for medical/mobility reasons). For one thing it will work out very expensive if you are walking all the way to the Pyrenees (and even more so if you are continuing on to Santiago all in one go). Also, you will probably find it a much more 'pilgrim' experience if you travel as light as possible and carry everything

with you all the time. A number of pilgrim-only places of accommodation along the Le Puy route do not accept walkers using baggage transport services anyway (except for disability reasons); and if you carry everything on your own back you will not be tied down to a rigid schedule that will prevent the kind of flexibility described in 'Booking ahead', above. It is therefore suggested that you carry your own rucksack wherever possible.

PLANNING THE DAY

Long-distance walkers in Britain usually operate on a 'nine-to-five' basis, leaving their accommodation shortly after breakfast and returning in time for an early evening meal. There may be few, if any, places of

Pilgrim road in the Lot (Section 2)

historical, religious or cultural interest, such as churches, cathedrals or stately homes, directly on the path that require a detailed indoor visit (as opposed to historic bridges, fortifications, market crosses and so on that can be inspected fairly quickly from the outside), and those that do normally work 'nine-to-five' anyway, so that combining walking and

Chapelle Sainte-Foy, Conques (Section 1)

sightseeing is usually incompatible. Therefore, walkers in Britain tend just to walk.

In France, however, not only are there an enormous number of places well worth visiting along the Le Puy route, of outstanding artistic, architectural, cultural or religious interest, but they are also open at convenient times for the walker: as well as 10am to midday, they normally open in the evenings from 4 or 5pm to 7pm. Churches in the *départements* of the Haute Loire, Lozère, Aveyron, Lot, Tarn et Garonne, Gers and the Landes are usually open all day long from April to October, but in the Pyrénées-Orientales those in small villages were almost always firmly closed when this guide was being updated, unless a service was taking place.

In July and August in particular it is extremely hot during the day, especially in the *causse* before Cahors, with temperatures well up into the 90°sF, although in many areas there is often quite a lot of shade. When walking in hot weather it is important to avoid becoming dehydrated by drinking plenty of water before you set out, as once you realise you haven't had enough to drink it is too late to do anything about it, even if you have supplies with you (top up your water bottle whenever you can).

It is difficult to do, but if you can drink at least half a litre of water as soon as you get up (as well as any tea/coffee available) you will find the hot weather affects you much less. The best way to avoid walking in the heat is to get up before it is light and set out at daybreak (but not earlier). At this time of day it is cool and pleasant, with the added advantages of watching the sun rise as you walk and enjoying the scenery in the early morning light.

In this way, even with stops, you should be able to reach your destination by the early afternoon, when you can then rest up awhile before going out sightseeing or visiting in the (relative) cool of the early evening. It is also a good idea, in large towns and other places of any size, to go for a walk in the evening and check your route out for the next day, so as not to waste time or get lost the following morning.

OTHER PRACTICAL INFORMATION

Shops Shops (for food) are normally open until midday or 12.30pm, and then from 2.30 or 3pm until about 7pm. Those in small villages (where they still exist) are usually shut not only on Sundays but often on Monday mornings (and sometimes afternoons) as well, so considerable organisation is needed when following the GR65, particularly if you are doing your own cooking. There are now, however, an increasing number of *points multi-services* along the way – a hybrid type of establishment selling fresh bread, newspapers, limited groceries and so on, often located next to petrol stations.

Public holidays There are more of these in France (*jours fériés*) than in Britain: 1 January, 1 and 8 May, Ascension Day, 14 July, 15 August, 1 November, and 11 and 25 December. Shops, including those for food (but not bars, restaurants or bakeries), will be closed on these occasions.

Meals In France meals are available between midday and 2pm and from 7–9pm. (If you are a vegetarian you will probably find eating out very difficult.) Breakfast (in hotels and so on) is usually available from 7 or 7.30am onwards. **Cafés and bars** may open as early as 7am in summer along the pilgrim route (check first if you want breakfast before setting out) and may well close by 10pm in large towns and much earlier in small places.

Changing money It is usually possible to change money in post offices in France, even in quite small places. There is also an increasing number of cashpoints (*distributeurs de billets de banque*, 'ATM' in the text), even in fairly small towns, which accept Visa, cash cards bearing the Cirrus/Maestro logo, and so on. Banks' opening hours are similar to those in Britain.

Post offices These (the 'PTT') are open from 8am in large places, 9am in small places, and until as late as 7pm (12.30 or 1pm on Saturdays), and many of them have cashpoints too. If you want to send things to yourself further along the route (such as maps and guides) you can do this via the *poste restante* system whereby you collect your mail (on presentation of your passport) at the post office. Address the letter or parcel to yourself (surname first), Poste Restante, postal code and name of town. The most likely places you will need will be the following: 43000 Le Puy-en-Velay, 46100 Figeac, 46000 Cahors, 82200 Moissac, 40800 Aire-sur-l'Adour and 64220 Saint-Jean-Pied-de-Port. There is a small fee for each item collected, but note that it will only be kept for 15 days before being returned to the sender.

Telephones Most public telephones (where they still exist) operate with *télécartes* (phone cards), except in some rural areas. All phone numbers in France consist of 10 digits, with 01, 02, 03, 04 or 05 placed at the start of the previously eight-figure numbers, according to the region they are in (06 is reserved for most mobile phones, 07 and 09 for others). (Note that if you phone from Britain you do not use the '0'.) The emergency number in France for all services is 112.

Mobile phones are becoming increasingly essential (for booking/confirming accommodation, for example), but note that they do not always work in rural areas. There are now only very few telephone boxes (*cabines téléphoniques*) or *points-phones* along the route; you will therefore almost certainly need to take a mobile phone with you. However, you will probably find it a much more 'pilgrim' journey if your friends and relations back home cannot contact you at all hours of the day or night to tell you, for example, that the central heating doesn't work, that the cat next door has been run over or that your mother-in-law has broken her spectacles… So you may prefer to keep your mobile either on 'silent' or switched off, and inform your family, for example, that you will only have it switched on between specified times each day/evening or use it for emergencies only.

Internet/Cybercafés These are not nearly as easy to find in France as they are on the Spanish section of the route and as their availability changes frequently they have not been listed in this guide. However, they are indicated in the *Miam Miam Dodo* guide and tourist offices can usually tell you where to find one too.

Launderettes These can be found in all large French towns (unlike Spain, where they often do not exist) and, as indicated above, many gîtes d'étape now have washing machines.

Buvettes or **pauses-café** Stalls/places selling drinks and snacks, and sometimes local produce as well, are becoming increasingly available along the Le Puy route, often run by farms or by local people, particularly in isolated areas. You can also eat your own food there, provided you buy a drink. They are not listed in this guide as their availability changes frequently, but their enterprising owners normally post notices well in advance to alert you to their existence.

Drinking water There are many places along the way with a *point d'eau*, either taps or fountains, and marked '*eau potable*' when it is safe to drink. These are indicated in the text with a tap symbol (♣). There are also many public WCs, particularly in small places, often in or near the *mairie* (town hall).

Church services Although many churches are open all day, as explained above, apart from in large towns there is often only a mass there once a fortnight, or once a month in really small places. A list of mass times and where they will be held in the local area is normally posted in churches for the current and following month.

Medical assistance Make sure that you obtain an **EHIC (European Health Insurance Card)** before leaving Britain. Application forms are no longer available from the post office as this service is now dealt with either online (www.nhs.uk/ehic) or, alternatively, by telephone (tel 0300 330 1350). This is a Europe-wide document entitling you to free or reduced medical (but not dental) treatment under the French and other countries' health systems. If you already have one, check its expiry date before departure. Note, however, that the EHIC does not cover transport home, for which you will need separate travel insurance. Note, too, that these were the regulations in force 'pre-Brexit'; at the time this guidebook was being updated ('post-Brexit') no information was as yet available regarding any subsequent changes to the system, so you will need to check this before you travel.

Snakes have been seen on the stretch from Le Puy to Cahors, and also between Saint-Palais and Saint-Jean-Pied-de-Port. They may not be very common but if you do meet them (usually when it has been very hot for a while) it will be when you are off your guard (stick useful).

Hunting season When this opens (1 October onwards), be particularly vigilant when walking through forests and stick to the paths, especially at weekends and on public holidays, when pheasant shooting and other game hunting is extremely popular.

Dogs Their owners nearly always tell you that 'he won't hurt you' ('*il n'est pas mechant*') but this is often hard to believe. They may tell you, too, that it is the rucksack that bothers them (and as dogs are reputed to see only in black and white there may be some truth in this, faced with mysterious hump-backed monsters on two legs) but it is not much comfort when faced with an aggressive one. They live all along the route from Le Puy to the Pyrenees (as well as on the Spanish section of the route), are often (but not always) tied up, hear you ages before you have any idea where they are and are frequently enormous. (The small ones are, in fact, a greater nuisance, as they have a nasty habit of letting you pass quietly by and then attacking from behind, nipping you in the back of your ankles.) A stick is very useful – even though you might not usually walk with one – not to hit them with, but to threaten. Be warned!

USING THIS GUIDE

Waymarking

The route described in this book follows the GR65 through France, ending at the border town of Saint-Jean-Pied-de-Port, in the direction of the (modern) pilgrimage. It is described in one direction only. (Those who would like to walk the Way in reverse or return on foot will have no trouble in France as the route, unlike in Spain, is waymarked in both directions.) Waymarking (*balisage*) is in the form of pairs of horizontal red-and-white stripes (*balises*), one above the other to indicate that you should continue ahead (see diagram). Turns are indicated by bent red-and-white arrows, often preceded by broken waymarks to prepare the walker.

A useful feature is also the 'wrong direction' sign, a red-and-white cross telling you which direction **not** to take, especially in situations where it is hard to mark the correct option for lack of suitable trees, rocks and so on, on which to paint them. If you wonder at times why information about other routes is given in the description of this one, it is because all French long-distance footpaths (the *Sentiers de Grandes Randonnées* or 'GRs') have the same waymarking system and you should be alert to (usually short) sections that the GR65 has in common with, for example, the GR4. When they separate again you need to know which turning is the correct one as there is not always an indication next to the waymark.

You will also see, however, increasingly frequently in the early stages of the route, the yellow arrows familiar to those who have already walked the *Camino* in Spain: the

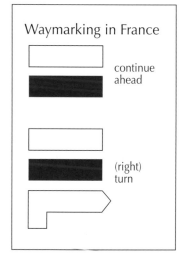

Waymarking in France

continue ahead

(right) turn

*Pilgrim waymarking in
Le Puy (Section 1)*

European shell logo on a blue background (often with the number of kilometres still remaining to Santiago) and, in the Landes and Pyrénées-Atlantiques, yellow stickers/markers with the blue shell motif.

Note, however, that the GR65 has not been waymarked with the long-distance pilgrim (as opposed to the holiday walker) in mind: that is, someone who is going to walk, if not all the way to Santiago in one go, then at least as far as Saint-Jean-Pied-de-Port, and thus wants to take the most direct route possible without walking on busy roads or missing essential monuments and places of interest. Instead the GR65 caters more for the needs of hikers or ramblers who are probably only doing a short section of the entire route or are just out for the day (and so do not need to go shopping for food suppies, for instance) or a weekend and thus have the time to make 'scenic' detours in order simply to have good plunging views of the next town (when approaching Saint-Côme-d'Olt, for example).

The GR65 also goes to some lengths in places to make sure that the walker avoids tarmac at all costs, doing 'loops' that involve going round three sides of a square when a short section on a very minor road (with little or no traffic) would be much more direct, or up and down steep hills on tracks parallel to a road. Such places are indicated in the text with alternative strategies suggested, for instance in bad weather. It is therefore important to read through the description of the following day's walk ahead of time and decide which option you would like to take in such cases. The GR65 also studiously avoids shops and bars at times, making life difficult when you need to purchase food supplies, but again alternative tactics are suggested when available.

Maps

Michelin 725 is a single map covering the whole of southern France, but maps in the IGN (Institut Géographique National) lime-green Top 100 Tourisme et Découverte series are recommended for walkers as the GR65 and its *variantes* are all marked on them. The scale is 1:100,000 and only five are required (as against 25 in the blue 1:25,000 Carte de Randonée series), given here in route order: 156 (St-Etienne–Le Puy-en-Velay), 162 (Rodez–Millau), 161 (Montauban–Albi), 159 (Pau–Mont-de-Marsan) and 166 (Pau–Bayonne).

These are available from Stanfords map shops in London and Bristol, from The Map Shop, Upton-upon-Severn (see Appendix F) or from many general bookshops, but make sure you get the latest edition.

Users of previous editions of this guide have often asked why 'proper' Ordnance Survey-type maps are not provided in this book. Unfortunately, problems of copyright and reprinting make it extremely complicated.

Chapelle Saint-Roch, Montbonnet (Section 1)

Instead, to aid the pilgrim or walker in planning his or her journey, it has only been possible to include sketch maps of the route in this guide.

Textual description

The text is divided up into four sections, split at Figeac, Moissac and Aire-sur-l'Adour: these are all places where the walking pilgrim can reach or leave the route easily by public transport, if they wish (or need) to complete the route in shorter stages. Each of the main places along the route appears in **bold**, preceded by the distance walked from the previous place and followed by a description of the facilities available, a brief history where applicable and an indication of the places of interest to visit. (Those wishing to spend time in any of the larger towns should obtain information leaflets and a street plan from the OT there.)

The text of each section is – deliberately – not divided up into daily stages, as in this way the pilgrim can decide the distances he or she would like to cover each day. (It is suggested that you go through the text in advance and mark in possible overnight stops with a highlight pen.) The figures after each place name heading indicate the height in metres where known and, in parentheses, the distance in kilometres from both Le Puy and Saint-Jean-Pied-de-Port. In the case of large towns (Cahors, for example) the distances to/from them start/end in their centres, normally at the cathedral.

Place names appear in the text in **bold type**, as do other names that help in wayfinding, such as street names, the names of prominent buildings, rivers and so on.

Abbreviations used in the text

L indicates that you should turn/fork left; R that you should turn/fork R. (L) and (R) mean that something you pass is to your left or right. KSO = keep straight on. KSO(L) or KSO(R) = keep straight on L or R. FB = footbridge, FP = footpath, > = becomes, // = parallel. Km = kilometre. N followed by a number (such as N135) refers to the number of a main road, D to that of a local road. AP = *accueil pèlerin*, CH = *chambre d'hôte*, K = kitchen/cooking facilities. OT = tourist office, PTT = post office. RE = reservation essential. X = closed/except, ♣ = drinking water available. ATM = cash dispenser. SNCF is the abbreviation for the French national railway network. HT = high tension (cables).

A comfortable pace

Unlike pilgrimages to Lourdes, Fatima or other locations where miracles are sought, where help for specific problems is often requested, and where being in the pilgrim destination itself is the most important factor, on the Way of St James it is the journey that is the pilgrim's principal concern, the arrival in Santiago being only a conclusion to the rest of the undertaking. It is not a 'map and compass route' either, although the walking along the Le Puy route is often strenuous. Timings have not been given from place to place, but 4km per hour, exclusive of stops, is often considered average, especially when carrying a heavy rucksack. However, a comfortable pace may often be more than this – a fit walker may well be able to maintain a speed of 5–6km or 3½ miles per hour.

WHEN TO GO

The route is practicable, but not necessarily recommended, all through the year. In winter there is often snow on the Aubrac plateau and nearly always in the Pyrenees, it rains a lot in the Basque country – something it does on all parts of the route in spring – and much of the accommodation may be closed at that time of the year.

If you are not restricted to a particular time of year then May or early June or the autumn are best – dry, but not as hot as in summer, with long hours of daylight, although accommodation is naturally becoming increasingly crowded then.

Traditionally as many people as possible aimed to arrive in Santiago for the festivities on 25 July, St James's Day, particularly in Holy Years. Many still do.

THE ROUTE

Pilgrim road beyond Varaire (Section 2)

SECTION 1
Le Puy-en-Velay to Figeac

LE PUY-EN-VELAY 625M (0/742)

Population 19,976. All facilities. SNCF (trains from Paris via Saint-Etienne-Châteaucreux. Several hotels and numerous CH (see *Miam Miam Dodo*). Three gîtes d'étape: a) Le Relais du Pèlerin Saint-Jacques, 28 Rue Cardinal de Polignac (near cathedral, tel 06 37 08 65 83), open 1 Apr–15 Oct from 3pm and run by former pilgrim volunteers from the Association des Amis de Saint Jacques du Velay, 27pl, pilgrims only, no fixed charge but donation; b) for both pilgrims and walkers in the Maison Saint-François (also near cathedral, tel 04 71 05 98 86, 19pl, K), 6 Rue Mayol, open all year X Xmas to New Year; c) Gîte d'Etape des Capucins (and adjoining Appart'Hôtel) is on the route out of town at 29 Rue de Capucins (tel 04 71 04 28 74, open all year X mid Dec to mid Jan, 19pl, K). Youth hostel (tel 04 71 05 52 40, open all year but closed w/ends 31 Oct–31 Mar, 50pl, K) in Centre Pierre Cardinal, Rue Jules Vallès, also in the upper part of town, as is the Association Grand Séminaire Accueil Saint Georges, 4 Rue Saint Georges, which also takes pilgrims (tel 04 71 09 93 10, open all year, 160pl but is often full with very large groups). Campsite (Camping Municipal de Bouthezard), Chemin de Roderie, Rocade d'Aiguilhe (tel 04 71 09 55 09), is to NW of town, on an island in the river (25 Mar–30 Oct).

Pilgrim stamp (and *créanciale* – pilgrim passport – if desired) available from the cathedral sacristy (10am–midday, 2–6pm Apr–Sept, 10am–midday and 3–5pm at other times). Mass in cathedral at 7am every morning (conducted by the Bishop of Le Puy whenever possible), followed by pilgrim blessing (stamp also available then). The Accueil Pèlerins El Camino, 2 Rue de la Manécanterie, many of them former pilgrims, holds an information session with a '*verre d'amitié*' (informal drink) every evening from 1 Apr–15 Oct, 5.30–7.30pm, where they also issue (and stamp) pilgrim passports.

Le Puy (its inhabitants are known as *ponot(e)s*) is an ancient town in a volcanic landscape, dominated by rocky peaks rising from the valley floor. One is crowned by the chapel of Saint Michel d'Aiguilhe (the Needle), built by Godescalc, Bishop of Le Puy, after his pilgrimage to Santiago in AD951 (it is worth climbing the 267 steps to visit it). An enormous statue of Notre-Dame de France overlooks the town from a rock high above. It is worth spending at least half a day visiting Le Puy. Ask at OT (2 Place du Clauzel) for a walking tour plan of the town. Musée Crozatier, Eglise du Collège, first 'Jesuit-style' church in France, 13th-century Eglise

St James as a pilgrim, Le Puy Cathedral (Photo Marigold Fox)

Saint-Laurent, Chapelle des Pénitents, Baptistère Saint-Jean, Chapel of Monastère Sainte-Claire, Tour Pannessac. Le Puy is also famous for its lentils and its bobbin-lace making. (If you are interested in the latter, the Atelier Conservatoire National de la Dentelle du Puy-en-Velay, 36 Rue du 82e Reg. d'Infanterie – free of charge – is worth a visit.)

The Romanesque Cathedral of Notre-Dame (open 6.30am–7pm daily), now fully restored, is surrounded by the narrow twisting streets of the old town, with many interesting houses. Inside the cathedral: 11th–12th-century cloisters and 17th-century statue of the Black Virgin, which was originally in the former Chapelle de St Maurice du Refuge. This replaces a cedar statue from Egypt, brought back by King Louis IX (Saint Louis) after the seventh crusade but burnt by ultra-revolutionaries on Whitsunday 1794.

There are various theories as to the origins of the Black Virgins. Once considered to have come only from Coptic Africa, they have also been thought to be local, and 'black' either because of a life of hard work in the fields and the open air or 'black' because of being sinful (Mary Magdalene would therefore fall into this category). Whatever the explanation, the black Virgin in Le Puy plays an important role in the life of the cathedral and possesses a complete liturgical 'wardrobe', changed, along with altar cloth, vestments, and so on, according to the seasons of the church's year.

Le Puy has been a pilgrimage centre since the Middle Ages, not so much, as is often thought, as a starting (or assembly) point for French pilgrims and the many 'feeder' routes and/or those coming from further afield en route to Santiago, but as a pilgrimage destination in its own right. Pilgrimages to Notre-Dame du Puy began in the 10th century and the shrine has its own 'Jubilee' years, those in which the Feast of the Annunciation (25 March) coincides with Good Friday. The first was in 992 (thus predating the first Holy Year in Santiago, in 1179) and is the third oldest after Jerusalem and Rome. There were three such Jubilee years in the 20th century – 1910, 1921 and 1932. The first one in the 21st century fell on 25 March 2005; the next one was in 2016 but the one after that is not until 2157. The Rue des Pèlerins and the Hôtel des Pèlerins were therefore not used initially by pilgrims to Santiago, as is often supposed, but by those on pilgrimage to the shrine of Notre-Dame du Puy.

Despite the fact that one of Le Puy's 16 town gates (many of which were named after a saint) was the Porte Sainct Jacme (from where pilgrims left to go to '*monseigneur Sainct Jacques le Majeur en Compostelle ou Galice*'), Le Puy's connection with the pilgrimage to Santiago de Compostela was not common knowledge until the 19th century when, after the departmental archives of the Haute-Loire were reopened and the innumerable documents confiscated during the French Revolution became available, it was discovered, for example, that Godescalc, Bishop of Le Puy, had made the pilgrimage to Santiago in 951. This was something only known initially to a small circle of erudite research workers, however, and there was no mention of the hordes of pilgrims Godescalc was supposed to have incited to follow in his footsteps. Inventories in these archives also revealed that in 1253 the town of Le Puy possessed several hospitals, dedicated to different saints including Saint James, while the first Latin translation of Aymery Picard's *Pilgrim Guide* in 1882 mentioned the town as one of the 'four historic routes' to Compostelle, passing through Conques and Moissac.

The popularity of Le Puy as a departure point for pilgrims bound for Santiago is, in fact, a mid 20th-century phenomenon, encouraged in part by one or two bishops interested in the subject but mainly by the creation of the GR65, a long-distance footpath established by the forerunners of the present FFRP (Fédération Française de la Randonée Pédestre, the French national walking organisation) in the early 1970s to 'reinvent' a pilgrim route from that part of France. But although the *Via Podensis* or route from Le Puy-en-Velay was mentioned as one of the four main departure points in France in Aymery Picard's guide (see above), it was much less travelled in the past than the Paris/Tours, Vézelay and Arles routes (nowadays the reverse is true) and with much fewer pilgrim-related monuments and associations.

The idea at the time, as recreational walking began to become popular in France, was to create a route through wonderful scenery (the Velay region, the Aubrac, the Margeride...), avoiding towns at all costs, as well as roads with a lot of traffic (even if they were historically appropriate), passing as many places with Jacobean and other pilgrim references (St Roch chapels, for example) as possible and opting for a route where accommodation was available. The result was a scenic long-distance footpath, far from direct, with a lot of detours, that addresses the needs of walkers with plenty of time to spare, rather than pilgrims who need the most direct, safe and traffic-free route to a final desination many hundreds of kilometers away. The GR65 has become increasingly popular all the same, not only as a starting-point for those beginning the pilgrimage in France but also as an interim halt for those coming from Geneva on its extension from there, from other parts of Switzerland, from Germany and beyond.

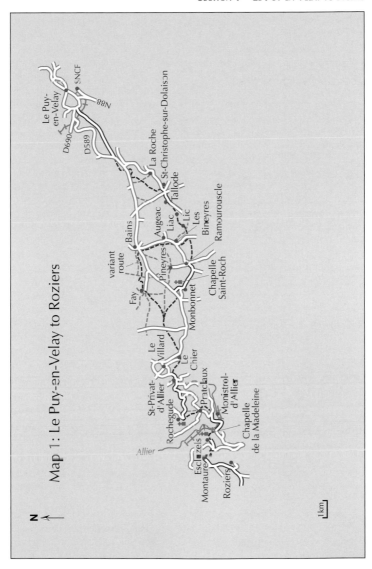

Map 1: Le Puy-en-Velay to Roziers

N ←

Le Puy-en-Velay

SNCF

88N

D690

D589

La Roche

St-Christophe-sur-Dolaison

Tallode

Bains

Augeac

Liac

Lic

Les Bineyres

Ramourouscle

variant route

Pineyres

Monbonnet

Chapelle Saint-Roch

Fay

Le Villard

St-Privat-d'Allier

Le Chier

Rochegude

Pratclaux

Monistrol-d'Allier

Allier

Esclzels

Chapelle de la Madeleine

Montaure

Roziers

1km

When planning your first day, remember that from Le Puy (625m) to the Lac d'Oeuf (1206m) the 20km stretch between Montbonnet and Saint-Privat-d'Allier is all, continuously, uphill…

Starting from the inside of the cathedral and with your back to the main altar *(note statue of St James the pilgrim on pillar to LH side of aisle, facing altar – this dates from the 15th century but was only purchased for the cathedral, by public subscription, in 1990)*, go down the main staircase ahead. Go down the long flight of steps outside and then down the **Rue des Tables** ahead *(note old houses with statues in niches at first-floor level)*. Turn L after the fountain (des 'Choristes') into the **Rue Raphaël**. KSO to the end and continue, veering R, down **Rue Chènebouterie** to the **Place du Plot**, the traditional pilgrim starting-point. Turn R at end into the **Rue Saint-Jacques** *(statue of St James the pilgrim in niche above chemist's shop on corner of this street and the Place du Plot, plaque of 'Amis de Saint-Jacques' on wall on L)*. Cross **Boulevard Saint-Louis** and KSO uphill, climbing steeply *(several benches en route)*, up the **Rue des Capucins**. At the top there is the first clear waymark and large wooden statue of St James pilgrim on L: turn R and then L after 50 metres up the **Route de Compostelle**, continuing to climb steadily. KSO(L) at fork and at bend in road turn R up FP by sports field and then L up a flight of steps back up to the road, where you turn R. *(Handy seat at top, positioned with a good view back over Le Puy.)*

When you reach the top (modern factory building on R), KSO(L) at fork down wide gravelled lane alongside high stone wall, passing below octagonal building on LH side. The lane then > an unsurfaced road. *Good views all round*. At the crossing of five tracks KSO, passing stone wayside cross (to your L, with notice telling you there are 1695km to Santiago – although these, and subsequent indications of this sort, are not necessarily entirely accurate). KSO, climbing gradually, and ignoring turnings to L and R for 2.5km until you reach the D589.

5.5km La Roche 872m (5.5/736.5)
Junction with GR3, which coincides, going SW, with the GR65 for a short distance.

Either turn L along D589 for 800 metres or, as the *balises* indicate (and to avoid walking on the road), cross over and KSO on walled lane for 800 metres then turn L for 400 metres back to road (making a triangular detour). Then either turn L (from road) or cross road (from track) onto a very minor tarred road and then turn hard R onto upper of two paths. KSO, ignoring turnings, and then descend slightly (lane > FP) to join another tarred lane below you and follow this round to the R behind houses.

About 50 metres before you reach the road again, turn L down grassy track, slightly downhill, which then > a FP. KSO, avoiding turns and maintaining your height, as the path winds its way along the shoulder of the hillside, // to the river *Gazelle* in the valley bottom below you to the L. *(TV mast on skyline ahead.)* Path follows low wall on your R for a while *(be careful in foggy weather as although it is fairly wide there is a steep drop to your L – you are walking along a ridge).* Path then goes on to open grassland. When you come to a T-junction with a farm track (1km later, coming from the R) KSO(L), descending slightly to small wayside cross on L.

There are a lot of wayside crosses in this area marking the pilgrim routes, but although they may seem like the equivalent of our modern waymarks, in centuries gone by they were often used to mark the site of a local shrine or pilgrimage. KSO(R) here at fork *(this is where the GR65 and the GR3 separate),* taking the uphill/level track to the R (the GR3 goes L downhill here) and KSO along grassy track that > a shady walled lane before it begins to descend slowly to cross small humpbacked bridge over stream. KSO again, along tree-lined lane rising gently until you reach the **Place de l'Eglise** in the village of...

3km Saint-Christophe-sur-Dolaison 908m (8.5/733.5)

Bar/tabac (doesn't do food but you can eat your own if you buy a drink), L'Auberge du Grand Chemin (X Mon, does meals Tues–Fri midday and Sat evening), Café du Soleil (X Thurs am), boulangerie + limited groceries, ⚓ by *mairie.* 12th-century church built of pink basalt rock, with interesting bell-tower and statue of St Roch pilgrim inside, château/*seigneurie.*

Pass to LH side of church *(mairie, phone box, ⚓ and PTT all on your L on road),* turn L (**Rue du Château**) and then turn R along the D31, passing remains of communal bread oven on RH side. About 100 metres later on turn R (**Place du Lavoir,** *seats, picnic tables)* at small junction down minor road marked 'Tallode 0,5km', skirt the *seigneurie's* perimeter wall, go under main road (D906) and KSO(L) by wayside cross on other side. Continue through hamlets of **Tallode** *(0.5km, CH, gîte de groupe X Dec/Jan, 14pl, tel 04 71 03 17 78 & 06 18 11 38 06)* and **Liac** (0.7km further), turning L at end after wayside cross on R by house on L then R down walled lane (track ahead of you continues as grassy track) marked 'Lic 1km'. Continue to hamlet of **Lic** (1km, lane enters open plateau land) and at end, as lane turns L, turn R at side of building up stony track which then opens out to grassy field and KSO alongside low wall on your L, later with low walls on *both* sides. After 400 metres turn second L down similar lane at right-angle junction and cross very minor tarred road 200 metres later. *(Variante via **Bains** – three CH, bakery, restaurant, shop on Route de Saugues. Church of Sainte-Foy de Conques*

– *begins here). KSO on other side. (Montbonnet visible on hillside ahead.)* At staggered junction of five similar tracks turn L (not hard L – *TV mast now ahead on skyline)* and 200 metres later fork R. KSO along this lane until you reach the D621 and turn R along it at the entrance to the village of…

5.5km Ramourouscle 1030m (14/728)

⚓ by junction, 17th-century wayside cross (with seat) and, on L, the first of several *métiers à ferrer les boeufs* that you will see along the way – a device for holding oxen in place while they were fitted with shoes.

In centre of village turn L onto smaller road marked 'Montbonnet 2'. KSO for 1.5km, ignoring turns, until you reach the…

1.5km Chapelle Saint-Roch (15.5/726.5)

Early 13th-century Romanesque chapel, the first of many along the way dedicated to the patron saint of pilgrims. It was originally dedicated to St James, then St Bonnet (a local saint) and then, in the 17th century, to St Roch. Inside there are two engravings of St Roch as a pilgrim and one statue. Chapel is normally open.

Continue on road for 500m, passing the **Croix des Pélerins** to the village of…

0.5km Montbonnet 1108m (16/726)

Two gîtes d'étape: a) Gîte d'étape privé l'Escole (tel 04 71 57 51 03 & 06 22 71 90 09, 1 Mar–4 Oct, 15pl); b) Gîte d'étape La Grange/Bar Bar Saint-Jacques (tel 04 71 57 54 44 & 06 20 74 47 43, open 7/7 May–Oct X first week in Jul). CH La Barbelotte (tel 06 50 93 54 07) on main road to L on entry, run by two ex-pilgrims, open all year.

Continue on road, following it through village, uphill, to junction with D589. (Turn R for gîte.) Turn L on road and 150 metres later turn R up gravelled lane just before the bar. *(From here to the* **Lac d'Oeuf** *the GR65 and GR40 coincide.)* About 1km later turn R at junction, uphill towards woods. Fork L at next fork, turn L at next junction and then, when track levels out, follow path to a T-junction.

When you reach a tarred forest road turn L along it. After 100 metres fork R down grassy track, descending gradually all the time. Reach a road, cross it and turn R down a second road (behind D589) leading into hamlet of…

Pilgrim path between Liac and Lic

4.5km Le Chier 1050m (20.5/721.5)
♣ by *mairie*. CH La Remise, tel 04 71 57 29 37 & 06 60 38 25 34, open all year.

KSO(L) in centre at tall wayside cross (where road bends round to R) down tarred lane alongside a *couderc* (a sort of village green). Lane > walled, continuing to descend, with fields on either side. Fork R 200 metres later down wide FP, descending steadily all the time. Pass turning (back L) marked 'Croix du Grand Rocher' and KSO. Around 200 metres later, when track starts to go uphill, turn L down wide FP, which > a narrow walled lane then a forest path, winding its way steeply down to the valley bottom where it crosses a wooden bridge by an old mill over the **Ruisseau du Rouchoux**. *(NB This section could be very slippery in wet weather.)* Continue on other side, passing in front of houses. Tarred lane climbs gently and joins D589 coming from back R. Turn L along it into village of…

3km Saint-Privat-d'Allier 890m (23.5/718.5)
Shops, hotel, Gîte d'Etape La Cabourne at end of village (tel 04 71 57 25 50, open 15 Mar–15 Nov, 53pl K). Gîte-Bar le Kompost'L (tel 04 71 57 24 78, open all year 7/7 but X Mon Oct–May). Gîte-Bar-Snack l'Acrobat, tel 04 71 06 17 47 & 0 50 93 29 20, open all year). Gîte d'Etape Le Château (tel 04 71 02 10 55 & 06 17 41 31 41 76, mid Mar to end Dec, 10pl). Gîte La Petite Place

Chapelle Saint-Jacques, Rochegude

(tel 04 71 57 23 95 & 06 63 12 20 54, May–Sept. Municipal campsite (tel 04 71 57 22 13, 1 May–15 Oct), another bar (X Thurs), two shops (7/7 but X Mon out of season), OT, ♣. Romanesque church, remains of château.

To continue, KSO(R) ahead at junction in centre of village between café and bakery, pass *mairie* (R) then turn L at next junction onto another minor road, veering L then, at bend *(three very large crosses and picnic table to R)*, fork L onto FP along side of hill with wall to LH side. Reach D301 by iron cross, turn R then L 100 metres later, after town place-name board and large electric pylon, onto small FP downhill which > a small walled lane. Cross stream and go uphill again to road (short-cutting bend on road). *(In winter, however, or in very wet weather, you might consider staying on the road until the path crosses it again as the FP may be flooded, like walking down a stream.)* Reach small FB, cross stream and KSO uphill to road again. Cross over and continue on other side up to a minor road.

Turn R here, then L almost immediately at a crossing opposite a large house, up wide cobbled walled lane. About 200 metres later turn L onto tarmac lane past small groups of buildings *(this is **Combriaux***: *Gîte d'Etape L'Estou (tel 04 71 09 58 91 & 06 48 12 63 80, 12pl, all year, camping possible)*; 200 metres after that KSO at fork, and then 100 metres later, by bend in road, fork R up FP uphill. Reach minor road again shortly afterwards, turn R along it for 500 metres then, by sharp RH bend, fork R up FP into the woods, // to road below. Return to road 200 metres later and look out for FP to L *(view of tower in Rochegude suddenly comes into view ahead)* and fork L down it through woods. About 400 metres later emerge at crossing at entrance to…

3km Rochegude 967m (26.5/715.5)

Tower, tiny chapel dedicated to St James perched on top of rocky belvedere, the only surviving remains, apart from the tower, of a 13th-century castle complex. Wooden statue of St James pilgrim inside. Commanding views on a clear day. (Beware of straying too far away from chapel if foggy as there are very steep drops on two of its sides.)

To see chapel and tower go up grassy track ahead. To continue, turn L downhill.

Go down rocky FP, which descends steadily and steeply (the descent from here down to Monistrol can be very slippery in wet weather). KSO(L) at fork. When you reach a road (at entrance to hamlet of **Pratclaux** – ⚶ *Gîte d'Etape de la Ribeyre, tel 06 63 46 37 09, 13pl, 15 Mar–30 Sept; CH tel 04 71 57 21 45 & 06 61 51 71 10, Apr–Oct – here you can, in fact, continue on road for 1.4km directly to Monistrol), turn L for 50 metres then fork L (opposite a RH turn down a 'no entry' road) off road up short walled lane. At top turn L and immediately R onto tarred lane through hamlet. After last house on R, turn R down grassy walled lane, veering L, cross road at bottom and KSO down another walled lane on other side. Turn R onto road at end and 100 metres later turn L down unsurfaced track. At T-junction turn R down grassy lane which > a FP, winding its way steeply down to road (again cutting out zigzags). Turn L and KSO on road then turn R downhill. KSO. Pass turning to a small FP to L, indicating a direct route to the municipal gîte d'étape. If you are not taking this, KSO downhill into **Rue des Poseurs** *(named after those who worked laying the railway line, open 1870)*, veering R and leading to the D589. Pass *mairie* and veer L to cross box bridge *(built by Gustave Eiffel, of tower fame, in 1888)* over the river **Allier** into…

4km Monistrol-d'Allier 619m (30.5/711.5)

SNCF (Paris–Clermont-Ferrand–Arvant–Nîmes), Hotel-Restaurant Le Pain de Sucre (tel 04 71 57 24 50, Feb–Nov). Gîte d'étape at Centre d'Accueil, 1.5km before village on Le Puy road (tel 04 71 57 24, 12pl, open all year X Nov–Feb, K). Gîte d'étape & table d'hôte 'La Tsabone' (tel 04 71 06 17 23 & 06 15 15 38 39, 12pl, Mar–Oct, near church). Gîte d'étape/CH Le Repos du Pèlerin (tel 04 71 57 23 57 & 06 18 33 30 73, Mar–Nov). Municipal campsite by river, below railway station, (mid Jun– end Aug) Café, shop, PTT. Romanesque church, former priory of La Chaise-Dieu. Cross has carving of pilgrim. You are now in the region of the Margeride. *Note: from Monistrol-d'Allier (619m) to the road by the Domaine de Sauvage (1292m) it is 31km almost continuously uphill and from Monistrol to the separation with the GR412 after Montaure (6.5km) there is an ascent of 150m (nearly 1500ft); remember this when planning your next day's walk.*

Turn R on other side then L up **Rue des Lombards** (turn L here to visit church, then retrace your steps), veering R. Turn L at end then fork R down road at side of mill (signposted to 'La Madeleine, La Vallete'). Cross bridge over the river **Ance** and then KSO, climbing very steeply. *(Views over Allier gorge and beyond.)* The road zigzags its way uphill, passing first a stone wayside cross and then a metal one. At metal cross turn hard L up stony track to the **Chapelle de la Madeleine** (20m),

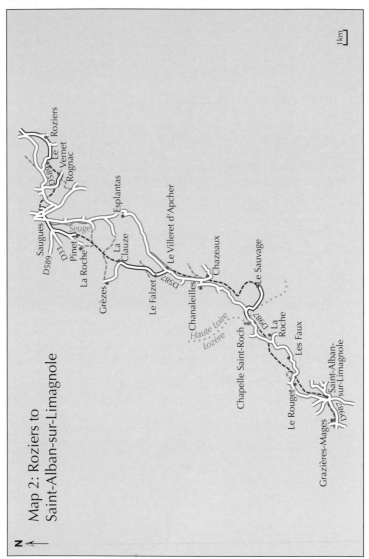

Map 2: Roziers to
Saint-Alban-sur-Limagnole

N ←

1km

thought to have been a grotto originally but faced with stone and made into a chapel in the 17th century.

Then continue very steeply up for another 200 metres to hamlet of **Escluzels**, turn R and then veer R after first house, pass *lavoir* (L) and another *métier à ferrer les boeufs* to R, with four pillars and remains of leather body and head straps. Turn L uphill on road and KSO. Around 800 metres later road forks: KSO(L) uphill again, but after 150 metres turn hard L up wide forest path, short-cutting hairpins in road. Cross road at top, go up narrow path and cross road again and fork L uphill off road on other side up another forest track. Continue uphill, zigzagging steeply, to…

Looking back over Monistrol-d'Allier

4km Montaure 1022m (34.5/707.5)
View over to Rochegude on opposite side of valley.

When you reach a road, KSO(L) ahead *(iron cross on R, ♣)*, veer L again at junction shortly afterwards (modern concrete wayside cross on R: this is the junction with the GR412). Continue on road (L) for 300m, then turn L onto track. KSO, ignoring turns, climbing gently all the time. *(Good views all round.)* When you reach the hamlet of **Roziers** *(1.9km, 1066m, ♣ by lavoir on entry)* KSO(R) on road through village. At a road junction after 0.6km turn R downhill *(the GR412 goes on ahead, to Pouzas)* to the village of…

3.5km Le Vernet de Saugues 1050m (38/704)
Fountain

Continue through village, turn L *(uphill)* at *fountain* and KSO(L). Around 30–40 metres later turn R by iron cross perched on top of large rock. KSO(L) along gravel track straight ahead, to LH side of woods. About 800 metres later track > FP through fields. KSO and reach road coming from back L at approach to hamlet of **Rognac**. KSO ahead, pass iron cross (L) and continue ahead uphill. About 700 metres later, when road bends round to R by some houses, KSO(L) down green lane towards HT pylon. Continue down it, descending gradually all the time until you reach the D589. *(Note the unusual wooden sculptures to LH side of road, made from single trees. You will also see several others in this area.)* Cross the road and descend, on the **Rue des Cimes**, into...

4.5KM SAUGUES 960M (42.5/699.5)

Population 2000. Two hotels, bars, restaurants, shops, banks (+ATM), PTT, OT 9 Cours Gervais. Gîte d'étape communal, Rue de la Margeride (in centre of village, tel 04 71 77 80 62 & 06 65 15 04 32, 15pl, Easter–Nov, K). Accommodation (+ meals if required) at Centre d'Accueil, Rue des Tours Neuves (tel 04 71 77 60 97, 40pl, 1 Mar–24 Oct). Gîte à la ferme, Rue des Roches (tel 04 71 77 83 45, 15 Mar–15 Oct. Several CH (see *Miam Miam Dodo*). Campsite by river (tel 04 71 77 80 62, Easter–1 Nov).

Detail of tree sculpture with St James, entering Saugues

Romanesque church of Saint-Médard (and treasury), diorama de Sainte-Bénilde (a local saint), 13th-century Tour des Anglais with dungeon, numerous old houses. Saugues was the meeting point of pilgrims coming from the Auvergne via secondary routes and had a 12th-century pilgrim hospital (now an old people's home near the Chapelle des Pénitents) dedicated to St James.

If you have not already come across this phenomenon before you may be surprised to encounter (from the south of France and onwards) the first of many church and other public clocks (on civic buildings, for example) that strike *twice* for every hour (and therefore 24 times at midday and midnight...). Since many of them do not have the 'ding-dong-ding-dong' prelude to the actual hour strokes that are customary on British clocks, the first series is, in effect, an announcement that the hour is going to strike – for the second time – after a couple of minutes' pause.

At entrance to town veer L along **Rue de la Demoiselle**, then turn R along **Route du Puy** (main street) into centre. Turn L into **Rue Saint-Gervais** and continue via **Rue Saint-Médard, Place Joseph Limozin, Rue de la Margeride** (D589 in direction of *Le Malzieu*) and **Route Mont du Mouchet** *(campsite below R)*. Cross D585 at bottom *(note another very large wooden sculpture with pilgrim motifs)* and then bridge over river **Seuge**. About 150 metres later turn L down track. At road 700 metres after that turn L uphill, forking L at metal wayside cross 0.6km before hamlet of **Le Pinet** (1020m). KSO on road through hamlet. At last house road > track, veering R, climbing gently towards conifer woods ahead. About 200 metres later KSO(L) at fork. KSO, ignoring turns. After reaching a col the track levels out and then descends gently to cross stone bridge over the **Seuge**. KSO(R) on other side. Track > walled lane, climbing gently all the time. Ignore turns to L and R. At the top of a hill 700 metres later, enter...

7.5km La Clauze 1095m (50/692)
Gîte/CH à la ferme Au Repos d'Antan (tel 04 71 77 66 56 & 06 66 47 67 18, 15 Apr–15 Oct). Gîte d'Etape des Pèlerins de Margeride (tel 06 81 20 66 08, 6pl, 15 Mar–15 Nov). Refuge Maison de la Béate (shelter) opp fountain. Bar/shop. Free-standing tower is the only surviving remains of the late 12th-century castle.

At junction of five tracks at entrance to hamlet, KSO ahead on minor tarred road coming from back R. When you meet another (bigger) road coming from back R, near tower, KSO along it through village and continue on road (D335). At top of hill (five-way junction) fork L ahead downhill on minor tarred road to...

2.5km Le Falzet 1134m (52.5/689.5)
Gîte d'étape (tel 04 71 74 42 28, 7pl, 1 Mar–1 Nov, K). Picnic area behind gîte.

Continue through hamlet to road, turn L uphill and 40 metres later fork R up track leading to...

1.5km Villeret-d'Apcher (54/688)
Gîte d'Etape l'Auberge des 2 Pèlerins, run by two former pilgrims (tel 06 07 28 06 44, 19pl, 1 Mar–15 Nov, K). ♣

At entrance to village, track > tarred road. Cross D587 (slightly staggered junction) and go down narrow street on other side, opposite gîte d'étape, veering L, and then turn R downhill to cross river **Virlange** and KSO(L) ahead on other side, uphill. Continue uphill and near top, at crossing, turn R, veering L downhill.

Fontaine Saint-Roch

Reach T-junction with tarred lane ahead and turn L onto sandy track, continuing along side of hill. Reach small tarred road and turn R up to the farm at…

2.5km Contaldès 1143m (56.5/685.5)

Pass to L of farm, KSO(L) ahead up a walled lane, along a line of telegraph poles.

Village across valley to R, with cemetery, is Chanaleilles (1km, 1170m), with shop (7/7), Café du Pont (does meals; ask here for gîte d'étape, tel 04 71 74 41 63, 12pl, 15 Mar–15 Nov). CH/bar, Place de la Mairie (tel 04 71 74 41 74, all year). Interesting Romanesque church. To go there, fork R on tarred lane in Contaldès, instead of continuing straight ahead.

KSO to **Chazeaux** (800m, snack bar 7/7 Apr–Sept) and then turn L in centre of village, steeply uphill then turn R, still uphill but then levelling out. Reach junction with minor road then continue on other side on sandy track, undulating. KSO. Turn L at fork, veering R. KSO. Enter woods and KSO. Go through small gate and KSO. About 1.5km later go through second gate and turn L uphill on other side. Some 250 metres later turn R onto more level track and 300 metres after that leave woods. Around 250 metres later turn R through wooden gate onto farm track, winding its way through pastureland. *(The small isolated stone house to R is a buron, a shepherd's bothy used during the summer when cattle and flocks of sheep are brought up to graze in the high pasturelands.)* KSO and 600 metres later reach the…

5.5km Domaine du Sauvage 1292m (62/680)

A historic monument, the former Domerie (hospital run by a religious order) des Templiers, dating from the 13th century. Gîte d'étape, tel 04 71 74 40 30, 40pl, all year, K, no meals available but food for sale.

Pass farm buildings and then veer round to R by small lake and continue through woods. KSO to road by ski-chalet Saint-Roch and then turn L. KSO for 300 metres to **Fontaine Saint-Roch** *(site of 13th-century oratory as well as pilgrim hospital from 12th to 17th centuries, after which it fell into ruins)* with picnic site. About

300 metres later, at border of the *départements* of the Haute Loire (that you are leaving) and the Lozère (that you are now entering) reach...

3.5km Chapelle Saint-Roch 1280m (65.5/676.5)

♣ Also known as **Chapelle de l'Hospitalet du Sauvage**, this was a hospital for pilgrims and travellers, founded at this col in 1198, and originally dedicated to St James (chapel was next to present fountain). The chapel was rededicated to St Roch after the Wars of Religion (1562–98), but then fell into ruin. The new chapel built at the end of the 19th century was destroyed by a cyclone in 1897, and the present one was rebuilt in 1901. Usually locked, but a grille in the door enables you to see inside. Statue of St Roch with his dog above the altar. Sunday Mass 11.15am Jul–Sept and an annual local pilgrimage on 16 Aug, the feast day of St Roch. Refuge on road (clean and well kept, fountain at rear) is a useful place to rest, eat or shelter in bad weather.

About 100 metres later, when road bends R, KSO(L) downhill on wide grassy track. (Waymarks tell you there are now 'only' 1478km left to Santiago...) *The section from here down to Saint-Alban is easy walking.* Continue through semi-shaded woods. At end cross another track and KSO on walled lane. After 2km cross D987.

KSO on other side, gently downhill all the time. Almost at the valley bottom there is a junction with the GR4 *(you can also turn L here for the two gîtes)*, and the GR65 and GR4 continue for a short stretch in common. Cross the river **Gazamas** at the bottom and KSO uphill into pinewoods. At junction with forest road, gîte d'étape and also hotel accommodation at **Les Faux** signposted to L *(L'Oustal de Parent, 10min away, tel 04 66 31 50 09, 19pl, 15 Apr–30 Sept, K).* KSO(L) along wide forest road joining from back R *(here the GR65 and GR4 part company again).*

KSO, slightly downhill all the time. When the road veers L, KSO(R) ahead down grassy lane. This leads downhill all the time. At T-junction (and with road below you now) turn R and 700 metres later reach the D987 again (♣ at crossing) in the hamlet of...

6km Le Rouget 1017m (71.5/670.5)

Gîte d'Etape à la Ferme la Croix du Plô, on GR65 500 metres after leaving village (tel 04 66 31 53 51 & 06 33 55 61 03, 12pl, all year, K).

The village takes its name from the red stone in the area. From here onwards the style of building changes and the red-tile roofs characteristic of the area up to and including Saugues give way to grey slate. Picnic area 500 metres further on on GR.

Cross road and veer R down minor road which > track. At bottom (100 metres later), KSO(L) on minor road coming from back R, pass metal wayside cross and KSO. At bottom of hill (end of hamlet) turn R down track which passes under HT cables. When this bends L at farm building *(Gîte d'Etape La Croix de Plô is here)*, KSO(R) down smaller track which leads to the D987 (coming from back R) at entry to **Saint-Alban-sur-Limagnole**. At junction in front of you veer L down minor road marked 'Hôpital' and with football pitch on L (this is the **Chemin de Compostelle**). Turn R at end, veering L then R round to front of hospital, downhill all the time. Pass in front of château *(turn R up steps, then up more steps for OT inside)*, continue downhill then turn L down flight of steps. After that either go down a second set of steps into the **Grand'Rue** or turn R and then L into it.

3.5km Saint-Alban-sur-Limagnole 950m (75/667)

Small town (population 2000) with two hotels (all year), four CH (all year), shops, restaurants, bars. Gîte d'étape privé, 14 Grand'Rue (tel 04 66 31 58 69 & 06 32 24 43 17, 10pl, all year, K). Gîte d'Etape La Penote, 19 Route de Saugues (tel 06 88 24 51 32, 4pl, all year, K). Accueil bénévole La Maison du Pèlerin, 37 Grand'Rue (tel 04 66 45 74 33, 1 Apr–30 Oct, 13pl, donation). Gîte d'étape on top floor of Hôtel du Centre (tel 04 66 31 50 04, 10pl), bank (with ATM), OT (in castle, Rue de l'Hôpital). Campsite at end of town (1 Mar–1 Nov), 500 metres after GR turn-off. Romanesque church of Saint-Alban in town centre (red sandstone and polychrome brick). Château (various dates) is now part of the regional psychiatric hospital.

In **Grand'Rue** turn R in front of church, then L down its side (ie when facing entrance) and L down **Rue de la Tournelle** to the **Hôtel de Ville**. Turn L along road (**Rue de la Baysse**) to D987 and turn R along it for 400m, turning R at end of town up gravelled lane just after sports ground and town exit boards. *(Campsite marked 500 metres further on on road.)* Go up lane through trees, uphill to tall stone cross at top then downhill, ignoring turns, to road in hamlet of...

2km Grazières-Mages 930m (77/665) ⚓

Turn hard L along road, veer R *(at iron cross in front of you)* downhill and then veer L to cross river **Limagnole**. Cross D587 and veer R steeply uphill on gravel path through semi-shaded woods, levelling out onto an open plateau at the top. Reach road in hamlet of **Chabannes** (2km) and veer R along it downhill *(note stocks on RH side)*, passing (R) another of the tall stone crosses typical of the Lozère, and KSO.

Map 3: Saint-Alban-sur-Limagnole to Nasbinals

N ←

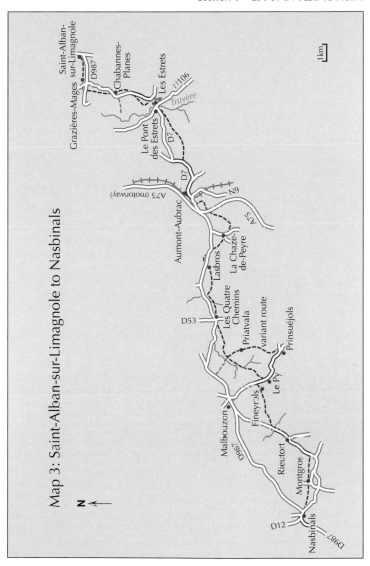

Saint-Alban-sur-Limagnole

Grazières-Mages

D987

Chabannes-Planes

Les Estrets

i/106

Truyère

Le Pont des Estrets

D7

A75 (motorway)

D7

N9

Aumont-Aubrac

N75

La Chaze-de-Peyre

Lasbros

Les Quatre Chemins

D53

Priatvala

Variant route

Prinsuéjols

Malbouzon

D987

Fineyrols

Le Py

Rieutort

Montgros

D12

Nasbinals

D987

1km

When road veers L at second stone cross (small), KSO(R) down shady lane along line of telegraph poles, then turn second R at staggered junction on track coming from road at back L. Continue on ridge *(good views)*, enter woods and descend, gradually at first and then more steeply, down to road, turning L and then R round church in...

5.5km Les Estrets 940m (82.5/659.5)

Gîte d'Etape Le Gevaudan (tel 04 66 45 61 90 & 06 88 90 97 89, 20pl, 25 Mar–10 Oct, also CH), Bar du Pont (X Wed, does food), phone box, fountain. Formerly a commandery of the order of St John of Jerusalem, controlling the passage over the Truyère; hence its name: 'détroit' = 'straits'. Present church dates from 1866, replacing previous one (although plaque on wall refers to 'chapelles' being rebuilt); statue of St Roch inside, and lectern has carvings of scallop shell, scrip and pilgrim staff.

Turn R along road (D7) *(church to R)* and continue through village *(note small stone cross with figure of Christ on LH side)*, veering L *(gîte signposted to R)* to D806. Cross over and veer R to cross old bridge over the **Truyère** in hamlet of **Le Pont des Estrets** (1km).

Turn L up track between two houses and continue steeply uphill. After 1km reach minor road at a bend *(iron cross)* and turn L downhill into hamlet of **Bigose**. *(Snack bar/hotel/gîte Les Granges de Bigose, tel 04 66 47 12 65, 15 Mar–11 Nov; picnic area.)* Veer round to R and KSO(R) along track, undulating along RH side of valley then veering to LH side before veering L uphill along side of woods, climbing steadily all the time. Enter wood and continue to climb uphill continuously.

Emerge into small clearing at top and KSO(R) along similar track coming from back L by modern wayside cross, slightly downhill. Continue ahead, pass metal wayside cross and then start climbing again until, 1km later, you reach the...

4km Route D7 1096m (86.5/655.5)

Turn R along D7 for 100 metres then turn hard L on gravel track. Opposite an industrial building fork R down shady walled lane with small stone cross with scallop shell at start, // to road. *(Note the prayer and scallop shell on tree to L.)* After 1km reach road again at iron cross, turn R down minor road (**Route de la Margeride**) for 400m, rejoining road again by junction with iron cross. KSO and at bend continue ahead down some steps into **Rue du Barri Haut** (gîte d'étape on RH side), cross over main road by large iron cross, continue on other side, go down **Rue du Prieuré** and turn L down side of OT to church. Turn L uphill *(note 1708 Mater Dolorosa in niche at first-floor level on L)* and go up to **Place du Portail (Hôtel de Ville)** in the centre of town, where there is a statue of the Bête du Gévaudan, *the beast renowned in the area as being responsible for the mysterious disappearance of some 50 people between 1765 and 1768; a lynx killed near Saint-Flour in 1787 was thought to have been the culprit.*

Chapelle de Bastide, Lasbros

3km Aumont-Aubrac 1050m (89.5/652.5)

Small town (population 1111) with two hotels; shops, cafés, bank (ATM by PTT), OT Rue du Prieuré. a) Gîte d'étape & CH La Ferme du Barry at entrance to the town, 9 Rue du Barry (tel 04 66 42 90 25 & 06 71 83 17 46, 30pl, all year). b) Gîte d'Etape Les Sentiers Fleuris, 7 Place du Portail (tel 04 66 42 94 70 & 06 42 64 80 02, 20pl, 15 Mar–31 Oct), also CH. c) Bar-gîte d'Etape Le Calypso in Aubrac Hôtel, Place du Forail (tel 04 66 42 99 00). d) Gîte Chemin Faisant, 15 Avenue du Peyre (tel 06 24 83 19 36 & 06 86 52 57 47, 14pl, all year). Two CH. Municipal campsite, Route du Languedoc. SNCF (train service now replaced by buses) to Clermont-Ferrand.

Former Benedictine Priory and Romanesque church of Saint-Etienne; restored in 1994, it now has splendid modern stained-glass windows.

Continue ahead on main road (that is to your R, **Avenue du Peyre**) and then fork R at war memorial on **Route d'Aubrac**. Go under railway line and turn L along minor road alongside it. About 200 metres later fork R up fenced lane leading to side of woods *(iron cross to L)* and KSO uphill, passing under HT cables. Turn R at top along road for 300 metres and then fork L to track (just after town name board). After 150 metres turn L and then R to go under motorway via a specially placed 'pilgrim tunnel' *(referred to locally as the 'Saintjacqueduc')*. Turn R on other side and then L to continue on a level track leading to woods. Continue along it, descending gradually to the **Route de la Chaze** (3.5km, *stone cross*, 1016m). Turn R along it for 1km (tip of church spire visible), KSO(R) at fork by cemetery and enter village of…

4.5km La Chaze-du-Peyre 1040m (94/648)

⚓. Two crosses in square in front of church, one 18th-century, the other 19th. Church of varying periods including St James's chapel.

Continue through village on road, passing church and veering R uphill, forking L between drinking trough and iron cross onto minor road signed 'Lasbros'. After 1km, at junction with D987 *(the old Roman road from Lyon to Toulouse – the* Voie d'Agrippa *– that would have been used by pilgrims in centuries gone by)*, reach the tiny **Chapelle de Bastide** *(not always open), begun in 1522 but reworked several times and sometimes referred to as 'La Chapelette'. (Shortly afterwards there is a wooden bus shelter, useful for a rest in bad weather, with another in the hamlet of Lasbros ahead.)* Continue on D987 into the hamlet of…

2.5km Lasbros 1091 (96.5/645.5)

Gîte (tel 04 66 47 08 94 & 06 75 37 20 21, all year, K). Fountain.

At end of hamlet fork L down minor tarred road. Continue downhill, KSO(R) at fork and continue uphill, road > track. KSO, fork L at T-junction, then turn L along minor road which also > a track. KSO, gently uphill all the time *(and watching out carefully for hunters with shotguns in the open season…)*. Pass first turning (L) to **Prinsuéjols** *(waymarked in red and yellow)* and KSO, veering R at very end to road junction known as…

4km Les Quatre Chemins 1174m (100.5/641.5)

Gîte d'Etape Aux Quatre Vents (tel 04 66 45 72 16 & 06 64 19 34 03, 13pl, 20 Mar–15 Oct). Café 'Chez Régine' (picnic with own food possible if purchasing a drink), sandwiches, all year.

Continue ahead on road to join D587 coming from back R then turn L down forest track. KSO 100 metres later down track fenced in with barbed wire through grassy plateau land, undulating, with occasional shade. *(In bad weather some parts of the track are very boggy.) Like other areas of the Margeride and the Aubrac, this is a paradise of wildflowers in the springtime.* Shortly after, track > a walled lane. You reach a T-junction with another walled lane to L, opposite cattle pen on R and with grove of trees ahead.

If you want to sleep in the gîte d'étape in **Prinsuéjols** *(1205m, 3.8km due south, bar/restaurant, tel 04 66 32 52 94, 50pl, all year) you can turn L here and follow the red-and-yellow balises of the GR du Pays known as the 'Tour des Monts d'Aubrac'. If so, you do not need to retrace your steps the following morning but can take the D73 northwards from Prinsuéjols in the direction of Malbouzou,*

Communal oven, Rieutort d'Aubrac

passing through the hamlet of **Pratviala**; *this road crosses the GR65 further to the west, just after the Ferme des Gentianes.* Otherwise, KSO. Go through four *cledos*, cross road leading to L to **Pratviala** and KSO. Track > unsurfaced road (more *cledos*). When you reach a bend in the road *(iron cross ahead, the Croix de Ferluc)* continue to road (farm to R) and KSO on minor tarred road. About 100 metres later reach crossroads with the D73 at the...

5km Ferme des Gentianes 1192m (105.5/636.5)
Farm (tel 04 66 32 52 77) does meals, has gîte d'étape (19pl, 1 Apr–30 Sept, K, camping possible) and CH.

KSO ahead, go through hamlet of **Fincyrols** (♣ *and picnic area to L; CH La Rose de l'Aubrac, tel 04 66 45 78 55 & 06 08 31 55 61, all year*) and fork R uphill at end (> track), wending its way through grassy plateau land strewn with big boulders. KSO, ignoring turns. Track > grassy walled lane, climbing gradually across the deserted Aubrac plateau. *(Splendid views on a clear day.)* At the top of the plateau (1273m, **Roc des Loups**) KSO alongside wall on L, descending gradually. This is the **Grande Draille**, *a historic drove road*, veering R (to become walled lane again) and then L. At T-junction with gravelled lane turn R, and 200 metres later turn L along minor road at the **Pont sur la Peyrade** and KSO to...

4.5km Rieutort d'Aubrac 1158m (110/632)

♣ CH 2km to L at Marchastel, on GR65A, tel 04 66 32 53 79. Note two granite drinking troughs, communal oven and the remains of another *métier pour ferrer le boeufs*.

A 20km variante route to Aubrac or directly to Saint Chely d'Aubrac – the GR56A plus GR6 and/or GRP – turns L here via Marchastel, Lac de Saint-Andéol, *Gallo-Roman site* Ad Silanum *and* Pendouliou-de-Fabrègues, *1359m. It is marked on the green series maps but is not waymarked and is an even more deserted route, only recommended in good weather and for experienced walkers.* Otherwise, continue on through village, veering R and KSO (1.8km) to junction with D900 at the **Pont de Marchastel** over the river **Bès**. Turn R over bridge and 60 metres later turn R up track. When you reach a road, veer R up it into village of…

3km Montgros 1234m (113/629)

Private gîte d'étape/hotel-restaurant La Maison de Rosalie (tel 04 66 32 55 14, 14pl in gîte, nine rooms in hotel, café).

Continue on road to end of village and at crossroads *(iron cross)* KSO ahead down track undulating between fields. Cross minor road and KSO uphill ahead. At crossing continue downhill to road *(stone cross)*. Turn R along D900 to…

3KM NASBINALS 1180M (116/626)

Three hotels, municipal gîte (Maison Richard, Rue Principale, tel 04 66 32 59 47 & 04 66 32 50 17, 19pl, 1 Apr–31 Oct, K), Gîte d'étape privé La Grappière (next to pharmacy, tel 04 66 32 15 60, 15pl, 15 Mar–15 Oct, K). Gîte d'étape in Centre d'Accueil (tel 04 66 32 50 42, 38pl, all year). Gîte de Caractère Lô (tel 04 66 32 92 69 & 06 80 28 51 12, 20pl, all year X 15 Nov–20 Dec, K). Gîte-Centre équestre des Monts d'Aubrac (on D12 500 metres towards Chaudes-Aigues, tel 04 66 32 50 65 & 06 77 51 03 25, 22pl, all year, RE). Camping municipal, Route de Saint Urcize (tel 04 66 32 51 87 & 04 66 32 50 17, 1 May–30 Sept). OT (tel 04 66 32 55 73, 7/7 in season, X Sun pm Oct–Jun), pharmacy, bank, *boulangerie, épicerie*, bars.

11th-century Romanesque church in local stone and style (statue of St Roch inside, together with wooden statues of various other saints): monument with a pair of crutches on its base is to Pierre Brioude ('Pierrounet'), a 19th-century bonesetter and manipulator of joints who is said to have treated over 10,000 people a year.

Map 4: Nasbinals to St-Pierre-de-Bessuéjouls

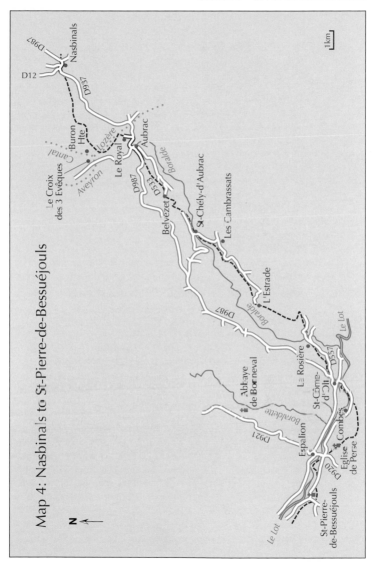

Modern sculpture on entering Aubrac

Cross D987, KSO down small street, veer R and then L around side of church (on D987) and follow road round uphill (municipal gîte d'étape on R) out of town in the direction of Aubrac. At the end (at **Le Coustat**) turn first R uphill onto tarred road which > stony track through woods. Veer L uphill (> walled lane). KSO(R) when you meet another track coming from back L, across undulating plateau land in direction of woods ahead.

About 1km later (at fork marked 'Nasbinals 3km, village 4km') fork L along wooded walled lane. At next fork turn R, cross bridge (**Pont de Pascalet**) over the river **Chamboulièe** and continue uphill. Around 100 metres before farm building ahead, turn R over stile, go uphill up side of field alongside wall (to your L), and 100 metres later turn L through gateway and continue alongside wall. Go over second stile and continue ahead uphill (away from wood to L), following line of tall wooden marker posts, to the…

6km Buron de Ginestouse Bas 1303m (122/620)
Another *buron* (bothy) used during the summer months when shepherds and their flocks were up on the plateau, returning to the valleys in the autumn.

Two small stone houses to R. Go over another stile and KSO ahead, in direction of small group of woods ahead and three small buildings away up the hill to your R ahead *(Ginestouse Haut)*. When you reach a wall, go through fourth stile and KSO alongside wall (on your L). *(NB All these stiles have cledos next to them but while they are easy enough to open they are often very tricky to shut!)* When the wall veers L at woods, follow it round and then KSO above (and // to) woods to your L. Then veer R slightly uphill to follow another wall (again on your L) uphill. Follow wall round to your L, pass between two wooden gateposts.

The blunt, cone-shaped hill above R is the Trois Evêques, the border of three bishoprics in the old days, and today the borders of the départements of the Cantal, the Lozère and the Aveyron, as well as of the old regions of the Auvergne, the Aubrac and the Midi-Pyrenees. From here you leave the Lozère and until just past Conques you are in the Aveyron.

Go through cattle pen (gates at both ends) and KSO alongside wall to your L. Go downhill slightly, through a *cledo* and then KSO ahead uphill (shelter – *abri* – at top) up a very wide walled lane, the **Grande Draille** again. Continue ahead on this, descending to the road *('Village de vacances Royal-Aubrac', a former sanatorium, to R, tel 05 65 44 28 41, open all year, also has gîte d'étape)*. Cross road and continue on path on other side. *(Modern sculpture, erected 2006, has text 'dans le silence et la solitude' on its LH side and, on R, 'on n'entend plus que l'éternité').* At crossing 300 metres later, turn R uphill for church, tower (with gîte d'étape communal inside) and village of...

3KM AUBRAC 1307M (125/617)

Hôtel-restaurant de la Domerie (tel 05 65 44 28 42, X 15 Nov–15 Dec), two other restaurants (summer only), café (4 Apr–11 Nov), OT. Gîte d'étape communal in La Tour des Anglais (tel 05 65 44 21 15, 16pl, open mid May to mid Sept only, K). CH with 14pl dormitory (tel 05 65 48 78 84, X 15 Nov–15 Dec). CH 'La Colonie' with small *épicerie* (tel 05 65 51 64 79, all year).

The village of **Domerie d'Aubrac** was founded in 1120 by a Flemish knight, Adelard de Flandres, who was attacked by bandits on his way to Santiago and who almost died there in a storm on his return journey. In gratitude for his deliverance he founded Aubrac as a place of refuge for pilgrims. Church of Notre-Dame des Pauvres has a large panel painting in two parts on the inside wall (1993–94), depicting the history of the Domerie d'Aubrac, from its founding to the late 20th century. The church, plus two other buildings now privately owned, is all that remains of the monastery. Tour des Anglais, botanical garden.

From here you have the option of a 26km route, waymarked in light blue, direct to **Espalion** via the Cistercian **Abbaye de Bonneval** (simple gîte d'étape, attended by volunteer *hospitaliers* during Jul and Aug, 6pl, in its Tour Saint-Jacques, tel evening before on 05 65 44 48 83, donation; maps at end of *Miam Miam Dodo*). Otherwise, from here to Saint-Chély-d'Aubrac you descend steeply, dropping some 500m in 8km. The scenery changes after this, the vast open plateau giving way to gorges and more woods before entering the Lot valley in Saint-Côme-d'Olt.

Leave Aubrac along the D987 (west). After 800 metres fork L off road down grassy track. KSO, descending steadily all the time, KSO twice when track joins from back R.

The yellow-flowered plant, approximately 1m high and seen growing everywhere around here, is gentiane, whose root is used to make Suze (a liqueur). After large wooden cross fork L on grassy track then at junction fork L downhill, becoming

Large wayside cross near Belvezet

a walled lane *(view of hamlet of Belvezet below and remains of castle perched on top of pillar-like rock)*. When you reach two extremely large rocks on hill immediately in front of you, fork R down FP, veering L and then R to road in hamlet of…

4km Belvezet 1144m (129/613)

Turn L along road and then hard R down lane 100 metres later. Then turn R and veer R down narrow walled lane downhill. Reach crossing of similar tracks and KSO. About 1km from Belvezet, cross the **Aude** and continue L on other side, descending steadily all the time. About 1.5km later pass farm on L (**La Vayssière**) and track > a tarmac lane. *(If you want to go to the Gîte Saint-André or the campsite in Saint-Chély, look out for FP on L leading downhill straight there.)* Reach road 200 metres later at a U-bend in it. Turn L, and KSO down it to junction with main street in **Saint-Chély** and turn R along it. To continue, turn L by PTT. To go to municipal gîte (further along street on L), KSO.

4KM SAINT-CHÉLY-D'AUBRAC 808M (133/609)

Small town with two hotels, restaurants, shop, bar, OT Rue de la Tour, PTT (+ATM), ♿. Gîte d'étape communal, Route d'Espalion (tel 05 65 44 21 15, 26pl, 1 Apr–31 Oct, K). Gîte d'Etape Saint-André (on L at entry to village, tel 05 65 44 26 87, 20pl, Mar–Oct, K). Bar Le Relais Saint-Jacques gîte & CH (tel 05 65 44 79 83 & 06 47 32 04 08). Gîte (6pl) & CH La Tour des Chapelains (tel 05 65 51 64 80 & 06 69 14 33 38, all year, next to OT). Camping municipal (15 May–31 Sept).

15th-century church has gold statue of St Roch pilgrim to LH side of wall behind altar (with a lot of scallop shells on his lapel, stick, hat, dog and gourd), a stained-glass window of St Roch pilgrim to the L of the apse and an unusual statue of St Peter with a cockerel at his feet.

From Saint-Chély-d'Aubrac to Figeac the GR65 and GR6 share the same route. Turn L by PTT (**Rue de la Mairie**), veering R into **Place Joseph-Bond** (in front of the *mairie*), turn L down side of the **Ecole Publique** into the **Rue du Pont des Pèlerins** (turn L here into **Rue de l'Eglise** to visit church then retrace your steps) and KSO down narrow street winding its way down to cross the old bridge over the **Boralde**. *(Note 16th-century cross on bridge with tiny pilgrim sculpted in its base, with his stick and rosary.)* Veer L, R and then L on other side to cemetery and then turn hard R at 'stop' sign onto a track leading uphill behind cemetery, which then > a walled lane, climbing steeply to the road (D19). Turn R uphill and 300 metres later (at L bend) KSO(R) downhill on minor road (signed 'Les Combrassats 2') through hamlet of **Le Recours**. About 200 metres later fork R off road down walled lane, which then > clear forest track, undulating through woods for 2km. KSO, then track climbs uphill again, > FP and rejoins road again. *(Note cross just below road.)*

Turn R along road (just before hamlet of **Combrassats**, 919m). KSO(R) at fork at entry to hamlet, then turn L behind first building on L down a walled lane, undulating, until you reach a disused farm at **Foyt**. Turn L up grassy lane to minor road and then turn R. KSO on ridge *(good views)*, ignoring turns to L and R, descending gradually. After 1.5km pass RH turning to **Bessières** and 150 metres later fork R off road by small wooden wayside cross onto grassy lane which continues along a ridge. KSO, veering L at end, to hamlet of…

5.5km L'Estrade (138.5/603.5)

Gîte d'étape 20mins off route (tel 06 75 59 00 91, 17pl, Apr–Sept). ⚐, shelter on R (with tables) in former communal oven.

Turn R along road *(handy seat)* which > unsurfaced track along ridge, descending gradually before veering L downhill through woods and later > walled lane between fields. About 4km later veer L at fork and then immediately, at junction with forest road, R (a staggered junction) down through woods again, descending fairly steeply until you cross **Le Cancels** (stream) via FB. Go uphill for 100 metres on other side and turn R on D557 (by 'stop' sign). About 100 metres later, at U-bend in another road, KSO ahead on other side by modern wayside cross between the two, down shaded track, forking R shortly afterwards down

Twisted church spire, Saint-Côme-d'Olt

FP leading to road. Turn L, cross bridge and KSO on road. Just after a bend and before a bridge you will see a sign pointing you steeply uphill on a sandy track. Here you can:

a) KSO ahead on road (D557, little traffic) for 3.5km to Saint-Côme-d'Olt, via the hamlets of **Martillergues** and **La Rigaldie**, an option suggested in bad weather, joining the high-level route when the **Rue de la Draille** joins the **Route de Castelnau**;

b) turn R uphill (very steep, signed 'La Rozière, Saint Côme'). *This option is a 'scenic detour', 2km longer and only worth it (on account of the views) in very clear, bright weather.* Go uphill, veering L, very steeply to **La Rozière** (fountain) at top. Turn L, go through hamlet and KSO(L) at end down walled lane. Around 300–400 metres later fork R down narrow walled lane, widening out. Follow it downhill, then up again, and after 500 metres at farm (**Grèzes**) continue on tarred lane. About 100 metres later turn L, then 50 metres after that turn L again onto sandy lane, until you reach the hamlet of **Cinqpeyres**. KSO(L) downhill at fork and continue towards road *(view of church spire ahead)*, but just before you reach road fork L to LH side of house down walled lane. Reach minor road and turn R along it, then L 200 metres later down **Rue de la Draille**.

At bottom turn R (**Route de Castelnau**) – *twisted spire of the church in Saint-Côme visible ahead from here* – and 20 metres later cross D987. *(Turn R here if you want to sleep in the Espace Angèle Mérici, Couvent de Malet, 500 metres before town on D987, phone ahead on tel 05 65 51 03 20, donation, rooms with 2–3 beds, 15 Jan–15 Dec).* Otherwise, KSO down lane on other side, veer L near end, turn R along minor road and then L through tunnel under road. KSO up **Rue Mathat** to **Place de la Porte Neuve** in...

10.5KM SAINT-CÔME-D'OLT 385M (149/593)

Hotel, shops, two restaurants, PTT, bank +ATM (Avenue d'Aubrac). Gîte d'étape communal del Romiou in Tour de Greffe (former prison, tel 06 35 59 16 05, 18pl, 1 Apr–31 Oct, K). Gîte La Halte d'Olt, 15 Route de Boraldette (tel 06 76 26 69

89 & 06 74 84 32 75, 8–10pl, Mar to 1 Nov, K). Gîte L'Antidote, run by former pilgrim, 22 Chemin des Plantiers (tel 06 41 90 62 89, 11pl, all year, donation). CH & 5pl gîte Le Jardin d'Eline, 3 Avenue d'Aubrac (tel 05 65 48 28 06 & 06 82 64 04 49, Mar–Nov). Camping Bellerive, Rue du Terral, near bridge (tel 06 98 22 91 59, 15 Apr–30 Sept, also rents caravans per night), OI.

Olt is the old name for the river Lot. Medieval town with very few modern buildings. 16th-century church of SS Côme and Damien has twisted spire (similar to the one in Chesterfield), 10th-century Chapelle des Pénitents, formerly with pilgrim hospital dedicated to St James adjoining, Ouradou (pilgrim oratory). 15th- and 16th-century houses, 14th-century château is now Hôtel de Ville. Gothic bridge. Historic information on street plaques: walking tour available from OT. Street names are given in both French and Occitan (eg Carrièra la Glèisa = Rue de l'Eglise).

Cross **Place de la Porte Neuve**, go under archway and turn L down **Rue du Greffe** to church. Continue (church L) through next arch (**Porte Théron**), turn L, cross **Place de la Barryère** and go down **Rue du Terral**, veering R at iron cross to cross old bridge over the **Lot**. (Stone cross on bridge.) Turn R almost immediately down minor road marked 'Combes'.

After 1km along river and after bridge you have a choice between a high-level detour to visit the **Vierge Notre-Dame de Vermus** (a viewpoint over the whole of the Lot valley with a statue of the Virgin on top, worth the climb in splendid weather but not otherwise), or continuing along the road to Espalion (little traffic – although this way you will miss the opportunity to visit the Romanesque Eglise de Perse unless you do a detour). If you decide to do this (ie not visit the Vierge de Vermus), KSO on road (marked 'Combes') which goes along the river **Lot**. Pass entrance to campsite just outside the town, join the **Rue de Perse** then go through park to riverside walkway, pass gîte d'étape (on R, in **Rue Saint-Joseph**) and reach the **Place du Plô** in the centre of **Espalion**.

Otherwise, to visit the Vierge de Vermus, fork L uphill up cobbled walled lane. Go through two gates and continue uphill (**Font-dels-Romieus**, a fountain used by pilgrims, to L uphill), veering R onto more level track and KSO. At meadow to R and three ruined buildings start climbing steeply. About 300 metres below the top, turn L onto wide forest track (uphill), passing under telegraph poles. At top turn R along grassy lane along ridge, which then descends gradually, veering R at end onto minor tarred road on hill. Turn R along it, undulating along ridge and passing under two sets of telephone/HT cables. (Good view over the Lot valley.)

Ignore RH fork and KSO steeply uphill all the time (track now > unsurfaced road), and at bend to R KSO ahead (marked 'Vierge de Vermus') up FP before descending (ahead) through woods on gravelled lane, turning L down narrow FP 20 metres later. After passing along LH side of fields, re-enter woods and KSO downhill all the time on wider, rocky FP. (To visit Vierge – 15min each way – turn R up steep but clear FP halfway down.) Emerge by house and KSO downhill along gravelled lane. *(View of Espalion ahead and château on hilltop.)* Cross bridge at bottom, behind the...

5km Eglise de Perse 353m (154/588)

Romanesque chapel of Saint-Hilarion (built on site near where he was beheaded by the Saracens in the eighth century) in red stone, former pilgrim halt and priory affiliated to Conques. Very fine carvings on outside, but church is often locked.

To visit church: turn L up side of it and enter via cemetery. To continue: KSO ahead into **Espalion**, via the **Chemin de Perse** then the **Rue de Perse** to the **Place du Plô**.

1KM ESPALION 342M (155/587)

Busy town (population 4614) with two hotels, four CH, shops, cafés, nine restaurants. Gîte d'Etape Au Fil de l'Eau, 5 Rue Saint-Joseph (tel 06 77 58 53 08 & 06 24 83 19 36, 20pl, K, all year). Gîte d'Etape Pont Vieux, 21 Rue Arthur Canel, tel 06 65 51 10 30 & 06 77 58 53 08, 8pl, K, all year). Gîte d'Etape La Halte Saint-Jacques, 8 Rue du Dr Trémolières, (tel 06 28 30 38 30, 18pl, 1 Apr–1 Oct). Gîte d'Etape Obrador, 7 Rue Arthur Canel (tel 05 65 48 71 52, 8pl, Apr–Dec). Gîte d'Etape La Sourse Saint Hilarien, 21 Rue de Fontsange (tel 05 65 44 12 29 & 06 81 73 98 98, 24pl, all year (200 metres before Chapelle de Perse)). Hotel-Restaurant de France, 36 Blvd Joseph Poulenc (tel 05 65 44 06 13, all year). Gîte-type accommodation, K, also available in the Centre d'Hebergement Municipal de Boraldes, 1.5km outside town on Route de Saint-Pierre (tel 05 65 48 04 08 & 06 07 27 68 67, all year). Camping municipal Le Roc de l'Arche, Le Forail, 2 May–3 Sept, also has caravans to rent per night. OT 23 place du Plô (tel 05 65 44 10 63).

Pilgrim bridge over the Lot, built in the reign of St Louis by the Frères Pontiff (a monastic bridge-building order). Renaissance château (1572) and Musée Vaylet, local museum.

From the **Place du Plô** continue ahead R on **Rue Arthur Canel** and reach **Rue Droite**. Cross the end of it (the old bridge is now on your R) and continue along **Quai du Lot**. Cross **Boulevard Joseph Poulenc** (new bridge on R) and continue along riverbank (400–500 metres) until you reach a wayside cross on R. Turn L up **Rue Dr Jean Capoulade** and then R into **Rue Eugène Salette**. KSO to very end of road where it > a lane after last house on L. KSO then turn L 100 metres later and then R, before lane goes uphill to become a tarred road leading to junction with D556. Turn R along it (quiet) for 1.5km then turn L up minor road at wayside cross, shortly before hamlet of **Coudoustrimes** ahead. KSO (500 metres), ignoring turns, to the…

Church of Saint-Pierre-de-Bessuéjouls

3km Eglise de Saint-Pierre-de-Bessuéjouls 335m (158/584)
One of the oldest churches on the route, 11th-century chapel of Saint-Michel on first floor of bell tower, with ninth-century altar and interesting capitals. Good place for a rest outside, ⚓. Gîte d'étape (6pl)/CH (tel 05 65 48 20 71, Mar–Oct X 20 Jun–5 Jul).

KSO on road then turn R over bridge *(fountain to L)*, R again beside *mairie* and immediately L uphill, passing to RH side of house, and continue up narrow FP which zigzags its way very steeply up hillside through woods. *(In very bad weather, however, when this route will be slippery, you can continue on the road, turn L 500 metres later and rejoin the GR65 in Verrières via the D556.)* Continue to climb very steeply (FP > wider, rockier/stonier, before becoming a stony track). *(Good view of Espalion to rear.)*

Shortly before the top it levels out and then joins a road at the top. Turn L along it, along ridge for 1km to hamlet of **Griffoul**, veer L at end and 200 metres later turn R off road onto level earth track *(splendid views)* which then undulates before becoming a walled lane along ridge. Later on it descends, gradually at first and then steeply. Turn hard L at T-junction, turn L at fork and 400 metres later reach gravelled lane by **Château de Beauregard**. Turn R downhill for 100 metres and turn L along minor road to junction by **Trédou** church *(⚓ by cemetery gate)*.

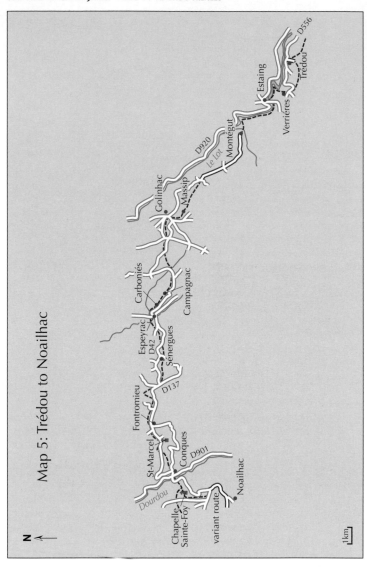

Map 5: Trédou to Noailhac

N ←

1km

D556
Trédou
Verrières
Estaing
Montégut
D920
Le Lot
Massip
Golinhac
Carboniés
Campagnac
Espeyrac
D42
Sénergues
D137
Fontromieu
St-Marcel
Conques
D901
Dourdou
Chapelle Sainte-Foy
variant route
Noailhac

Turn L by cemetery* (ie just before church) down minor road into hamlet of **Les Camps**. At end turn R onto tarmac lane between fields. About 300 metres later, at crossing, KSO ahead on other side on gravel track. Turn L at T-junction then reach minor road and turn R along it, into **Verrières**.

*You can, however, continue ahead to the church, veering R behind it and then L onto the D556, rejoining the GR65 1.5km later at junction by cross** in...

6km Verrières 460m (164/578)

KSO ahead down minor road, veering R, then turn L at junction *(cross**)*. Veer L and then R downhill, forking R *(note building with bell on top to L)* to cross bridge over stream, with shelter (and seats) opposite. Turn R and 100 metres later at junction with D100 turn L down it.

About 500 metres later, after turning to **La Roque**, either KSO on D100 to Estaing or fork very steeply uphill on stony track, which levels out after a while, becoming FP through woods, more or less // to road below you to R. Descend to the D100 and after 800 metres reach...

2KM ESTAING 320M (166/576)

Small town (population 1000) with two hotels, cafés, restaurants, shops, PTT +ATM. OT, 24 Rue François d'Estaing (tel 05 65 44 03 22). Hospitalité Saint-Jacques, 8 Rue du Collège (small lay community offering lodging to pilgrims, 16pl, donation, no reservations X families with children under 12 & groups (max 10pl), Apr–Oct, prayers morning and evening). Gîte d'étape communal (tel 06 44 95 52 14, 22pl, Apr–Oct, K). Gîte d'Etape Chez Anne, 3 Rue François d'Estaing (tel 07 87 96 68 75, 14pl, Mar–Oct, K). Gîte Chez Michèle, 3 Rue du College (tel 06 34 64 00 71, 6pl, May–Sept, K). CH 100 metres after bridge on GR65 (tel 05 65 44 71 51 & 06 70 38 42 01, Mar–Nov). CH 5 Rue François d'Estaing (tel 06 80 66 77 79, May–Sept). Camping municipal La Chantellerie, 2km north of town on D167 (tel 05 65 44 70 32, May–Sept).

Gothic bridge over the Lot. 15th-century château of the Counts of Estaing is now a convent. 15th-century church of Saint-Fleuret has stone cross outside depicting tiny pilgrim.

The GR65 does not go into the town, so to visit: turn R over bridge. To continue, energetic pilgrims have the option of a (4km) shorter route to Conques on the old GR6 via **Saint-Genies des Ers**, **Campuac** *(restaurant all year, shop, modern church*

Estaing

with fine stained glass) and **Larrigue**, rejoining the GR65 in **Campagnac** *(restaurant all year, shop)*, 3.5km before Espeyrac. To take this option, leave Estaing on minor road (marked 'Campuac') to LH side of chapel at end of bridge.

Otherwise, turn L and then immediately R at small chapel on L by bridge (staggered junction), down quiet shady minor road marked 'La Roquette'. This continues for 3km, undulating along the L bank of the **Lot**. At junction (**La Roquette** to R) KSO(L) on same road which then descends to cross bridge over the **Luzanne**. Turn R along road and 100 metres later turn hard L up very steep narrow FP through woods, the first of several shortcuts in the road's many hairpin bends. Turn L at top on road again uphill and 20 metres later, after hairpin, turn hard L up another FP, zigzagging up to road at a cluster of houses in…

5km Montégut 400m (171/571) ♠

Turn R for 20 metres then L up another narrow FP, which > forest track, to road at **Montégut Haut**. Turn L on road and continue uphill, climbing steadily. Pass turning to **Rion del Prat** (hard R) and then fork R to **Campredon**. At junction with road from back L just before hamlet of **La Sensaguerie** (530m, *pump to LH side of road*), road begins to level out *(splendid views if clear)*. Continue on road, undulating, mainly shady, then slightly downhill, ignoring turnings. Pass *lieu-dit* **Le Mas**. KSO(L) ahead at R turn to **Castilhac** and shortly before reaching hamlet of **Falguières** fork L uphill off road up grassy track to woods, which > forest track. Climb gradually on and through edge of woods. Cross minor tarred road and KSO ahead down grassy lane, entering woods again, undulating mainly, otherwise climbing steadily.

When you reach a junction at exit from woods (3km after leaving road), turn L uphill. This > a forest road leading, after 1km, to road in hamlet of **Massip** *with gîte d'étape L'Orée du Chemin (tel 05 65 48 61 10 & 06 71 38 07 57, 20pl, Apr–Oct, K)*. KSO on road for 200 metres then turn L into woods, just before bend. Reach road again, cross over and continue very steeply downhill on FP through woods to another road below. Turn L and shortly afterwards KSO(R) along lane through woods when road bends L. At T-junction with wayside cross 1km later, turn L uphill and then KSO(R) along road to hamlet of **Le Radal ⚓**. KSO for 300 metres to road and turn R along it in…

11km Golinhac 650m (182/560)

Shop, Camping Bellevue and Le Hameau de Saint-Jacques, with three gîtes d'étape (tel 05 65 44 50 /3, 43pl, 4 Apr–20 Oct, K), and bar-snack are all on L at entry to village, also CH (tel 05 65 51 63 68, all year).

Church of St Martin (statue of St Roch with *coquilles* inside) on site of foundations of ninth-century Benedictine abbey (note cross at entry to village with tiny pilgrim and staff on base).

To continue, pass shop *(gîte and campsite behind it)* and KSO on road to church, turn L and then hard L behind war memorial and immediately R up very minor road, forking L behind houses. Go up walled lane by last house, then up tarred lane, then at minor road turn R. At crossing KSO down grassy walled lane, veering L to road junction of D42 and D904 in hamlet of **Le Poteau**. KSO ahead along D42 (marked 'Espeyrac 9'). Around 400 metres later fork R onto grassy lane leading into the woods and uphill on forest track. *(There are a lot of wayside crosses in this section.)* At road in **Les Albusquiès** turn R and 50 metres later turn L downhill, L again, veer R and KSO(R) down grassy walled lane downhill, continuing between fields to road (1.5km). Turn L *(picnic area to R below)* and 500 metres later, at junction at top of hill, turn R (signed 'Espeyrac', *good views if clear)*. Continue on road, zigzagging down through hamlets of **Campagnac** (593m), **Le Soulié** *(Accueil Chretien du Soulié de Saint-Jacques, tel 05 65 72 90 18 & 06 42 35 69 01, 11pl, Easter to end Oct, donation)* and **Carboniés**. Continue L on road then, at bend, fork R onto FP through woods (**Camin d'Olt**) downhill again. KSO(R) at fork shortly afterwards, follow track round, cross bridge over river, veering L at fork on other side. Continue on walled lane, turn L onto small street at entrance to Espeyrac and reach road by *mairie*, church and gîte d'étape in…

8.5km Espeyrac 369m (190.5/551.5)

Hotel/bar/restaurant (tel 05 65 69 87 61, X 15 Oct–20 Mar), café, shop (behind hotel), fountain/♣ by church. Gîte d'étape communal behind *mairie* (tel 05 65 72 09 84 & 06 89 08 72 29, 12pl, all year, K).

Church of Saint Pierre has almost life-size statue of Saint-Roch pilgrim on L inside and also unusual statue of St Peter with a cockerel at his feet (on R inside).

Turn L, follow road round side of church to small square with restored well, then turn hard R, passing shop and hotel. Cross road and KSO on other side down road leading to cemetery, pass to L of it and continue on FP to cross FB over the river. Turn L on other side up FP winding its way uphill to minor road 800 metres later at staggered junction with wayside cross. KSO ahead and then KSO(L) at U-bend in another road. About 100 metres later fork L down grassy track, cross river again by new footbridge and turn R along D42 for 510 metres to hamlet of **Célis**. Turn L and then R up RH side of farm and KSO(R) up steep shady FP (> walled lane) and continue uphill; pass cemetery and enter village of…

3.5km Sénergues 506m (194/548)

Café (X Wed), PTT and other shops. Private gîte d'étape in Domaine de Sénos, large house on LH side of road at entry to village (tel 05 65 72 91 56, 33pl, 1 Feb–1 Nov, K). Picnic area with ♣ by church and pilgrim shelter (with ♣) on leaving village. Gîte l'Oustalet 400 metres from GR on leaving village (tel 05 65 69 83 96 & 06 79 69 02 75, 10pl, K, Apr–Oct).

Church of St Martin (statue of St Roch pilgrim inside on back wall, nice modern stained-glass windows) on site of ninth-century priory. Tour Carré.

Turn R up narrow lane to church *(shady square at side is a good place for a rest, good views)*. Pass church, turn L down main street and KSO(L) to end of village. Just after petrol pumps turn R up narrow FP by bus shelter and electricity transformer, cross road at top and KSO uphill up gravel lane. KSO ahead up another road at top, passing 'Abris Pèlerins' on L *(with WC, picnic seating, sink and wash basins, all under cover)*. Enter woods, climbing steeply all the time (this is the **Forêt Départementale de Sénergues**). Veer L on lane alongside edge of woods *(fields to R)* and track begins to level out.

On leaving woods KSO(L) along lane, undulating between fields. KSO until you reach road, turn L, 20 metres before five-way junction with D42 and D137 *(large modern wooden wayside cross)*. If you are tired or the weather is bad you can continue straight ahead on the D42, picking up the GR65 again 1.5km later (marked*, not much traffic) after it has done a 'loop'.

Turn R (at junction) along D137 for 750 metres and at RH bend turn L onto grassy lane along ridge between fields. Descend through woods to join unsurfaced track coming from back R and fork L almost immediately afterwards along grassy track through fields to rejoin D42*. Turn R (not much traffic) and KSO for 2km, almost level, on a ridge-like road with splendid views, until you come to the junction above the hamlet of…

5km Fontromieu 591m (199/543)

Here the D42 turns L but you KSO along minor road to…

1km Saint-Marcel 570m (200/542) ⚲

Church of Saint-Marcel (a pope, martyred in 309), but nothing is left of the original Romanesque building except the chapel; the present church was rebuilt in 1561 but only finally finished in 1875. The statue of St Roch as a pilgrim, with hat, scallops, stick and gourd (that was inside the church when an earlier edition of this guide was being prepared) seems to have disappeared. Stained-glass window above door has three scallop shells. There was a leprosarium here in the 17th and 18th centuries and a Chapelle St Roch built in 1629, at the height of the plague. This is the original pilgrim route, which ran along the ridge before descending to Conques in the valley below.

Leave Saint-Marcel and continue on ridge road for 1.5km to isolated farm at the *lieu-dit* **La Croix Torte**, a five-point junction at a place where several sets of telegraph poles and wires intersect. Turn L steeply downhill on gravel lane as far as a pair of gates, then pass to RH side of them down shady, narrow rocky walled lane, descending all the time. Path gradually widens out as you go. Reach a road on the outskirts of **Conques**, cross over to take *second* RH turn (cul-de-sac sign). KSO(L) at fork down pedestrianised **Rue Emile Roudié** and at next fork either KSO(R) on level for municipal gîte d'étape or KSO(L) downhill for abbey.

3KM CONQUES 280M (203/539)

Hotel, three CH, shop, bakery, restaurants, PTT +ATM, OT Rue du Chanoine Benazech (tel 05 65 72 85 00). Accueil Abbaye Sainte-Foy (Communauté des Prémontrés) in abbey has dormitory accommodation for pilgrims plus rooms (tel 05 65 69 85 12, 96pl, open all year, phone ahead). Gîte d'étape communal, Rue Emile Roudié, in former gendarmerie (tel 05 65 72 82 98, 30pl, Apr–Oct,

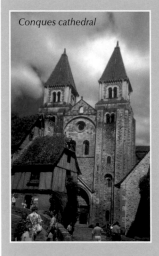

Conques cathedral

K). Camping Beau Rivage by river (tel 05 65 69 82 23 & 06 61 17 47 73, gîte in mobile homes, Apr–Sept).

The whole town is a historic monument so the *balises* are very discreet: wooden squares, carved, so watch out for them carefully. Abbey church (cathedral) of Sainte-Foy (Saint Faith): its origins date from the eighth century although the present-day building is from the 11th. Tympanum of the Last Judgement scene on the main doorway is a very fine example of Romanesque sculpture and the abbey also has a medieval treasury. The abbey became famous when the remains of Sainte-Foy (martyred in AD303 and famous for her ability to cure eye disorders) were brought here from the church on the outskirts of Agen (where she came from and was buried) by one Arivisius, a monk from Conques. He had apparently spent several years in Agen with the religious community whose duty it was to guard her remains. Gradually he gained their confidence, until one day an opportunity arose to steal the casket containing them and take them back with him to Conques. Here the relics attracted enormous numbers of pilgrims and led to the expansion of the cathedral to accommodate them.

Detail of tympanum, Conques cathedral (Photo: Marigold Fox)

From the church, fork L down the **Rue Charlemagne** *(paved)* and continue downhill, under the **Porte du Barry**. Pass turning (L) up to **Chapelle Saint-Roch** *(perched up on top of hill above L, good views back over Conques in evening sunlight)* and continue steeply down to the bottom of the hill. Cross the road and continue across old pilgrim bridge over the **Dourdou**. On other side continue on road for 200 metres then KSO ahead up FP through woods, climbing steeply. Cross road and continue uphill on other side to...

Modern stained glass of St James, Chapelle Sainte-Foy

1.5km Chapelle Sainte-Foy (204.5/537.5)
Site of a local pilgrimage, chapel built by a spring whose waters were reputed to be miraculous cures for eye complaints. Modern stained-glass window of St James as pilgrim inside. View of Conques.

Continue on FP, climbing until you come out onto a ridge. Then, at a junction of similar tracks 1.5km after the chapel, the GR65 divides into the main route and the *variante* (both waymarked):

a) What is now the main route is, in fact, another 'scenic detour', 5km longer than the more direct *variante* and involves 900m of *dénivelés* (changes of height). It is also less pilgrim-oriented as it misses out the Chapelle Saint-Roch and the Stations of the Cross leading up to it. Turn R here if you want to take this option *(in exceptionally fine weather, as it has good views)*.

b) For the *variante* route via Noailhac, KSO ahead alongside fence and 150 metres later turn L onto a minor road. KSO along it for 1km until you reach a junction with the D606 and turn L along it. KSO for 1.5km to junction with D580; turn hard L on it then veer R and KSO into village of...

4km Noailhac (208.5/533.5)
Gîte d'étape communal 100 metres before village (tel 05 65 72 91 25 & 06 12 75 30 09, 18pl, all year, K). Café-restaurant-shop Chemin Saint-Jacques does demi-pension for pilgrims staying in the gîte.

Pass church of **Saint-Jean-Baptiste** *(restored in 17th century on site of 15th-century building)* and at junction continue straight ahead uphill (marked 'Decazeville').

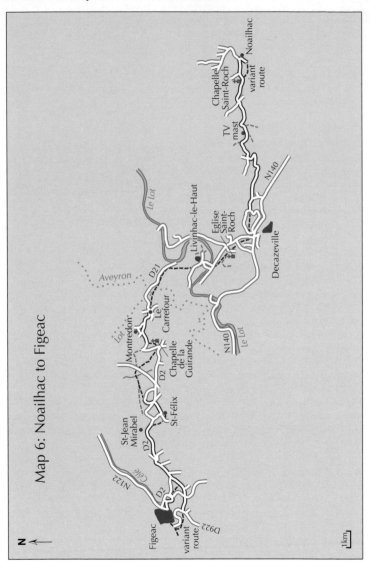

Map 6: Noailhac to Figeac

N

Noailhac

variant route

Chapelle Saint-Roch

TV mast

N140

Le Lot

Livinhac-le-Haut

Eglise Saint-Roch

Decazeville

N140

Le Lot

Aveyron

D21

Le Carrefour

Lot

Montredon

D2

Chapelle de la Guirande

St-Félix

St-Jean Mirabel

D2

Célé

N122

D2

Figeac

D922

variant route

1km

Then, when road veers L, KSO(R) up lane (signposted 'La Merlaterie' and 'Chapelle St Roch'). Pass 13 large wayside crosses (track continues as a walled lane after the fourth), forming a *Via Crucis* (Stations of the Cross – the fourteenth and last is next to the chapel), leading up to the D580 at the...

3km Chapelle Saint-Roch 595m (211.5/530.5)

Chapelle Saint-Roch

Picnic area; splendid views looking over Conques in valley below. The chapel has statue of saint as a pilgrim outside in the tympanum above the door and another (as a non-pilgrim) inside above the altar. The chapel is the focus of a local annual pilgrimage on 16 August, St Roch's Day; this began between 1847–9 when, due to a typhoid epidemic, a procession of local people made its way to the top of the hill, where public prayers were addressed to the saint, invoking his help. As a result the number of those inflicted with the disease is reported to have decreased rapidly and the custom has continued ever since. The chapel was built on the site in 1884. It also contains two modern stained-glass windows, donated by the artist in 1997 and 2000.

Continue on road for 500m, uphill, to TV mast (640m) and very large wayside cross. *Panoramic views and orientation plan.*

KSO (road descends after TV mast), and at five-point junction 3km after Noailhac KSO on D580 (marked 'Decazeville'). About 300 metres after turning to **Fonteilles** fork L up sandy lane. *(Noticeboard at start explains the* Méridienne verte, *the line North Pole– Paris– South Pole, which was planted with a line of trees in 2000 to mark the millenium.)* KSO, with fence to L, through fields, then descending gradually down side of hillside with valley below you to LH side. Cross a minor road and continue on grassy track on other side. *(View of Decazeville ahead; the big scar on the landscape to your L is the remains of the opencast coal mine.)* About 200 metres later track splits: KSO to *R*-hand side of fence, heading for woods ahead. Go through small gate and just before you reach the woods fork L down FP leading downhill to large green industrial building on RH side. Continue ahead on gravel track and KSO(L) ahead behind farm buildings, downhill all the time. Reach a road coming from back R and KSO along it.

At junction (**Le Plegat**, gîte d'étape at Le Buscalie indicated ahead at entrance to cul-de-sac) KSO on road, veering R. At junction by farm (**Fromentals**) fork L downhill, descending steadily all the time. Pass **La Gaillardie** and then **La Combe** (seat). Pass entrance to **Le Madieu** (on L) but KSO(R) on road ahead. At fork (with seat, picnic area, ♣) KSO(R) ahead (**Route de Vivioles**; Ecogîte Le Mineur Paysan at house no 760, tel 05 65 43 33 44 & 06 23 20 29 97, 14pl, K, camping, Apr–Oct). At end of this KSO ahead on **Route de Montarnal** and continue downhill all the time, through residential area, and reach road with a 'stop' sign (**Avenue Marméjours**, bar opposite) on the outskirts of…

11km Decazeville 225m (222.5/519.5)

Medium-sized town (population 7000) with all facilities, OT (Square Jean Segalat, tel 05 65 43 18 36). Gîte d'Etape Les Volets Bleus, 3 Rue Camille Douls (on GR65, tel 06 46 89 97 16, 15pl, 1 Apr–15 Oct, K). Gîte Au détour du Chemin, 11 Rue del la Quatrième République (tel 06 42 46 25 64 & 06 16 35 31 76, 4pl, K, Mar onwards). Hôtel (open 7/7) Restaurant Foulquier, 14 bis avenue Victor Hugo (on GR, tel 05 65 63 27 42, X w/ends). (If you intend to sleep in Livinhac on a Monday, buy food here.)

The town takes its present name from the Duc de Decazes, Minister of Industry under Napoleon and responsible for the promotion of large-scale mining in this area. Decazeville had the largest opencast coalmine in Europe, La Découverte (visits possible).

Turn L first then R (**Rue Camille Douls**, Gîte 'Les Volets Bleus' at no 3), then at traffic lights turn R uphill (**Avenue Laromiguère**, but unmarked at start, house no 13 has sign 'eau potable' outside). Turn R at traffic lights and then 20 metres later turn L up steep hill (**Route de Nantuech**) which turns R 200 metres later up very steep hill, veering L and climbing continuously. At the top, road levels out and at end of village (**Nantuech**) KSO(R) along road joining from L (wayside cross and seat). About 100 metres later turn hard L (**Chemin de Boutigou**, uphill again!) and KSO, emerging at staggered junction (another wayside cross and seat) in a residential area. KSO ahead (still on **Chemin de Boutigou**). Pass cemetery (L) and reach…

2km Eglise Saint-Roch 353m (224.5/517.5)

Gîte Sentinelle (accueil chrétien), Montée de Saint Roch (tel 05 65 43 49 52, 7pl, donation, all year X Sat, prayers morning/evening).

A parish church, rather than the usual chapel or hermitage dedicated to this saint. Three statues of him inside the church, one above the main altar in full pilgrim gear, another large statue as pilgrim but minus hat in side chapel and a third small (alabaster?) statue of the saint as a non-pilgrim at the side of the altar in the side chapel. There is also a modern drawing of St Roch the pilgrim walking with his dog by his side in front of the chapel at Noailhac, but here his cloak is down and his wound covered up as he is on the move.

KSO on D157 for 1km then turn R down grassy lane opposite farm in **Pomayrols**, veering L and descending steadily all the time, zigzagging down to the D21 opposite the modern bridge over the **Lot** at the entrance to…

2km Livinhac-le-Haut 220m (226.5/515.5)

Café, bakery, shops, PTT, ♣ by *mairie*. Gîte d'étape communal, Place du 14 Juin by church (tel 05 60 80 84 82 & 06 76 86 94 77, 29pl, Mar–Oct, K). Bio Gîte la Vita é Bella, 85 Place du 14 juin (tel 06 77 55 78 33, 13pl, mid Mar to end Oct). *Accueil paroissial* for pilgrims (behind church, 5.30–7.30pm daily, end Apr to early Oct, hot/cold drinks, cake, but no sleeping facilities). Five CH: a) Podiensis, Impasse des Esplagnes (tel 05 65 63 36 97 & 06 72 07 64 03, 15 Apr–15 Oct); b) Le Potager du Peyssi, 530 Route du Peyssi (tel 05 65 63 35 92 & 06 37 98 01 35, K, Mar–Oct); c) 470 Rue des Esplagnes (tel 09 51 57 54 66 & 06 62 83 27 04, all year); d) 215 Rue du Couderc (tel 06 83 35 26 96, all year); e) Sur le Chemin Place du 14 Juin (tel 06 89 55 55 32 & 06 16 98 44 77, all year). Camping le Roquelongue by river at entrance to town (tel 05 65 63 39 67, all year, restaurant-bar, rents caravans per night).

Cross bridge and turn first L up long street (**Rue Camille Couderc**, but no name at start), cross a more major road and fork L ahead (**Rue de la République**) to **Place du 14 Juin**.

Cross square and go down **Rue Camille Landes** to R of *mairie*. Turn into **Rue du Couderc** and continue to road junction (D627 and D21). Cross over and go down D627 (signed 'Capdenac'). About 300 metres later, in hamlet of **La Planque**, fork R by wayside cross and 20 metres later on, at farm building, KSO ahead up narrow lane to minor road junction (**Peyrols**, *seat, gîte to L*).

KSO up road, ignoring turns, to hamlet of **Le Thabor** and then turn hard R at bend down gravelled lane. When this veers R, KSO(L) ahead along grassy lane to road junction (marked 'Le Poux', 'Chaunac'). Turn L along D21 and 50 metres later turn R up minor road (marked 'Le Feydel'). About 150 metres later turn L up tarred lane marked 'Le Feydel' and 100 metres later turn R up grassy lane for 100 metres to farm at U-bend in minor road. KSO(L) ahead, uphill, then along ridge.

About 800 metres later join minor road coming from back R then turn L onto D2 *(picnic area with ♣)* at entrance to…

6km Montredon 396m (232.5/509.5)
♣ *Accueil paroissial* in room behind church for pilgrims (8am–6.30pm daily, hot/cold drinks, cake, but no sleeping facilities). CH 'La Mariotte' on GR65 on leaving village (tel 05 65 34 38 20, Apr–Oct).

Hilltop village with Chapelle Notre-Dame at crossroads (replaces older chapel, has 14th-century *pieta* above altar) and Church of Saint-Michel on site of former priory. You are now in the *département* of the Lot.

Turn R on D2 and continue uphill to church. Veer L past it and continue downhill on road, turn R at junction (pass 'La Mariotte' on L and 200 metres later, at staggered junction, KSO ahead uphill. Turn L 100 metres later (marked 'Tournié'), following road round through hamlet of **Tournié** and KSO ahead at crossroads, downhill.

Turn L into hamlet of **Lacoste** *(note well on L; Gîte-Accueil Pèlerin Lacoste, tel 07 83 77 73 99, 3pl, Apr–Oct)*, continue down unsurfaced road and 200 metres later turn R downhill on green lane. Turn L at bottom onto road and L again at fork. About 200 metres later on at road junction reach…

3km Chapelle de Guirande 277m (235.5/506.5)
Romanesque chapel of Sainte-Madeleine with late 14th-century murals of the four evangelists over altar (in good condition).

Turn R and pass to RH side of cemetery ♣ to road. *From here the GR65 does quite a few 'loops' to avoid the road, something made more difficult by numerous tracks in private ownership, so from here to Saint-Félix those in a hurry or in bad weather may prefer to continue on the D2 from the chapel (3km) instead of taking the (6km) 'scenic route' via a reservoir and various green lanes, some of which may well be very boggy. Turn L for Saint-Félix when you get to La Ragoulie.*

The GR65 turns R again 100 metres after the chapel up a minor road to hamlet of **Guirande**. At T-junction turn R down lane lined with oak trees, which then turns L onto track at small aerodrome. KSO(L) along side of fields downhill to road. KSO then turn first L downhill by wayside cross in hamlet of **Le Terly**, leading down to reservoir *(plan d'eau)*. Cross it by a causeway, KSO ahead on other side, passing to L of farm, and continue ahead, downhill along line of trees. Around 300/400 metres later turn L down similar track. Continue on road (in hamlet of **Bord**, CH *(tel 05 65 10 66 71 & 06 18 62 25 24, Apr–Sept) with picnic area and pilgrim shelter (all year))*, and then turn R. At end of hamlet veer R down

Saint-Félix, church of Sainte-Radegonde, tympanum with Adam and Eve

grassy lane, then L, then R onto fenced-in lane leading to road in hamlet of **La Cipière**. KSO(R) along it to road (D2, *watch out here for rerouted FP direct to the church in Saint-Félix*) and after 300 metres turn hard R at junction (V9) along road for 1km to…

6km Saint-Félix (241.5/500.5)

Romanesque church of Sainte-Radegonde has Adam and Eve with tree and serpent on its 11th-century tympanum. Early 20th-century stained-glass window of St James.

Fork L after church (behind restaurant, not always open), passing between buildings onto a narrow FP. At top (**Le Puech**, bend in road to L) turn R along tree-lined lane to road. KSO(R) along it then turn L at crossroads. About 100 metres later turn R up grassy lane then KSO up minor road. Turn R at next junction uphill to road in hamlet of **La Causse**. Turn L at top and 80 metres later, just before village entrance boards for **St-Jean Mirabel**, fork R (opposite fire hydrant) down lane leading to D2. Cross over and KSO ahead on other side then, at staggered junction, turn L past *salle communale* (on L) with a sculpture of an enormous bicycle outside. *(Halte pèlerin near the mairie, free, open 7/7, WC, shower, place to sit and eat.)*

Turn R here for 200 metres *(and then retrace your steps)* to visit the Eglise de Saint-Jean Mirabel – Romanesque, recently restored. Framed painting of a very

Saint-Jean Mirabel, bicycle sculpture outside salle communale

sturdy looking Saint Roch (with stick, dog and bread) inside on R. A modern stained-glass pilgrim window (above the altar) has a rucksack, stick and gourd while the tympanum frieze over the west door (the original entrance to the church when it was still only a chapel) dates from the 13th century and depicts scenes concerning St John the Evangelist in the top row and St Jean the Baptist in the lower row of sculptures.

Turn R onto the D2 at the end and KSO. At brow of hill by RH bend (place marked on map as **Bel-Air**) fork L down walled lane to road. Turn L for 80 metres then R (marked 'Les Crouzets' and 'L'Hôpital'), and 300 metres later turn R up green lane.

Emerge onto gravel lane and KSO(R) to D2 by junction, turn L and then L again to D210 *(leading to **Lunan**, 1km, whose church of St Martin is a historic monument, 200m)*. Turn R down tarred road 1.2km later, at entrance to **La Balme**, which > an unsurfaced track, descending to crossing of paths, the...

4.5km Carrefour des Sentiers 327m (246/496)

Turn R up green lane, veering L and rising slowly up to road 800 metres later. Turn R for 150 metres to D2 then turn L *(view of Figeac ahead)*. About 100 metres later fork L, KSO(L) at fork and 800 metres later reach the junction with the GR6A just after the *lieu-dit* **Pipy**. Turn R for Figeac here *(see below)*, opposite a farm (**Fournamantane**).

Here you have the option of a) continuing ahead straight to **La Cassagnole** *(gîte d'étape, see details on page 91 below) via the GR6A, picking up the GR65 again after the Aiguille du Cingle (an obelisk); or b) turning R to go into* **Figeac**.

a) To go directly to **La Cassagnole** *(with green walker symbols)*, KSO ahead for 150 metres, then turn R at junction onto another minor road. At the next junction, 300 metres later, turn R *(turn L for Centre Leclerc with large superstore: food, cafeteria and ATM)*. Continue ahead, cross D840 *(new roundabout layout)* and continue on other side marked 'Fumat' *(café/restaurant on corner)*. KSO ahead then 800 metres later fork L up grassy track with high(ish) wall to LH side.

Cross minor road (water tower to R) and KSO on walled lane. Cross another minor road (follow *green* signs here as GR6A turns R here) and KSO ahead along another walled lane, veering R to D922. Turn L along it and 250 metres later turn L (before roundabout sign) along minor road (signed R to 'L'Aiguille' and 'Monument du Cingle') and the GR65 from Figeac joins at next crossing from R below *(obelisk and shady picnic area with* ♣*)*. Turn L here, veering R along boundary wall and fence to a roundabout *(waymarks with a yellow walker on a green background)*. Cross over, go down D822 for 100 metres then fork R (marked for 'La Cassagnole') past factories in an industrial estate. After bend in road fork R down minor road marked 'Z.I. Aiguille' and continue as described below* (see page 91).

b) To go into **Figeac**, turn R here down walled lane *(dovecote to L)*. At field at end turn L down walled FP, skirting it, and KSO. Cross track and KSO downhill to D2 and turn L down to junction with N140. Cross it (carefully) and 20 metres later turn L up green lane and then R along road, uphill, // to N140 (to your R below). KSO(L) along road coming from back R and descend to cross railway line. Continue down **Rue de Londrieu**. Turn L along **Allées Victor Hugo**, then R and either KSO and cross bridge over the river to visit Figeac or turn L immediately down **Avenue Jean-Jaurès** to continue on GR65.

5KM FIGEAC 194M (251/491)

All facilities. SNCF (Paris, Brive, Toulouse), five hotels (see *Miam Miam Dodo*, also for smaller gîtes), 20 restaurants, OT (Hôtel de la Monnaie, Place Vival, tel 05 65 34 06 25). Gîte/CH Le Soleilho, 8 Rue du Prat (tel 05 65 38 42 62 & 06 75 89 96 53, 6pl, all year, K). Gîte du Carmel, 9 Ave Jean Jaurès (tel 06 14 32 05 51, 8pl, phone 48hrs ahead, donation, May–Sept). Gîte d'Etape du Gua, 14 bis Ave Joffre (tel 05 81 71 50 28 & 06 74 73 22 69, 15pl, all year). Gîte le Coquelicot, 20 Ave du Faubourg du Pin (tel 05 81 71 55 93 & 06 27 58 67 54, 14pl, all year). Gîte Chemin des Anges, 30 Allées Victor Hugo (tel 06 10 30 55 90 & 06 07 12

35 63, 112pl, all year). CH Les Pratges, 6 Avenue Jean-Jaurès (tel 05 65 50 01 42 & 06 07 05 07 92, all year). Camping-Restaurant Les Rives du Célé, Domaine du Surgié (tel 05 61 64 88 54, Apr–Sept). Accueil Spirituel Association 'Sur les Chemins de Compostelle' in Eglise Saint-Sauveur, Jun–Sept, 4.30–6.15pm, Tues–Fri, Mass and Benediction (blessing) 6.30pm; no sleeping accommodation.

Busy town on river Célé (population 10,500) with network of restored medieval streets (ask in OT for walking tour leaflet), worth half a day's visit. Former abbey church of Saint-Sauveur, consecrated 1093, with ambulatory characteristic of pilgrim churches. Churches of Notre-Dame du Puy and Saint Thomas. Formerly an important pilgrim halt with six hospitals (one still exists). Musée Champollion (Egyptology), Musée du Vieux Figeac, Gothic Hôtel de la Monnaie (mint – for coins), Maison des Templiers.

To continue: turn L down **Avenue Jean-Jaurès**. About 150 metres later turn (second) L up street (marked 'Cingles Bas') alongside high wall, veering R then L under railway line. Turn R and then fork L uphill. Road > forest track through woods, climbing steadily up side of hill and veering L, passing TV mast to reach war memorial, *an enormous concrete cross, with the names of the 145 Jewish people deported on 12 May 1944. Picnic area with view over town of Figeac.*

Continue ahead on road, mainly uphill, for 1.5km to second monument *(obelisks marking limits of eighth-century Benedictine abbey, another picnic area)*: this is the place where the GR65A *variante* meets up with the GR65 again*.

To continue on GR65, turn R (the waymarks ahead are those of the GR65A). About 200 metres later KSO(R) along D922 and 100 metres later fork R down wide road past factories and marked 'Z.I. Aiguille'. KSO along level road on ridge, ignoring turns to L and R. *(On the skyline you can see the water tower in Faycelles as a reference point.)* KSO(R) at next junction and continue along road, passing **Malaret**, passing above **Buffan** and just after a crossroads KSO to...

5km La Cassagnole 311m (256/486)
Birthplace of Louis the Pious, son of Charlemagne and second Holy Roman Emperor. Gîte d'Etape Relais Saint-Jacques, tel 05 65 34 03 08, 33pl, all year, K, limited food supplies for sale, also CH.

KSO(R) at fork and continue on road through **Ferrières**, KSO(L) at junction *(with modern stone cross)*. KSO(R) at next junction *(note dovecote to R)*. Join road from back L *(another dovecote to R)*. Cross D662 and continue into village, veering R uphill to church in...

4km Faycelles 319m (260/482)
Bar/restaurant/shop 'La Grillade' with CH on main street (tel 05 65 34 65 09, all year but X Tues 1 Oct–30 Apr). CH La Caselle (tel 05 65 34 05 68 & 06 31 83 20 98, all year). CH Bleu Lumière, Mas de Rou (tel 06 86 71 13 14, Feb–Nov).

Continue ahead L, past church, uphill, KSO(L) up walled lane at bend, reach D21 and turn R along it. *(Viewpoint with picnic tables. Good view over Lot valley.)* KSO(R) at junction.

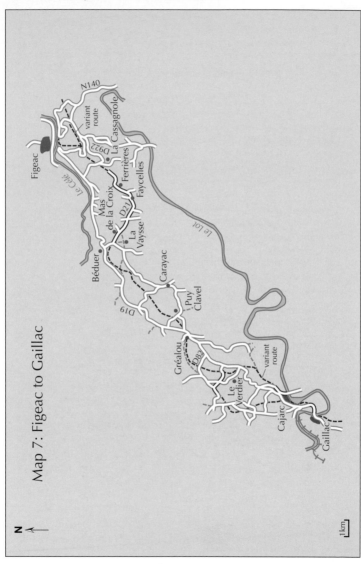

Map 7: Figeac to Gaillac

N

1km

Note caselles *in this area. Also steeply pitched barns, two storeys, with grassy ramp leading up to first-floor entrance.*

Continue on D21 for 2km until just past RH turn for **Ayrens** (hard R, *Restaurant Le Bar de l'Eté, 11am–3pm Sat, May–Sept*), then fork L down shady lane (to side of bar/restaurant) for 300 metres to road. *(200 metres ahead on L is La Planquette, a gîte d'étape, tel 05 65 40 01 36, 10pl +8 in marquee in summer, campsite, Apr–Sept).* Turn R and then R again almost immediately down FP and at end turn R onto D18 just before its junction with the D21 in hamlet of...

3.5km Mas de la Croix 327m (263.5/478.5)

This is where the GR651 starts, the (waymarked) variante *route along the Vallée du Célé: see Appendix C.* CH (tel 05 65 11 40 86 & 06 38 94 10 47, all year).

a) For GR651. KSO on D21 to Béduer (800 metres) Bar/resto, bread, 7/7. Two CH, both on Chemin du Chateau: a) La Coquille (tel 05 65 11 40 18 & 06 60 03 71 93 & 06 88 16 66 15, K, all year); b) La Mythié (tel 05 65 34 22 25 & 06 42 47 92 93, K, Mar–Oct).

b) For GR65: fork L by bus shelter down minor road, pass above château and then, at small crossing *(base of stone wayside cross to R)* turn L up narrow walled lane which then > a minor road. When it bends R downhill turn L down a (wider)

Two-storey barn, typical of the Lot

walled lane and KSO, ignoring turns, as it wends its way downhill *(large lavoir/ fountain, the Fontieu, to R)* and then up to minor road).

Turn L and immediately R uphill at junction (marked 'Surgues') then turn L down gravel track 150 metres later at bend and KSO *(note caselle/gaviote to L)*, ignoring turns. When it > a walled lane (farm of **Combes-Salgues** to L) KSO. At crossing of paths 100 metres later turn R for 2km along another walled lane.

KSO, ignoring turns, to road (D38). Turn L for 300 metres then turn R down track. KSO. In a grassy clearing where track forks L, fork R up grassy lane. KSO ahead at crossing and continue uphill to road in hamlet of **Le Puy Clavel** *(Gîte Ecoasis, tel 06 71 00 48 30 & 09 50 07 74 66, 26pl, limited groceries, 1 Apr–31 Oct, on GR itself).* Turn R and 100 metres later turn L onto a walled lane, and turn R uphill to D19 *(Gréalou place-name boards to L).* Cross over and KSO *(large iron cross to L).*

In this area the footpaths are often broken by roads/staggered junctions/short stretches on road, hence the complicated instructions.

Turn hard L 300 metres later after waterworks building, then R at junction and arrive at the church in...

The oldest wayside cross in the Quercy, near Gréalou

9km Gréalou
374m (272.5/469.5)

Gîte de l' Atelier des Volets Bleus, Place de l'Eglise (tel 05 65 40 69 86 & 05 65 10 69 35 & 06 84 37 64 73, 8pl) Gîte near school (tel 05 65 40 66 00 & 06 07 09 59 85, 4–6pl). ♣ in picnic area.

Romanesque church of Notre-Dame de l'Assomption. There are a lot of dolmens in this area.

Turn R at church, pass cemetery (R) and continue on lane. At junction with road and small iron cross KSO(L) ahead on track along ridge, continuing along open heathland to small stone cross *(thought to be the oldest such cross in the region)*. Opposite a dolmen veer L down green lane alongside wall and continue down to road (D82) and KSO on other side down walled lane, ignoring turnings. KSO ahead at junction and continue until you reach a road. Turn R and then at a T-junction turn R again to hamlet of…

4km Le Verdier 316m (276.5/465.5)
CH/Gîtes Le Chant du Verdier, tel 05 65 11 25 39 & 06 86 82 94 88, all year.

In bad weather you may want to take the variant route through the woods to Cajarc *(2km shorter, via the GR65A, waymarked)*. If so, KSO on here on road then turn L onto a minor road leading to the D21. KSO(R) then KSO along it for 1km. Then, just before the junction with the D19, fork R onto path. Turn R on D19 and 50 metres later turn L onto wide gravel path. KSO, following it round, and at T-junction with similar paths, turn R. Follow track down for 2km and at T-junction at very bottom turn R ('no entry' sign). Tarmac at first then grassy FP downhill. Cross tarred lane and KSO on other side (**Chemin de la Salle**). Reach a bigger road* marked 'Centre Ville 400m' to R and turn R here. When you reach the **Boulevard de la Tour de la Ville** turn R to the **Place du Forail** in the centre of **Cajarc**.

*Note: the GR *variante* continues ahead here (still the **Chemin de la Salle**), goes under the railway line, turns R along the river and then rejoins the main GR65 but without taking you into the town centre.

Dolmen, near Gréalou

Otherwise, to continue on the main GR65, turn R into hamlet and KSO on road, uphill for 500 metres, to crossroads *(iron cross)*. KSO ahead (marked 'Chemin des Vignes'), continuing to climb until you reach another road. Turn L and 150 metres later fork L up unsurfaced road and KSO through fields, track then becoming a green lane. At crossing KSO ahead (level) and continue to road. Cross over and continue on other side on track which > walled lane, descending until you reach a T-junction with ruined building on L.

Turn L along track and KSO, ignoring turns, uphill to road. Cross it and continue ahead down green lane, descending to join road coming from back L. KSO(R) for 20 metres then KSO(L) (at bend to R in road) down walled lane. This > a tarred lane, descending all the time.

About 150 metres after road joins from back R, turn R along green lane under the cliffs *(Cajarc below L)*. This > a stony track that descends continuously in a straight line until you reach a field at the bottom. Turn R alongside a wall on a grassy path and then KSO along minor road at end and turn L onto D922.

The GR65 does not enter Cajarc either. *To visit town:* KSO. *To continue:* turn R immediately (after turning L onto D922).

6km Cajarc 160m (282.5/459.5)

All facilities. OT (Place du Forail, tel 05 65 40 72 89). Gîte d'étape communal, Rue de la Cascade (tel 06 14 66 54 89, 20pl, Mar–Nov). Gîte d'Etape Le Pèlerin, 11 Rue Lacauhne (20pl, Apr–Oct, K). Gîte Chez Annie et Claude, 8 Impasse des Lilas (tel 05 65 40 61 00 & 06 30 65 43 26, K, 1 Apr–15 Oct). Four CH, two hotels, seven restaurants. Camping municipal du Terriol (tel 05 65 40 72 74, on GR out of town, May–Sept). Accueil Spirituel Association 'Sur les Chemins de Compostelle' in Eglise Saint-Etienne, 15 Apr–15 Sept, Mon–Fri 5–6pm, Mass 6pm (no sleeping accommodation).

Town situated in a 'circus' of chalk cliffs. Pilgrim bridge over the Lot built in 1320 and a hospital existed in 1269. Chapelle de la Madeleine (only the chancel remains, known as 'Chapelette de Cajarc' today, the chapel of former 13th-century leprosarium).

Note: after Gaillac the causse begins, with no food or water until Cahors, except in Limogne and Varaire, so stock up on both before leaving Cajarc.

To leave from town centre (**Place du Forail**, facing OT) turn L, continue on **Boulevard de la Tour de Ville** and turn R into **Avenue de la Capalette** then second L into **Rue de Cuzoul**, picking up the waymarks again, and KSO past campsite. Continue alongside railway line (on LH side) and just before *second* tunnel underneath it turn R along side of garden and then L up stony FP to road *(D922, above R under cliffs)*. KSO(L) ahead and then KSO(L) again at junction with

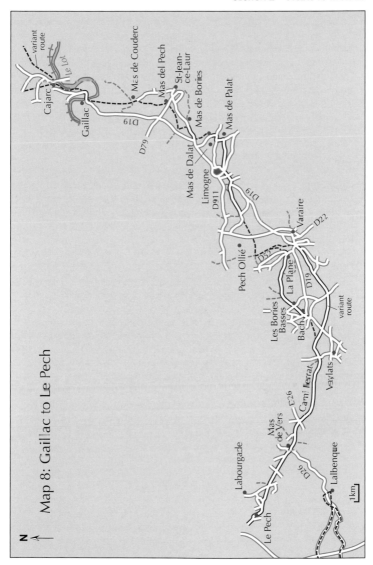

Map 8: Gaillac to Le Pech

the 'Capelette' *(on L, 11th and 15th centuries)* and huge wooden cross (on R). *Picnic area.*

KSO(L) here (**Chemin de la Route Veille**) and fork R 100 metres later. KSO(R) and after 1km *(CH on GR itself, partway down on R, 1.5km after Cajarc, tel 05 65 40 70 00 & 06 24 11 11 69, Apr–Oct, K)* and descend to five-way junction. Take second R *(brickworks to R. Note very large cages on L, used for drying corn on the cob)* then join D19 (**Route de Limogne**) coming from back R.

(Church in Gaillac up on clifftop ahead of you.) Cross suspension bridge over the **Lot** and turn L on other side, continuing uphill on road to entry to…

4km Gaillac 180m (286.5/455.5)

At RH bend on entry to village fork L steeply up short FP and KSO(L) up minor road, KSO(L) at fork and continue ahead on level grassy lane. At junction KSO(L) on track from back R and enter woods, uphill, veering L. KSO(R) at fork and then fork R again (the centre of three) almost immediately, continuing on stony track. *(Watch out carefully for waymarks as there are no distinguishing features in the* causse *and no views through or over the trees, which are not very tall and mostly old and untended.)*

Turn L at crossing near brow of hill and KSO ahead along track coming from back L. KSO along track coming from back R and fork L almost immediately afterwards. KSO, mainly uphill, then ahead at crossing. Reach minor tarred road coming from back L and KSO(R) along it, uphill, passing the entrance gates (L) to **Mas de Couderc** (a farm) some 700 metres later. Pass turning (L) to Salvagnac and Cajarc on bigger road and KSO(R) ahead; then, by wayside cross fork R down grassy track which > a walled lane. Track joins from back R; KSO. Reach large pond surrounded by stone wall and pass to R of it (♣). *(Gîte d'Etape du Mas de Jantile on GR shortly before fountain, before Saint-Jean-de-Laur, tel 06 88 85 07 18, 10pl, K, 1 Apr–30 Sept; AP by fountain, 28 Apr–15 Oct, 8am–1pm)*. Turn R onto road, reach junction with wayside cross and continue ahead on tarred lane on other side. KSO(L) in hamlet of…

6km Mas del Pech 339m (292.5/449.5)

Gîte d'Etape Les Deux Pigeonners (tel 05 65 40 70 13 & 06 09 93 05 48, 7pl, 1 Apr–15 Oct, reservation recommended). CH at entrance to hamlet (tel 05 65 11 46 95 & 06 21 09 60 61, all year).

KSO ahead down narrow walled lane. About 1km later reach T-junction with wider walled lane and turn R and then fork L 50 metres later. Follow lane round for 1km, veering L by farm and reach road *(lavoir L, another pond surrounded by stone walls, waterlilies, R)* in hamlet of…

2km Mas de Bories (294.5/447.5)

Turn R. Continue ahead on road for 1km, pass wayside cross (L) and KSO. At T-junction and bend turn L up small shady walled lane, gradually uphill. Near top turn R, veering L, to very minor tarred lane by entrance to farm (**Mas de Teule**). Turn R.

KSO(R) uphill at T-junction and reach another T-junction with wayside cross in hamlet of **Mas de Dalat** *(Gîte Dalat'Etape (tel 06 07 31 69 61, 15pl, K, 20 Apr–30 Sept)*. Turn L, veering R 50 metres later, then turn R at bend 100 metres after that onto walled lane, veering L up into woods. About 300–400 metres later turn L at junction, gently downhill, and shortly afterwards reach the D143 and turn L along it uphill into **Mas de Palat**.

Fork L onto tarred lane, turn hard R *(turn L for CH 'La Hulotte,' tel 05 65 31 58 51 & 06 17 38 84 47, all year)* and KSO ahead at fork past iron cross. Continue on raised path between fields, veering L uphill on shady walled lane. Similar track joins from back R; KSO ahead on shady walled lane. Continue ahead (**Chemin de Malecargue**) *(this is also a sentier botanique, with labels on plants and bushes to either side of it)*. Reach a road, KSO along it and then turn R 50 metres later *(wayside cross)*, gently downhill through residential area *(shady seat to R)* to junction of D911 and D19 at entry to town. Turn L along it, passing gîte d'étape 100 metres later on RH side of road and continue into the centre of…

6km Limogne-en-Quercy 300m (300.5/441.5)

Small town with shops, cafés, restaurants, OT 55 Place d'Occitaine (tel 05 65 24 34 28). Gîte d'étape communal, Route de Villefranche (tel 06 12 84

Lavoir *outside Limogne*

86 47, 19pl, all year, K). Gîte La Maison en Chemin, 99 Rue de Lugagnac (tel 06 65 23 24 41 & 06 77 57 83 64, 11pl, 15 Apr–15 Oct). Four CH. Camping Municipal Bel-Air on edge of town (on D911, tel 05 65 24 32 75, limited groceries, 1 Apr–3 Oct). *Point internet* in tabac-bazar, 14 Avenue de Villefranche.

To leave: watch out carefully for the waymarking as the GR65 has been re-routed to go through the town (rather than skirt it). Leave on the D19 and then continue ahead on a wide walled lane, semi-shaded, for 2km, descending gradually to road just before farm in **Ferrières**. Turn R and continue uphill, then fork L at junction with wayside cross. About 150 metres later KSO(R) down walled lane (another farm to L) and 500 metres later, as you begin to descend, turn R through a *cledo* onto FP through trees.

Watch out carefully for waymarks throughout this section; it is easy to be lulled into a rhythm and forget to pay attention.

Around 100 metres later go through a second *cledo* and turn L along narrow walled lane. After 500 metres cross road and continue on wider walled lane on other side. After 1km reach another road coming from R. Continue on road for 75 metres then continue straight ahead, taking LH of two green lanes at LH bend in road. About 200 metres later turn L into similar lane and KSO for 1.5km to junction with minor road. Turn R (on road, not hard R on track) and after 200 metres reach…

6.5km Junction near Varaire (307/435)

Here you have a choice of routes, depending on whether or not you want to go into **Varaire** (eg to sleep; see b) below) and/or take the *variante* along *Cami Gasco* (an old Roman road) or bypass it and continue on the main GR65. Both options are waymarked and join up again at the start of the *Cami Ferrat*, 1.5km after **Bach**.

a) To continue on the main GR65: turn R along walled lane for 400 metres, turn L along road for 200 metres and fork R up lane. Cross D52 and continue ahead on minor road, meeting the GR36 coming from back L 100 metres later. Veer L past hamlet of **La Plane** (1km) and KSO(L) down wide unsurfaced track, ignoring turns, for 4km until you reach an isolated house at…

4.5km Les Bories Basses 310m (311.5/430.5)

Continue on minor road. Just after farm the GR65 (KSO) and GR36 separate. KSO for 1km, ignoring turns, to village of…

1.5km Bach (313/429)

CH Le Mas de Jouge (tel 05 65 22 67 37 & 06 70 65 38 43, Apr–Oct, on GR 100 metres from *mairie*). Gîte d'étape/CH La Grange Saint-Jacques (tel 05 65 31 08 75 & 06 45 38 37 61, 10pl, all year, at entrance to Bach). Restaurant (but irregular opening hours).

The village takes its name from a German family who settled here in the 18th century.

Turn R on road (D19, marked 'Caussade'), cross D22 and 600 metres later fork L down a grassy lane. About 900 metres later turn R at a junction with a similar track coming from your L, the…

1.5km Junction of the GR65 with its *variante* (314.5/427.5)

b) *The GR65 variante, waymarked, passes to the south of the D19. It takes you along the course of the* Cami Gasco *on wide, almost flat lanes and the occasional minor road and, as explained above, joins the main GR65 at the start of the section on the* Cami Ferrat *(old Roman road) 1.5km after* **Bach***.*

KSO ahead at the junction before **Varaire** and reach the D19 in the centre of the village. *Shop (X Sun pm + all day Mon), café-restaurant-gîte d'étape Les Marroniers on main road (tel 05 65 31 53 85, 25pl, Apr–Oct, K). Gîte d'étape Clos des Escoutilles (tel 05 65 24 50 84 & 06 73 47 02 36, 12pl, 1 Apr–1 Oct), picnic area +* ♣ *at end of village 50 metres from GR.*

From the D19 (with the bar to your R and the shop to your L) fork L on minor road marked 'M. La Jamblusse', veering L, and then fork R at wayside cross up tarmac lane. KSO(L) at next junction. KSO ahead, KSO(L) ahead at next fork then, 2km after Varaire, at crossing with an isolated stone building, turn R 2km after that, cross the D22 and continue ahead on other side. KSO, ignoring turns to L and R and 2km later reach the D19. Cross over, KSO ahead on other side and 400 metres later the main GR65 joins from the RH side at the…

65km Junction of the GR65 with its *variante* (314.5/427.5)

Continue ahead and 100 metres later you reach a junction. *Turn L here if you want to sleep in the gîte run by the nuns in the Couvent des Filles de Jésus Association 'Jean Liausu' in Vaylats (2.5km, tel 05 65 31 63 51, open all year but reservation essential). Also CH by church, café/galerie de l'Orme (tel 05 65 31 68 47 & 06 86 93 53 69, all year). However, to continue the following morning you do not need to backtrack but can turn west along the D19 and after the last house (after the village exit board) a FP is waymarked 'GR,' leading you back onto the* Cami Ferrat *where you turn L.*

Otherwise, KSO ahead. *This is the* Cami Ferrat *('iron path' – it was originally paved) which the GR65 follows for 15km altogether. Like all Roman roads it is more or less straight, and linked Caylus with Cahors. It was not much used by pilgrims in the past, due to its lack of maintenance and its solitude, lending itself readily to ambushes and without easy access either to food or lodging. There are not many distinguishing features in the* causse *it passes through, and few buildings. It is level, in the main, and most of it is either shady or semi-shaded, with woods and/or fields to one side or another. At weekends you may meet people on mountain bikes but on the whole it is a very lonely route, although not as far from habitation, as a glance at a map will reveal, as you might suppose.*

KSO (quite literally!), ignoring turnings, for 7.5km, crossing successively the D42, the **Ruisseau des Valses** *(a stream that is often dry and where, briefly, the track ceases to be level)* and the D55, reaching the D26 in the hamlet of…

7.5km Mas de Vers 252m (322/420)

From here, if you do not want to go into Cahors, you have the option of a way-marked shortcut (along one, instead of two, sides of a triangle) that takes you directly to **L'Hospitalet**, saving you some 26km. To take this option turn L along D26 at the crossing by Mas de Vers to…

3km Lalbenque 282m
Gîte de Balat, 15 Place du Balat (tel 05 65 22 17 76 & 06 85 99 65 13, 4pl, K, all year). Gîte Mango, 67 Route de Puylaroque (tel 07 80 02 94 69 & 09 62 52 23 00, all year). CH La Vayssade (tel 05 65 24 31 51, all year). Restaurant, shops, OT Place de la Bascule (tel 05 65 31 50 08).

The 14km walking route is waymarked in orange from the PTT here to **L'Hospitalet**. Alternatively you can take the D19 via **Saint-Cevet** *(Gîte Le Balcon des Hugots, tel 05 65 21 00 35 & 06 32 09 20 20, 6pl, all year)*, **Ventaillac** and **Granéjouls** *(CH Le Pech d'Huguet, tel 05 65 21 05 28 & 06 82 43 56 77, camping possible, Apr–Oct)*, 12km.

Otherwise, at **Mas de Vers** cross D26 *(stone cross at junction)*. *(Gîte d'étape privé at* **Poudally**, *turn L here down D26, tel 05 65 22 08 69 & 06 60 09 88 30, 27pl, all year X 1–10 Jul, limited groceries, camping possible.)* The *Cami Ferrat* continues on other side as a minor road. Cross another minor road and the *Cami Ferrat* then > an unsurfaced road. Cross D10 and KSO *(turn L 1km later for Gîte d'Etape Le Gascou, 500 metres off route, tel 06 75 43 01 93, 8pl, Apr–Oct)*,

Map 9: Le Pech to Montcuq

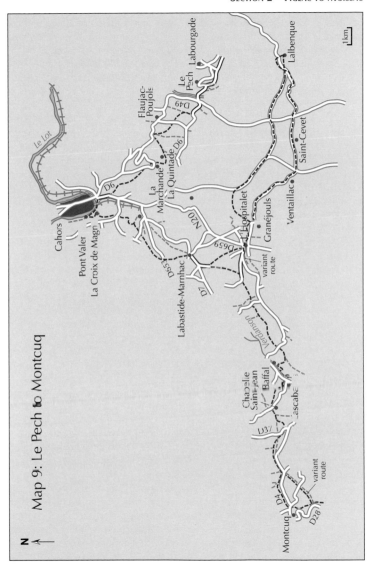

1km

N

Cahors

Le Lot

Pont Valer
La Croix de Magn

Flaujac-Poujols

Le Pech

Labourgade

D49

Lalbenque

D6

La Marchande
La Quintade
D6

Saint-Cevet

Ventaillac

N20

Hôpitalet

D553

Granéjouls

Labastide-Marnhac

D659

variant
route

D7

Vendenson

Chapelle
Saint-Jean

Baffal

Lascabanes

D37

variant
route

D7

Montcuq

D28

descending gradually to minor road 1km later at a large *lavoir (good place for rest/shelter in bad weather)*. Turn R shortly before bridge *(signposted for Gîte Privé Elisa at La Bouyssière (tel 05 65 31 60 46 & 06 69 58 01 32, 4–6pl, Apr–Oct, K)* and reach the…

6km Junction near Le Pech (328/414)

Turn L along road and KSO to a junction with a minor road *(turn R for 500 metres up steep hill for gîte d'étape at Le Pech, tel 05 65 24 72 84, 18pl, 1 Apr–15 Oct, K)*. At bend in road KSO ahead on lane, veering L towards road 800 metres later. Turn hard L uphill then turn R at 'stop' sign, go under motorway and KSO ahead uphill on other side (D6) for 1.5km. At sharp LH bend, at place marked 'Le Gariat', fork R off road onto stony FP uphill. About 250 metres later, at top of hill, turn R along tarmac lane on ridge, more or less level, then > gravel. KSO for 600 metres then turn L onto stony track. About 800 metres after that fork L at intersection of GR65 and GR6, uphill to woods on shady track, levelling out. Pass sports ground/stadium (on R, ♣ + picnic tables) and reach junction with C4, just after entrance board for Flaujac-Poujols. Fork L down shady lane, the **Chemin de Saint-Jacques**. This is tarred to begin with but > stony FP, down to valley bottom *(passing a fine example of a* caselle *over to L)*. Turn L (below road) along valley bottom, gently uphill all the time, for 2km. KSO(R) at fork, then R almost immediately afterwards, on shady path up side of wood. Emerge into the open and pass to RH side of **La Quintade** *(a group of three restored buildings)*, turn R on tarmac lane by its entrance gate, uphill to the D6 in the *lieu-dit* of…

7km La Marchande (335/407)

From here it is nearly all downhill to Cahors. If you want to bypass the town, however, you can turn L here along a 10km *variante* route leading directly to L'Hospitalet (not described here).

Turn R along D6 then fork R along **Route de la Marchande** then turn L down **Chemin de la Marchande**. Reach D6 again, cross over and continue ahead on **Chemin de la Cabridelle**. This then > a track, veering L to open grassland and continuing along a ridge (the **Mont Saint-Georges**).

About 2km later (radio mast to L) track begins to descend. Join minor road coming from back L and KSO. After passing a second radio mast (on L) you can see **Cahors** below for the first time as you begin to descend steeply. Turn R downhill at T-junction, zigzagging down to a railway line (on your L, on **Chemin du Pech de Fourgues**). Then turn L to go under it (the railway) when you reach a more major road which > the **Rue du Barry** *(turn R here for gîte/CH La Maison*

*des Pèlerins, 158 Rue des Cayssine, tel 05 65 30 03 06, phone ahead, 10pl,
evening prayers, K, 11 Apr–15 Oct, after 3pm)* in the **Quartier Saint-Georges**
in...

5KM CAHORS 122M (340/402)

All facilities. SNCF (Paris–Toulouse–Portbou). Two APs: a) the L'Octroi de Cahors
association welcomes pilgrims (almost) every day from Easter to mid Oct, 11am–
5.30pm, in the former tollbooth on the Pont Louis-Philippe; b) Association sur les
Chemins de Compostelle welcomes pilgrims in the cathedral 4–7pm, 7/7, Apr–mid
Oct (no sleeping accommodation). Gîte d'Etape Le Relais des Jacobins, 12 Rue des
Jacobins (near Pont Cabessut and Eglise du Sacré-Coeur, tel 05 65 21 00 84, 15pl,
20 Mar–16 Oct, camping possible, K, but not for groups). Gîte Saint-Laurent, 15
Rue Saint-Laurent (tel 06 13 37 70 02, 4pl, K, 15 Apr–30 Oct, 150 metres from
Pont Louis-Philippe, by lake). Association pour l'Habitat des Jeunes en Quercy, 129
Rue Fondue-Haute (tel 05 65 35 29 32, K, open all year X w/ends, phone ahead)
also puts up walkers/pilgrims. Résidence des Cordeliers-Auberge de Jeunesse, 222
Rue Joachim Murat (tel 05 65 35 64 71, 52pl, K, phone ahead, all year). Gîte Le
Papillon Vert, 51 Rue du Tapis is Vert (tel 05 81 70 14 09 & 06 75 80 58 42, 10pl,
K, 3 Apr–15 Nov). Three CH, four hotels. Camping Rivière de Cabessut, 1180 Rue
Rivère, by river to NE of town (tel 05 65 30 06 30, bar/limited groceries, Apr–Sept).
OT Place François Mitterand, tel 05 65 53 20 65.

Large town (population 21,000) surrounded on three sides by the river Lot.
Important pilgrim halt and a good place for a rest day. Cathedral of Saint-Etienne
with cloisters, several interesting churches and secular buildings. Pont Valentré
(finest fortified bridge in Europe), museum. Ask in OT for a town plan with walking route.

After turning l under railway line, turn R at traffic lights at end of **Rue du Barry**
into the **Place de la Resistance** (at side of main road), go up steps (L), cross over
main road and cross the river **Lot** by the **Pont Louis Philippe**.

*At the AP in the former tollbooth on the LH side of the bridge you can have
your pilgrim passport stamped, obtain information about accommodation and the
route ahead and have a cold drink.*

Then (the GR65 as such does not enter the town centre) you have a choice:

a) To visit Cahors: after crossing the bridge continue ahead along the
Boulevard Gambetta to **Place Aristide Briand** *(mairie, OT)*. To continue (and pick
up the GR65) turn L shortly afterwards down **Rue Wilson** which leads you (crossing railway line via an underpass at the end of this street) to the **Pont Valentré**. *(If*

you look up before you cross you will see the Croix de Magne on the skyline to the L.) Cross the bridge *(note 18th-century wine-press to L)*.

b) To continue without visiting Cahors: after crossing the bridge turn L along the **Quai Eugène Cavaignac**, continue along the **Allées des Soupirs** and then turn L over the **Pont Valentré**.

Note the sculpture of the devil on the upper RH side of the second tower. The story goes that when the bridge was first built, at the beginning of the 14th century, the master mason in charge of the work despaired of ever getting it finished in time. So he did a deal with the devil who, in exchange for the mason's soul, agreed to get the construction finished. However, when it was nearing completion, the mason, still hoping to save his soul, sent the devil off to a spring to fetch water for the building work – but in a sieve! Realising that he had been tricked, the devil backed out, but in revenge removed a stone from the central tower and cast a spell on it so that every time it was replaced it would dislodge itself again. When the Pont Valentré was restored in 1879 the architect noticed that there was still a stone missing, and decided to fill the space with the sculpture of a devil clutching at the cornerstone he tries desparately, but always in vain, to extract.

Pick up waymarks on other side of the bridge where, once again, you have a choice:

a) *'Passage sportif'* – the main GR65: turn *left* at end of the bridge, where a steep FP to your R, fitted with handholds to stop you slipping, zigzags its way

Caselle near Cahors

uphill (watch out carefully for waymarks) and then levels out a little. It passes the top of a water treatment tower and then > a bigger track. Follow it until you reach a minor road at radio masts. *(Very good views of Cahors and the Pont Valentré as you climb.)*

However, although the steep section is not very long, if you have a large/ heavy rucksack, if you are not very agile, if you don't like scrambling or if the weather is wet (and therefore slippery) you may prefer not to take the waymarked *'passage sportif'* up the cliffs but take the *'déviation équestre'*, an alternative, way-marked in orange. This is 1km longer, missing out the **Croix de Magne**.

b) *'Déviation équestre'* – turn *right* after crossing the bridge and immedi-ately afterwards fork L down a road closed to traffic from this end, the **Route de Lacapelle** (uphill – *do not follow the red-and-white* balises *here, which are for the GR6, not 65*), veering L to join a road coming from back R. About 300 metres later, at bend, turn L up **Côte de la Croix de Magne (C1)**, zigzagging uphill. At crossroads at top turn L (**Chemin de la Croix de Magne**) to go to the cross or KSO on road to pick up GR65 waymarks (which come from your L).

1km Croix de Magne 223m (341/401)

A very large cross, visible from the town near the Pont Valentré.

Turn R and follow this road to crossroads *(bus stops to R)* and turn L ('déviation équestre' *joins the route here)*.

Turn L at T-junction 100 metres later (road bridge to R) and follow road down to N20, ignoring turnings. Go through the tunnel under the N20 at bottom of hill.

Veer L on other side and turn L (over tunnel) and KSO on this minor road (**Route de Fontanet** to begin with > **Route des Matthieux**), ignoring turns *(occa-sional shade, not too much traffic)* for 1.5km along the valley. KSO uphill to junc-tion with iron wayside cross in hamlet of **Les Mathieux**. Fork R uphill on **Chemin de la Courounelle et des Mathieux**. About 150 metres later fork R onto FP uphill through woods, reach small tarred road and turn L. KSO. Continue on **Chemin du Pech de Gadal**. Reach another road opposite Gîte de la Domaine des Mathieux *(gîte d'étape & CH, tel 05 65 31 75 13, 28pl, Mar–Oct, K)*.

Turn L here but then immediately R, downhill, on rough track. Turn L to better track, downhill, but less steeply, go under bridge and reach road (D653). Cross over and KSO on small FP on other side, lined with young trees. Cross wooden FB (dried-up stream) and turn R onto grassy track that > shady gravel lane. KSO(R) at fork and R again at next fork, almost immediately. Reach track coming from back R and turn L uphill.

Near the top fork R (LH turn is marked 'propriété privée'). KSO then, when track levels out a bit, turn hard L at junction uphill again. When you reach the beginnings of a residential area, KSO ahead on road and reach junction with the D7 at the entrance to village. Cross over and KSO ahead on other side *(picnic table)* up towards church in…

8km Labastide-Marnhac 257m (349/393)

Phone box, ♣ behind church. Gîte de l'Eglise (tel 05 65 23 91 50 & 06 27 70 59 89, 5pl, K, 1 Apr–15 Oct). Gîte Villa Malique (tel 06 82 82 73 67 & 06 09 09 74 58, 5pl, K, 1 May–15 Oct, near church). Bar/resto/shop, Easter–1 Nov.

To visit **Saint-Remy**, *30min, a pilgrim hospital built in 1286, turn R after church, a variante GR, waymarked. To return to GR65 either retrace your steps or take the D67.*

To continue: KSO, pass church (L), *mairie* (L), join D7 and KSO(L) along it. About 50 metres later fork L onto track (by *caselle* on L). At crossing of unsurfaced tracks 500 metres later KSO. *(Around 2km after Labastide-Marnhac turn L for variante GR65 via* **L'Hospitalet***, 1.5km away, with CH, Domaine des Tuileries, Chemin de L'Hospitalet, tel 05 65 21 04 72, all year. From there, to return to the main GR65 turn R onto variante for 2km then continue on main GR65 coming from back R.)*

KSO, ignore RH turn, KSO(L) at fork, passing isolated house on R (**Maison Gâteau**). KSO(R) at fork and reach T-junction of similar tracks. *(All this stretch is fairly level.)* Turn L and 200 metres later reach minor road by farm (**Trigodina**, *Gîte d'étape à la ferme, tel 05 65 21 70 97 & 06 71 06 98 72, 10pl, K; picnic area with drinks machine and ♣ at junction with GR and variant route.)* Turn R along minor road. At crossroads 500 metres later KSO, after which road > unsurfaced after large isolated house on RH side.

KSO on ridge *(this is the old Hospitalet–Lascabanes road)*. After 3km, still on ridge, turn hard L (when you least expect it) onto another track, veering R. KSO(L) at fork and reach minor road, at the inside of a U-bend. Cross over and fork L (not straight ahead) down track. Another track joins from back L at opening on plateau; KSO ahead. KSO, ignoring turns.

When you reach another road *(iron wayside cross L, picnic area to R with covered seating)*, cross over and KSO(L) ahead, diagonally, along track. KSO. When track begins to rise slightly, fork R at junction to grassy track, veering L and then R downhill into wide bowl-like valley. When green lane joins from R, KSO(L) along it and downhill (> tarred) to minor road in hamlet of **Baffalie**. Turn R along it for 200 metres then turn L (by small wooden wayside cross) down grassy track along side of field, veering L at end by *lavoir*. Do not cross bridge (to D7) but KSO(L) ahead on very minor road and turn R at next crossing by large house in spacious grounds. Emerge on D7 by *mairie* in…

11.5km Lascabanes 180m (360.5/381.5)

Gîte/CH L'Etape Bleue, *lieu-dit* Durand (turn R 800 metres before Lascabanes, tel 05 65 35 34 77, 10pl, K, limited groceries, 15 Mar–2 Nov; rejoin GR65 1.8km later the next day by Chapelle Saint-Jean). Gîte d'Etape Le Nid des Anges in former presbytery (adjoining church, tel 05 65 31 86 38, 17pl, phone ahead, open from 1pm, all year). Gîte/CH Le Bouy 100 metres before village, by castle (tel 05 65 22 92 63 & 05 65 53 61 49 & 06 59 72 99 24). Accueil Association 'sur les Chemins de Compostelle': mass and pilgrim blessing in church every evening at 6pm. ♣ by church. Lascabanes had a pilgrim hospital in the 15th century.

To continue, either pass to RH side of *mairie*, turning R and then R again, or cross D7 and continue to church and gîte, then continue on minor road (marked 'St Géry/Sabatier') and 300 metres later (at bend) KSO ahead up unsurfaced road and then uphill into woods, along walled lane (note *gariotte* to R) until you reach a minor road (1km from Lascabanes). Turn R along it for 1km to junction with the **Chapelle Saint-Jean-le-Froid** on the LH side and then turn L. *(The chapel is always open, a good place for rest/shelter. Fête and Mass in Occitan last Sunday in June.)*

Continue ahead past chapel, pass to R of farm *(♣ to L)* and veer R uphill on unsurfaced track. KSO. When you reach a road at a sharp RH bend, turn hard L then immediately R onto track (in effect continuing in a straight line from where you have come from).

At junction of tracks on ridge in open heathland, KSO ahead. Reach junction with D37 *(turn R here for 250 metres to Gîte/CH La Grange de Grizou, tel 05 65 23 46 30 & 06 75 39 73 35, 8pl, all year)*. Otherwise, turn L and then 20 metres later turn hard R onto gravel lane alongside field that winds its way past more fields and then over heathland on ridge. KSO(L) at fork 700–800 metres later. KSO at next and at fork *(seat, splendid views)* fork L. About 400 metres later reach D4, turn R along it and KSO.

For the variante *GR65 avoiding Montcuq – shorter, waymarked – take second L 500 metres later onto minor road marked 'Barnac' and then turn R immediately through fields. This rejoins the main GR65 1.5km south of Montcuq, just before the D28.*

Otherwise, KSO(L) at fork then 200 metres later fork R onto minor road marked 'La Mothe 0,7', veering L, and continue on ridge. Road > unsurfaced after a while, descending gently at first *(FP to Gîte Le Souleillou on L, just before radio mast)* and then more steeply, veering L at end into **Place du Sol**, a square *(with ♣ and remains of another* métier à ferrer les boeufs*)* opposite a church in...

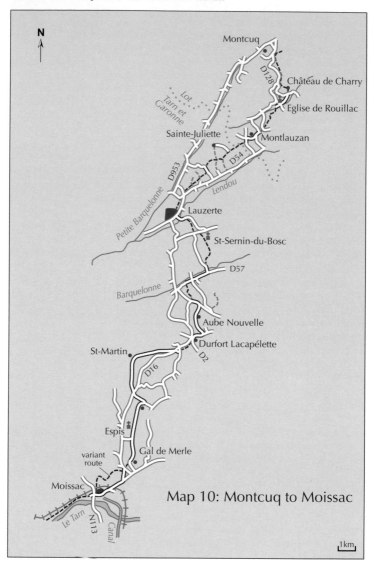

N

Montcuq

D128

Château de Charry

Eglise de Rouillac

Lot

Tarn et Garonne

Sainte-Juliette

Montlauzan

D54

D953

Lendou

Petite Barquelonne

Lauzerte

St-Sernin-du-Bosc

D57

Barquelonne

Aube Nouvelle

Durfort Lacapélette

St-Martin

D16

D2

Espis

Gal de Merle

variant route

Moissac

Le Tarn

Canal

N113

Map 10: Montcuq to Moissac

1km

9km Montcuq (369.5/372.5)

Shops, cafés, several restaurants. Gîte d'Etape Le Souleillou near entrance to town, 22 Rue du Souleillou (tel 05 65 22 48 95, 29pl, K, all year, camping possible). Gîte A l'Ombre de la Tour, 22 Rue du Faubourg Saint-Privat (tel 06 59 34 45 66, 14pl, K, all year). Gîte/CH Le Solelh, 1 Rue du Grimpadou (tel 05 65 23 90 33 & 06 83 04 90 15, 10pl, all year). Hotel, three CH, Camping municipal Saint-Jean (tel 06 30 98 37 38, 15 Jun–5 Sept). OT 8 Rue de la Promenade (tel 05 65 22 94 04).

Small hilltop town dominated by 12th-century keep. Church of Saint-Hilaire and a second church. More or less the halfway point between Le Puy and Saint-Jean-Pied-de-Port.

To visit town: KSO past church to R up **Rue du Faubourg** and then retrace your steps to continue. *(Useful town plan on board at entry.)*

To continue: turn L along **Rue du Pontet** (D28), cross bridge and 50 metres later fork L uphill up tree-lined lane. Continue on ridge at top on open track through fields and at wide track turn R and then 80 metres later turn L along D28. (Variante *rejoins main GR65 from L here (1.5km from Montcuq)).*

About 150 metres later at RH bend, KSO(L) down very minor road, descending gently and then turn R onto FP a few metres after road enters woods. Pass entrance gates to **Château de Charry** (L, *handy seat*) and KSO on FP through woods. Cross D28 (**Roux**, a farm, to L, and wayside cross – this is **Berty**) and KSO on other side, downhill down green lane. Turn R at bottom along minor road and then you can a) fork L uphill for 300 metres to visit church in **Rouillac** *(Romanesque frescoes on ceiling above altar)* and then retrace your steps, and/or b) KSO(L) ahead (marked 'Carros 0,6').

After about 1km turn L down unsurfaced track through fields, cross the **Tatuguié** (stream) by metal footbridge and continue ahead alongside fields, veering R, L and R again *(small lake to R)* uphill (slippery in wet weather) to road in hamlet of **Bonal** (1km).

Fork R along road *(Montlauzan ahead on hill)*. About 600 metres later KSO(L) at junction and continue on road *(another big lake to R)*. Turn R uphill at T-junction and KSO *(note topiary wayside cross to L)*, ignoring turns to…

7km Montlauzan (376.5/365.5)

You are now in the *département* of the Tarn et Garonne. For gîte & CH in former presbytery, 200 metres off route, turn hard R at top of hill (tel 05 65 36 04 02 & 06 73 44 26 39, 6pl, Apr–Oct, after 2pm).

Topiary wayside cross at entry to Montlauzan

The GR65 does not enter the village, so to continue do not turn hard R at top of hill but KSO downhill instead, on D256, to the D45. Turn L along it for 100 metres then turn R up path alongside vines at first, then continue on FP to L of hedge, uphill all the time into woods.

Emerge briefly onto open plateau *(more or less level with Montlauzan church behind you)* then re-enter (semi-shaded) woods. KSO, ignoring turns. After 2km reach minor road at bend and KSO(R) along it. KSO at junction *(L turn to Al Casse, R to Sainte-Juliette)* and then KSO(R) down unsurfaced track (at LH bend in road), alongside long wire fence. KSO for 1.5km on dead straight, shady FP until you reach a minor road at...

3.5km Le Pech-de-la-Rode (380/362)

Here you can either a) *(in bad weather)* turn L and then R on D45 and KSO to Lauzerte, or b) continue on FP ahead *(very slippery and dangerous in wet weather)* and reach minor road at a farm (**Raissou**). Fork R down a shady lane here, following it round along side of fields, gently downhill, until you reach the D54 2km later. KSO(R) along it to a roundabout *(large superstore on R, café, tabac/presse to L)* and continue ahead on D2 uphill.

Halfway up hill turn R up steep grassy lane. Turn R at top then immediately L up unsurfaced road *(Gîte/CH 'Les Figuiers' on R, tel 05 63 29 11 85 & 06 85 31 71 31, 30pl, all year, K)*, hard L at top onto road. Turn R, veering L into **Place des Cornières** in the centre of...

3.5km Lauzerte 221m (383.5/358.5)

Shops, cafés, restaurants, four CH, two hotel-restos. Gîte d'étape communal, Rue du Millial (tel 06 19 70 89 49, 17pl, Apr–Oct, ask in OT or café in Place des Cornières, K). Gîte d'Etape Villa Venou, *lieu-dit* Germa (tel 05 63 94 70 40 & 06 19 43 04 13 & 07 78 17 59 53, 12pl, K, all year, camping possible). Camping Le Beauvillage, Le Vignal, near large supermarket at entry to town (tel 06 67 31 20 19, Apr–Oct). OT Place des Cornières (tel 05 63 94 61 94).

Bastide hill town dating from 12th century. Medieval houses, two churches (Saint-Barthélmy, with modern statue of St James as pilgrim inside, and Eglise des Carmes).

Half-timbered dovecote

To leave: cross the **Place des Cornières**, KSO ahead on **Rue du Marché** then turn R down **Grande Rue/Rue de la Gendarmerie** past tower (L) and then turn L down steps (this is the **Impasse de la Brèche**) by **Maison de Retraite**. Cross road and go down small stone staircase, turn L on road and immediately hard R down slope. Cross minor road and KSO ahead alongside cemetery wall (on your RH side), veering L. Turn R and 60 metres later fork L off road down grassy track *(watch out carefully for waymarks)* leading to road. Turn L ('no entry') then continue on D953 for 200 metres before turning R down D81 (marked 'St Jean').

Cross three bridges (the third is over **Le Lendou**, a small river) then turn second R uphill (marked 'Péries') and KSO(R) up tarred road which > green lane *(lake to R)*, leading uphill (at times steeply) through woods (2km). *(Handy seat with good view back to Lauzerte at top.)*

Church of Saint-Sernin-du-Bosc

At road turn L for 300 metres to the (much-photographed) 'pigeonnier du Quercy,' a dovecote *(opposite* **Le Chartron**, *a big house)*, and 50 metres later turn R downhill on gravel track to small church in valley bottom

3km Eglise Saint-Sernin-du-Bosc (386.5/355.5)
Church of Romanesque origin, restored 1991 onwards.

KSO(R) uphill and 100 metres later turn R along minor road *(lake below to R)* and 200 metres later fork R along grassy lane

113

along side of hill then fork R again at next fork, leading down to minor road near farm (**Parry**). KSO(R), veering L. At junction KSO ahead on another minor road and reach D57.

Turn R along it for 1.3km and then (after passing small crossroads and opposite track to R and 100 metres after crossing stream) turn L up wide grassy lane leading along side of woods. Follow line of trees, veering R uphill to minor road by house.

Turn L on minor road for 300 metres then continue ahead on road to top of hill. Turn L here (**Mirabel**) then fork R 100 metres later before bending down lane between hedges *(old fountain to L)* leading downhill through fields. Turn R, L and L again (round three sides of a square) and KSO ahead on grassy track which > shady lane, to valley bottom. About 500 metres after turning L the second time, turn R over stream and continue uphill on muddy track veering L to farm. KSO(L) on minor road to the...

5.5km Auberge de l'Aube Nouvelle (392/350)
Hotel/restaurant (tel 05 63 04 50 33).

At junction 100 metres later turn R steeply uphill to road *(but KSO ahead, to L, for the Gîte Le Pigeonnier de Figué-Haut, tel 05 63 04 56 32 & 06 70 89 88 05, 12pl, all year, camping possible – tents provided, K)*. Turn L along minor road just before you reach the D22, then fork R on grassy track alongside fields. Turn R again, veering R to D2 and continue on FP to LH side of road, up to a roundabout. KSO on D20 to a junction with bakery and *bar/tabac/alimentation* in...

1.5km Durfort-Lacapelette 206m (393.5/348.5)
Bar/*tabac*/grocery store (X Wed), ♣ beside it, bakery (X Sun pm & Mon). Gîte du Soleil Levant (on GR65, in centre of village, tel 06 14 96 00 30, 6pl, K, all year).

Continue on D16 (towards Moissac) and after 1km turn R onto minor road to **Saint-Martin**, veering L. Turn L after 1.5km, passing church (to R), and descend to D16 again.

However, unless you want to sleep in La Baysse (gîte/CH, tel 05 63 04 56 03, 5pl, all year) it is not worth the detour as the route is all on tarmac and there is hardly any shade either. Instead it is suggested that you stay on the D16 until you see the waymarks indicating a left turn onto a minor tarmac lane.

Cross over and continue on small FP on LH side for 250 metres then turn L onto a minor tarred road, veering R, then at bend KSO(R) ahead on shady FP between hedges and fields. 1km later veer L, go up bank, turn R on minor road and 50 metres later return to the D16. Turn L onto FP below road and KSO.

Around 400–500 metres later turn L onto minor tarred road, veering R, and continue on clear grassy track through fields, // to D16 most of the time. About 800 metres later turn L up FP leading uphill through trees to gravel lane coming from L; turn R along it (farm to L) and 400 metres later (at **Fournaise**) turn hard R along a minor road and KSO along it on ridge, passing farm at **Carbonlères** (R), and continue to church (♣) and hamlet of...

9km Espis 152m (402.5/339.5)

Continue along ridge, ignoring RH turn before **Le Mole**, after which road begins to descend. KSO, going downhill to cluster of houses at...

3km Gal de Merle (405.5/336.5)

At junction at bottom of hill (HT pylons) KSO(R) ahead, cross footbridge over stream and 100 metres later reach D957 and turn L along it *(bench on L with shell on top, just before you reach the road, ♣).* Turn L onto road (D957) just before town entrance boards and continue to a roundabout. Continue ahead here (FP on RH side of road, ♣ at start).

From here there is a *standard route* into Moissac and a *variante,* both waymarked.

a) For the *standard route,* take the fifth turning R (opposite end of cemetery wall) into the **Chemin des Vignes**. This leads you, after some 1.5km, to the **Avenue du Chasselas**. Turn R along it for 300 metres then fork R (just before tunnel under railway line) up **Chemin de Ricard** (to RH side of tracks) and 300 metres later turn L over level crossing. Continue ahead (**Côte de Landeruse**) and then 100 metres later turn R. Go along **Faubourg Ste Blanche**, **Rue Général Gras**, **Rue Malaveille** and then turn R up **Rue de la République** to the abbey.

b) For the 'scenic route' (the *variante,* which has very good views, although you may not feel like it at the end of a long day), take the fourth R turn up the **Chemin de Malengane**. KSO for 1.5km and then turn L steeply uphill just before house no 643 *(waymark missing)* beside orchards for 150 metres to a minor road. Turn R and continue uphill again and onto a ridge, the **Croix de Lauzerte**. After 1km road begins to descend, KSO ahead at junction down the **Côte Saint-Michel**, descending steeply down grassy track *(plenty of seats)* and a tarred road to the old section of the town and the abbey.

2.5KM MOISSAC 76M (408/334)

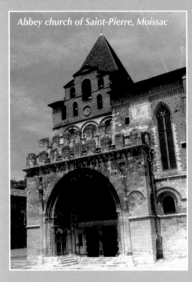

Abbey church of Saint-Pierre, Moissac

All facilities. Population 12,354 (twinned with Astorga, on the *Camino Francés* in Spain). SNCF (trains to Agen, Bordeaux, Montauban, Toulouse). Accueil de la Communauté Réligieuse de Marie Mère de l'Eglise, 20 Boulevard Camille Delthil (phone ahead 10am–midday, tel 05 63 32 28 87, 7pl, Easter–1 Oct, K). Gîte d'Etape in the Ancien Carmel, 5 Sente du Calvaire, high up on hill above the abbey (tel 05 63 04 62 21 & 09 64 48 71 99, 66pl, all year, K). Gîte La Petite Lumière, 1183 Sente du Calvaire (below Ancien Carmel, tel 06 74 68 12 94 & 06 62 62 73 72, 6pl, Apr–Oct, K). Gîte d'Etape Les Etoiles, 4 Rue Falhière (in town centre, 300 metres from cloister, tel 05 63 94 22 47 & 06 25 63 00 16, 13pl, 10 Apr–1 Oct). Gîte d'Etape La Coquille, 4 Rue des Mazels (tel 06 78 04 90 11, 8pl, K, all year). Gîte d'Etape Ultreia +CH, 45 Avenue Pierre Chabrié (on GR opposite railway station, tel 05 63 05 15 06 & 06 71 74 03 14, 14pl in gîte (+K), four rooms B&B, open all year). Six CH, four hotels, 18 restaurants. Camping communal de l'Ile de Bidounet, 1km south of river (tel 05 63 32 52 52, Apr–Sept). OT 6 Place Durand de Bredon (tel 05 63 04 01 85).

Major pilgrim halt from the Middle Ages onwards. Abbey church of Saint-Pierre, former Benedictine monastery founded in the seventh century with impressive cloisters; first built in 1100, they contain 116 columns and 76 capitals, 46 of which tell Bible stories or the lives of saints: a guided tour of the abbey is recommended. Services (all in abbey): a) Mon–Sat: 8.30am Lauds, 6pm Vespers, Mass 6.30pm; b) Sunday: Mass 11am, Vespers 5pm. Musée Saint-Jacques is in the former church (of St James). Centre d'Art Roman (Romanesque art) in former convent buildings to north of railway line near Abbey. Try to allocate at least half a day to visit the town.

SECTION 3
Moissac to Aire-sur-l'Adour

To leave Moissac: from Abbey (facing the main entrance) turn L into the **Rue Marcassus/Carriera Sant Miquel** and turn L into **Allées de Marengo** (don't go up slope). Continue along **Avenue Pierre Cahabrie**, forking R up slope to railway station and then go down steps (L) ahead, cross **Avenue Gambetta** and then road bridge over the canal. Turn R along the **Promenade St Martin** on LH bank of canal. Continue along the canal towpath *(shady in parts)* to a lock, the...

3km Ecluse de l'Espagnette (411/331)

After that you have a choice:

a) The main GR65 *(not described here)* crosses the canal at the bridge and, presumably to vary the long, flat walk along the canal, goes up along a ridge, visible ahead of you, before coming down again in **Maulause**: strenuous but with good views over the 'lake' where the rivers **Tarn** and **Garonne** meet. The GR comes down briefly into **Boudou** before climbing up again. After **Maulause** (9km) you continue along the towpath as in b) below.

b) The *variante* continues along the LH bank of the canal towpath and is the route described here. *However, neither this nor the main GR65 is the historic route: that crossed the Tarn in Moissac itself and continued south via St Nicholas de la Grave, thus missing out Auvillar, but the construction of the Autoroute des Deux Mers in the early 1990s necessitated considerable rerouting of the GR65. Both options are waymarked with the normal red-and-white balises. The towpath is fairly shady, particularly later on, quiet, in the main (especially after Maulause) and slightly shorter, and is suggested as a change after the constant ups and downs of the route until now and because there are no significant 'sights' on the higher-level option anyway.*

Continue on the LH bank of the canal, pass a second lock 3.8km later (**Petitbezy**), go under the D26 road bridge *(picnic tables)* and pass a first brick bridge at **Ganneau**, at the beginning of Maulause, and then another bridge in...

7.5km Maulause 66m (418.5/323.5)

Gîte, 11 Avenue de Bordeaux (tel 05 63 39 64 23 & 06 79 44 09 77, 10pl, K).
CH, 28 Avenue de Bordeaux (tel 05 63 05 16 44 & 06 79 17 21 82, all year.
Bar/pizzeria (X Mon), shop (X Sun pm & Mon pm), bakery (X Mon) in village itself. Picnic tables on RH bank by the second (concrete) bridge.

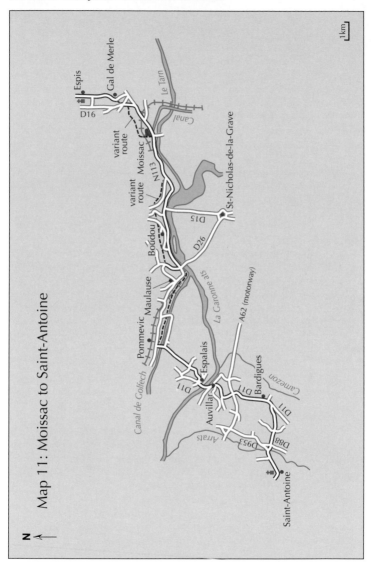

Map 11: Moissac to Saint-Antoine

At another similar bridge 1.5km later KSO ahead on LH bank. Pass a third lock and at the next bridge after that cross over the canal and continue on its RH bank for 400 metres to the **Pont de Pommevic** (a road bridge). *(About 100 metres before it, by seat, cross FB to village for shop, bar etc and then retrace your steps.)*

3.5km Pommevic (422/320)

Hotel-Restaurant-Bar La Bonne Auberge, 8 Avenue de Toulouse (tel 05 63 94 06 86, hotel 7/7, resto X Sun pm). 12th-century church in village, accessible by FP to R shortly before you reach the bridge.

Go under bridge and turn R immediately up a FP and then hard R to cross the bridge over both canal and river. *(Auvillar is visible on the hill ahead. Campsite (Capelinos, open all year) on LH side of road after crossing bridge.)* KSO ahead (marked 'Espalais 3'), KSO at crossroads and veer R just before entry to village of…

3.5km Espalais 63m (425.5/316.5)

Gîte-Accueil Pèlerin Le Par'Chemin, 34 Avenue de Monplaisir (tel 05 63 94 73 78 & 06 33 74 48 65, donation, camping possible, all year). CH Château de Lastours, 3 Route d'Espalais (tel 05 81 78 00 01 & 06 24 24 24 66, all year, 50 metres from GR).

Continue to end of village, pass church *(R, ♣, nice public garden with seats)* and turn L to cross road bridge (carefully) over the **Garonne.** Turn L on other side on **Espanade du Port**, fork R, pass Romanesque **Chapelle Sainte-Cathérine du Port** (R, ♣) and zigzag steeply uphill on **Chemin du Peyret**. At large renovated *lavoir* (R) turn hard L uphill on **Rue de la Fontaine** then R, passing gîte d'étape (R) and enter the **Place de la Halle** in…

1.5km Auvillar 108m (427/315)

Shops, cafés, restaurants. Gîte d'étape communal in former presbytery (18pl, K, 1 Apr–15 Oct, phone OT for access). Gîte d'Etape privé Le Clos d'Alange (tel 05 63 94 76 84 & 06 75 49 14 57, 6pl, K, all year). Gîte d'Etape privé, Chemin Neuf/761 Chemin du Moulin (tel 05 63 39 01 08 & 06 10 93 56 25, 3–4pl, K, Apr–Oct). Gîte d'Etape privé Chez le Saint-Jacques, 14 Place de la Halle (tel 05 63 29 14 21, 6–8pl, K, Apr–Oct). Gîte, 59 Chemin du Moulin (tel 06 63 15 86 18 & 06 95 63 91 82, 4pl, K, all year). Six CH, Hotel-Restaurant L'Horloge, Place de l'Horloge (tel 05 63 39 91 61, hotel open 7/7, 15 Apr–15 Oct, X Fri & Sat pm rest of year). OT 13 Place de la Halle (tel 05 63 39 89 82), ATM at PTT.

Small town on hilltop with circular medieval market hall, very well restored, in arcaded square. Church of Saint-Pierre, museum.

Continue R ahead along **Rue de l'Horloge**, passing under arch, and KSO ahead uphill (**Rue de la Sauvetat**, *the D11 to Bardigues*), veering R uphill. Turn L at top of hill, turn L onto minor road (marked 'Hautes Peyrières') just before town exit boards. Veer R at last house down grassy track leading downhill, then slightly up 500 metres later, to D11 again, by bridge over stream. Turn L, go under motorway and continue on D11 towards…

4km Bardigues (431/311)

Bar/restaurant by church (in village itself, to L of road, X Sun pm all year, also Mon off-season).

Continue on D11 for 350 metres then just before village exit boards turn R down minor road and continue on plateau for 1.5km to a T-junction. KSO *ahead* down unsurfaced track which > FP (overgrown to begin with) which leads in more or less a straight line downhill past farm (R, **Saint-Antoine** *visible to L ahead here*) and via a tarred road to D88 (1km). Cross over, marked 'Saint-Antoine 1,5', veer R and then turn L over bridge over the river **Arrats** and KSO on road (D953) for 1km to…

5km Saint-Antoine-de-Pont-d'Arratz 73m (436/306)

Gîte d'Etape & CH L'Oustal (tel 05 62 28 64 27, 30pl, Mar–Oct, to RH side of road on leaving village, camping possible). CH La Maison du Bois (tel 05 62 28 68 15, all year, after the church). Bar/restaurant/shop (7/7).

The village takes its name from the religious order of the Antonins, who set up a hospital (the present château) for people suffering from ergotism (a disease also known as 'St Anthony's fire'), which was very prevalent in the Middle Ages. It was contracted by consuming cereal products (such as rye bread) contaminated by the ergot fungus, and resulted in a gangrenous condition of the hands and feet. There was a similar such hospital further along the *Camino Francés*, the pilgrim road to Santiago in Spain, shortly before Castrojeriz.

The church has two murals, discovered in 2006: a) St George and the dragon, 14th century and b) the story of St Blaise (who was martyred by being skinned alive), 16th century.

You are now in the département *of the Gers, whose Conseil Général has made a strenuous effort to provide footpaths for pilgrim use alongside all its major roads*

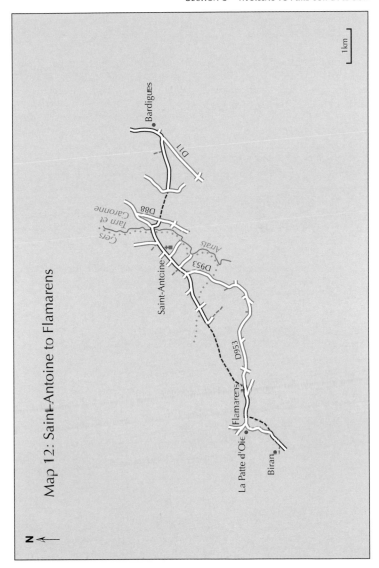

Map 12: Saint-Antoine to Flamarens

N ←

1km

Bardigues

D11

Tarn et Garonne

Gers

D88

Saint-Antoine

Arrats

D953

D953

Flamarens

La Patte d'Oie

Biran

used by the GR65 (until Aire-sur-l'Adour, where you enter the département *of Les Landes) and requests you to use them for both your own safety and that of other road-users.*

Continue through village, veering L, go under arch onto pedestrianised street, passing bar/restaurant/shop. At crossing 1.7km later *(CH/Gîte La Ferme de Villeneuve, tel 05 62 28 21 75 & 06 10 33 67 99, 15 Mar–15 Nov, on RH side of GR itself; CH L'Etoile d'Herberger, lieu-dit Hauron, 500 metres from GR to LH side, tel 05 63 32 38 40 & 06 52 16 74 38, all year)* KSO ahead then, at top of hill, by farm, continue ahead but then, almost immediately, fork R down grassy track ahead, downhill, down shady lane. Cross field, then stream, continue up on other side, pass farm, more or less in a straight line all the time, and KSO on minor road up to village of…

4.5km Flamarens 210m (440.5/301.5)

Accueil chrétien des pèlerins (tel 05 62 28 61 13 but only 48hrs ahead, 4–5pl, all year, donation, to LH side of route, 1km after village). ♣ by *mairie*. Castle (12th–15th century) is a historic monument, which can be visited during Jul and Aug (10am–midday and 2–7pm, X Tues). Eglise Saint-Saturnin.

The undulating countryside in this area consists mainly of cornfields and hundreds of acres of sunflowers, all lined up like battalions of well-trained soldiers who turn their heads towards the sun *en bloc*, according to the time of day.

Château de Flamarens

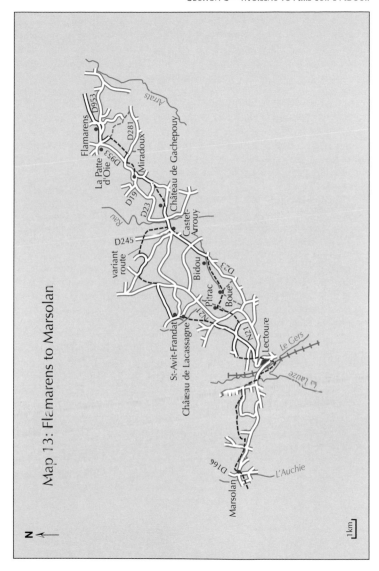

Map 13: Flamarens to Marsolan

N

1km

Turn R at 'stop' sign (D953) and then immediately L to church by large wayside cross. Go down path to R of castle to road and KSO along it, past another wayside cross, for 750 metres. Just before top of hill turn L down minor road (marked 'Gauran, Le Casse, Maynard') then 150 metres later, by fork, fork R down FP which > grassy track downhill, between fields, veering R to minor road then KSO(L) on FP to its LH side. Around 1.5km later pass *lieu-dit* **Biran** *(on R, small gîte d'étape, tel 05 62 28 64 65 after 7pm & 06 20 29 90 07, 7pl, camping, K, Apr–Oct)* then pass junction with D28. KSO ahead uphill, veering L to pass plantation of trees (on R).

Reach minor road on a ridge, at a U-bend. Fork L and KSO, downhill on FP to side of road. Continue (L) along D953 *(the* **Route de Valence***;* point d'accueil *and* info-pèlerin *at house on RH side)* to reach junction with D19 and turn L up it into…

4km Miradoux (444.5/297.5)

Bar/restaurant with rooms, 6 Route de Lectoure (tel 05 62 28 61 43). Gîte d'Etape Le Patio, 9 Place du Forail (tel 05 62 28 58 63 & 06 46 24 82 49, 10pl, K, 1 Apr–15 Nov). Gîte d'Etape Bonté Divine! 5 Rue Porte d'Uzan nord (tel 05 62 58 30 80 & 06 20 50 09 70, 12pl, Apr–Oct). Three CH: a) 3 Place de la Mairie (tel 05 62 28 84 35 & 06 75 57 49 29, all year); b) 16 Grande Rue (tel 05 62 28 69 19, Mar–Oct); c) 4 Place de la Halle (tel 05 62 28 69 19 & 06 46 24 82 49, all year). Bakery, *superette*, bank (+ATM), PTT, pharmacy, OT in *mairie* (tel 05 62 28 6308). ♣. Picnic area by Salle des Fêtes. Gothic church (modern statue of St James pilgrim inside). Fontaine de Condé.

Veer R, pass church and leave village on D953 (**Route de Lectoure**). About 200 metres after junction of D953 (to 'St Clar') and D23 ('Lectoure 14'), 1km from Miradoux, at bend, turn second L up minor road, marked 'Tucoula'. When this bends R 50 metres later KSO(L) ahead up grassy track and then turn R uphill. At three isolated chestnut trees on ridge, turn L along grassy track coming from farm to R *(view of Château de Fieux over to R)* and passing above **Château de Gachepouy**.

KSO at junction of similar paths by **Ferme de Gachepouy** (to R). Turn R at end of field along similar track coming from L. KSO(L) ahead when similar track joins from back R and go downhill to reach the D23. Turn L, cross stream and continue on FP to LH side of D23 for 500 metres. At entrance to village, just before its place-name boards, turn L onto minor road then R onto street, cross a road and continue ahead *(AP partway up on R)* to **Place de l'Eglise** in…

5km Castet-Arrouy (449.5/292.5)

Gîte communal *(mairie*, tel 05 62 29 28 43 & 06 84 92 73 96, 15pl, K, camping possible, Apr–Oct). CH Au Musée d'Albert (tel 05 62 28 73 97 & 06 22 18 42

76, opp restaurant). CH Chez Nat (tel 05 62 29 19 40 & 06 22 39 54 07, all year, *pause-pèlerin* with hot/cold drinks). CH A la Croisée de nos Chemins (tel 05 62 68 37 80 & 06 78 76 24 45, all year). Restaurant/shop 'La Plancha' opposite church (X Sun midday). Covered sitting area in church porch, with tables.

Village name means 'red castle', originally the site of a small fort. Church begun in Gothic times but with later additions has statues and newly restored 19th-century paintings.

To continue, KSO through village past church. KSO(L) on FP to LH side of D23 then change to RH side of road. KSO then, at end of woods, change back to LH side and KSO. Pass electricity tower, KSO and 700–800 metres later pass turning (R) to **Bidou**. About 100 metres later cross road and turn R uphill alongside fields, then through woods and KSO, following line of hedge.

Around 1km from leaving road, pass turning (L, over FB) to **Ferme Barrachin** *(gîte d'étape, CH, tel 05 62 68 84 57, 5pl, 15 Apr–1 Oct, no groups, K, camping, reservations only 2–3 days in advance)* and KSO ahead. Pass LH turning with bridge over stream by pond and KSO first to RH side of stream then to L. KSO; 1km later pass large rectangular pond (R) then turning to **Boué** *(farm, CH, tel 05 62 68 89 49, Mar–Oct, 100 metres from GR to R)* and KSO, gradually uphill, then 100 metres later, at crossing, turn R on grassy track, leading up into the woods. KSO and 1km after that reach lane by **Pitrac** (large house to R). Turn L uphill on very minor tarred road for 500 metres, leading to the N21.

Turn L along it for 50 metres then turn R down track *(passing house on L – this is the lieu-dit* **Tarisson***: CH second house on L after N21, tel 06 78 38 60 60 Mar–Oct)*. Continue on grassy track between fields *(view of Lectoure to R ahead)*, descending gradually but 150 metres before a farm turn R along side of field. Reach minor road, turn R then veer L 30 metres later. Around 400 metres after that fork L down lane. Fork L down grassy track at next fork, between fields, veering R alongside hedge. Reach minor road about 1km later and turn L downhill. KSO then go uphill, passing cemetery (on R, *handy seat*). Turn R by very large red wayside cross (**La Croix Rouge**) then, veering L, turn L (♣ *to L*) then turn R (**Rue Corhaut**: *Accueil Le Temps du Pèlerin, 2 Rue du Corhaut, tel 06 14 11 41 09, donation, reservation essential)*. Turn second R up **Rue Saint-Gervais** to the cathedral in…

10KM LECTOURE 186M (459.5/282.5)

Population 4000. All facilities. *Accueil chrétien* in presbytery (tel 05 62 68 83 83, reservations 24–48hrs ahead max, 10pl, 15 Apr–Sept, donation). Gîte'd'Etape

L'Etoile Occitane, 140 Rue Nationale (tel 05 62 68 82 93 & 06 74 45 11 17, 14pl, Apr–Oct after 2pm, K). Gîte, Résidence du Marquisat, 2 Chemin du Marquisat (tel 05 62 68 71 27, all year, K). Gîte à 2 pas, 56 Rue Nationale (by cathedral, tel 05 62 28 99 67 & 06 70 99 37 79 & 06 37 11 36 76, 10–12pl, all year). La Casa del Peregrino, 9 Chemin de Laucate (tel 05 62 68 58 49 & 07 78 35 13 30, pilgrims only, no suitcases, all year after 3.30pm). Gîte-CH La Halte Pèlerine, 28 Rue Sainte-Claire (tel 05 62 28 50 35 & 06 88 90 55 74, 8pl, all year, K). Six CH, two hotel-restaurants, OT Place du Général de Gaulle (tel 05 62 68 76 98 – ask here for walking tour leaflet).

One of the oldest towns in the Gers. Cathedral of SS Gervais & Protais, 17th–18th-century Hôtel de Ville, ramparts, many interesting old houses (Lectoure is also a spa town).

To continue, pass to RH side of OT (**Rue Fontelie**), veering L and then R downhill, down flight of steps, veering L past ramparts. Turn R onto **Chemin Claude Ydron** to junction of D7 and N21, turn L and 40 metres later go down minor road, the **Chemin de la Tride** (wedged between the N21 and the D7, to R), downhill. Turn R at bottom along D36 for 100 metres then turn L, go over level crossing and immediately turn R for 500 metres along minor road // to railway line. Just before *second* level crossing (to R), turn L onto D7. Cross the **Pont de Pile** over the river **Gers** and 100 metres later, before another bridge, turn hard R, veering L along wide grassy lane between hedges (semi-shaded).

Fork L at junction with similar track, reach the D36, cross it and KSO on minor road on other side. KSO(L) at junction and KSO, continuing on grassy track through fields after tarred surface ends at a farm.

Halfway up hill pass to other side of hedge and KSO. Just before farm *(over to R ahead)* turn L onto unsurfaced road, veer L 100 metres later up to road *(good views back to Lectoure as you climb)* in hamlet of…

4.5km Espasot 160m (464/278)
Gîte La Ferme d'Espasot (tel 06 37 64 89 80, 88pl, K).

Turn R *(useful stone seat 50 metres later)* and KSO for 2.5km along ridge *(very little shade)*. About 100 metres after a crossroads with a stone cross *(a croix de justice, picnic area with information board)* fork R down grassy lane. Track joins from back R, KSO. Pass another small stone cross on pedestal (R) and KSO. Cross track, KSO. After 1km reach tarred road at junction and turn L, passing cemetery in…

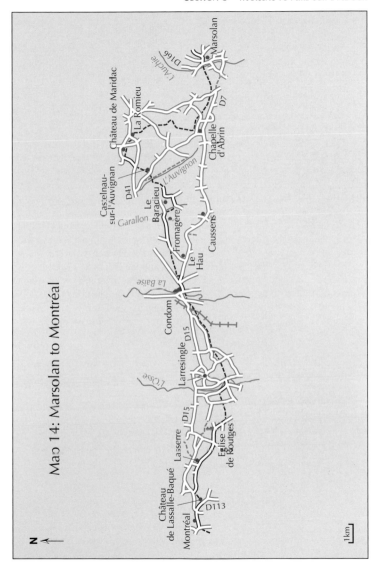

Map 14: Marsolan to Montréal

4.5km Marsolan 171m (468.5/273.5)

Gîte/CH L'Enclos du Tabus (tel 05 62 68 79 40, all year X Jul/Aug). Gîte Le Bourdon (tel 09 54 10 78 68 & 09 53 75 20 93, pilgrims with *crédenciale* only, either on foot, by bicycle or with a donkey, 12pl, K, Apr–Oct, last house on L on main street in village). Café/snack bar, shop, 7/7 Apr–Oct, otherwise Tues, Thurs, Sat 11am–1pm.

Remains of Hôpital Saint-Jacques at entrance to village. Shady square behind church good place to rest (♣ nearby). Covered rest area.

Enter by *mairie* and large wayside cross, pass to R of church and continue downhill to cross D166. Continue on other side, KSO at crossing 200 metres later then turn L, veering R at bend onto grassy track leading up through fields. Pass small lake (L) and continue up to minor road at bend (2.5km). KSO(R) along it, KSO(L) at junction and when tarmac stops at last house KSO along grassy track along ridge *(good views)* before descending to continue ahead (in more or less a straight line all the time) through fields. KSO. Join minor road coming from back R just before a farm (**Bertsuguières**), pass farm of **Montravail** and turn R down track (downhill), 100 metres before you reach the **Chapelle d'Abrin**.

However, if you want to go directly to Condom, missing out La Romieu (6km shorter), you can KSO ahead here for 4km, to the RH side of the river Auvignon, rejoining the GR65 500 metres after it leaves Castelnau-sur-l'Auvignon, where you turn L onto it. For a description of this option see page 130*.

Chapelle d'Abrin

5km Chapelle d'Abrin (473.5/268.5)

Former commandery of the Knights Hospitallers of St John of Jerusalem (now a private house), pilgrim halt at meeting of two routes (the other came from Rocamadour and Moissac via Agen).

Gîte Ferme de Gratuzous (turn R between the Chapelle d'Abrin and La Romieu and follow signs, tel 05 62 28 03 17 & 06 07 31 41 45, 6pl, K, Apr–Oct).

Pass lake (R), KSO(R) uphill at fork and KSO. After 800 metres at top of hill (track bends L) KSO ahead downhill along green lane, through fields and uphill into woods. Turn L at top of hill at T-junction, leave woods, reach road at bend and turn R for 80 metres. Turn L along track. Opposite farm (**Le Double**) turn hard R alongside woods onto another track and descend gently to **La Romieu**, veering R at entry, then turn L at T-junction and immediately R along the **Rue Surmain** (to visit town) or L along D41 to continue. *(Gîte de Beausoleil, Moncade, 500 metres off GR, 1km before La Romieu, tel 06 71 58 50 21, 35pl).*

5km La Romieu 478.5/263.5

Gîte d'étape privé Le Couvent de La Romieu, in former convent, next to church (tel 05 62 28 73 59 & 06 88 47 36 17, 15pl, 15 Mar–Oct, K, also rooms). Gîte le Refuge, Rue du Docteur Lucante (tel 06 80 05 09 31, 6pl, K, all year, opposite Collégiale Saint-Pierre). CH in former presbytery, 2 Rue du Docteur Lucante (tel 05 62 28 60 67). CH & Café-Restaurant d'Angeline, Place Bouet (tel 05 62 28 10 29 & 06 69 63 88 99, open 7/7 high season, otherwise X Wed). Four other CH. Camping-Restaurant Castel Le Camp de Florence (tel 05 62 28 15 58, May–Sept). Shop, bakery, restaurant. OT (Rue du Docteur Lucante, tel 05 62 28 86 33).

The village takes its name from the *romieux* (pilgrims) who passed through it on their way to Santiago. Like Condom and Lectoure, La Romieu also has an enormous church for its size, an indication of its former importance; the 14th-century Collégiale (built by Clement V, one of the Avignon Popes) is well worth a visit.

To leave: turn L on D41 then turn R down grassy lane (150 metres after *road* turns to R) through fields.

Three accommodation places near crossing of GR and D41: a) Gîte le Relais du Maçon (tel 06 16 93 84 70, 15pl, all year, limited groceries); b) Gîte/CH Domaine de la Rose des Vents, Le Bidon (tel 06 09 74 09 27, 30 Mar–10 Nov); c) Accueil bénévole l'Ancre sur l'Auvignon, Le Mourelot (tel 06 40 05 10 48, 9pl, K, donation, all year, on GR).

Turn R at bottom (on minor road) and 150 metres later turn L towards **Château de Maridac** and veer R alongside it 300 metres later down green lane and KSO to road. Turn L (ignoring first RH turn) uphill. Turn L at top and immediately R down unsurfaced track, veer L before farm and then KSO(L) downhill on grassy track to valley bottom. Cross the **Ruisseau d'Auvignon** and continue uphill ahead to road *(school to R, stone wayside cross)* at entrance to the village of…

5km Castelnau-sur-l'Auvignon (483.5/258.5)

Gîte/CH des Arroucasses in village itself (tel 05 62 28 12 24, 12pl, snack bar, Apr–Oct). CH La Maison du Lézard (tel 05 62 68 26 75 & 06 56 79 37 92, all year).

In this part of France (as in Castillian Spain), you can often see quite far ahead to where you are going next, as the landscape is very open.

Cross over and fork L downhill (continue line of path you were already on) down shady lane, then 200 metres later *turn* R and then *fork* R down green lane. Cut through minor road at 'S' bend and KSO over bridge over river **Auvignon** *(variante joins from L here, just before bridge)*.

* Variante *omitting La Romieu. This is also waymarked with the normal red-and-white* balises *but only adequately so. However, it is easy enough to follow.*

KSO ahead past the **Chapelle d'Abrin** *(now a private house)* on minor road then 300 metres later, at bend, KSO(L) ahead on earth track through fields. About 300 metres after that, just before a junction with a gravel track thet veers L, turn L (at right angles) downhill on grassy track. Turn R 100 metres later then fork L 50 metres after that, veering L downhill *(farm over to R)* through fields and then R to minor road at bend. Turn R along it. Around 300 metres later KSO(L) ahead on unsurfaced road. Continue ahead in valley, with river **Auvignon** // over to your L, passing **Touquet** *(farm)* and then the entrance to **La Maurague** *(farm)* to L. Some 4km after the **Chapelle d'Abrin** turn L, cross bridge over the river and rejoin the main GR65 coming downhill from your R.

After crossing the bridge continue ahead along green lane, fork L at junction and KSO to top of hill, passing to L of farm (**La Baraille**) and veering R on road to…

1.5km Chapelle Sainte-Germaine de Soldanum 168m (485/257)

Chapel from 12th–13th century, all that remains of former monastery (destroyed in the ninth century by the Normans), dedicated to a local saint. The church, now partially restored, is normally open when the cemetery is. ⚓ behind gate. Good (shady) place for a rest.

Continue on road to hamlet of **Baradieu**, turn L by pond and 400 metres later turn R by isolated barn down unsurfaced road to **Moras** (restored farm). Pass to R of it *(lake to R)*, veer L, cross stream (stepping-stones) and then turn R immediately along hedge and KSO alongside lake (**Bousquetara**). Veer L uphill onto tarmac lane, pass (on L) farm of **La Fromagère** and 1km later, at top of hill, cross D204. *About 1km before Condom there is a large gîte/riding centre (70pl, whether or not you have a horse) at the Domaine de Haou-Centre Equestre`L'Etrier Condomois (tel 05 62 28 09 41, all year: shortly after crossing the D204 turn L for 1.1km).*

Continue downhill, first on road, then on gravel lane, then on grassy track alongside field, descending, after 2km, to the junction with the GRP just before you reach the D7 (over to your R, at a house called **Bagatelle**). Turn L down shady lane, continuing as a minor road to junction with the D7 (**Avenue Rhin et Danube**) on the outskirts of **Condom**. Turn R over the river **Baïse** and continue R along the D7 (**Avenue Rhin et Danube**, becoming the **Avenue du Maréchal Joffre**) and then turn L (**Avenue des Anciens Combattants**) to war memorial. *(Turn R here to Rue Gambetta for shops, PTT, cathedral etc.)* Pass to RH side of it up **Rue Jean-Jaures** *(passing gîte d'étape in Centre Salvandy, R)* to **Place de la Liberté**. Continue along **Rue Buzon**, turn R onto **Quai Buzon** and either turn R here into **Rue Roques** for centre of town or turn L over **Pont des Carmes** to continue.

9.5KM CONDOM 81M (494.5/247.5)

Population 8000. All facilities. Gîte de Gabarre, 42 bis Avenue des Mousquetaires, on towpath on River Baïse, 200 metres off GR and 1km to south of town centre (tel 06 86 41 58 39, 40pl, 15 Apr–31 Oct, K). Gîte de l'Ancien Carmel (association), 35 Avenue Victor Hugo (tel 05 62 29 41 56 & 06 41 09 12 43, 50pl, all year). Gîte le Champ d'Etoiles, 18 Avenue de Maréchal Joffre (tel 06 08 05 26 84, 15pl, camping possible, Mar–Oct). Gîte Le Relais Saint-Jacques, 2 Avenue de Maréchal Joffre (tel 06 21 78 47 86 & 06 13 28 52 66, 15pl, K, all year). Gîte La Halte du Kiosque, 2 Square Salvandy (tel 05 62 68 37 76 & 06 84 32 30 01, 10pl, Mar–Oct, next to bandstand). Gîte le Refuge de Jean, 20 Chemin des Capots de Teste (tel 06 07 22 24 57, 8pl, K, camping possible, Apr–Oct). Gîte/CH, 9 Rue Roques/7 Rue Parguère (tel 06 64 54 81 86 & 09 66 97 69 17, all year with reservation). Gîte d'étape/CH Au Claire de l'Eau, 12 Avenue des Anciens Combattants (7pl, K, all year). Three other CH and three hotels. Camping municipal de l'Argenté à Gauge (tel 05 62 28 17 32, Apr–Sept). 19 (!) restaurants. Cyber café Jeux m'Inform, Rue Jules Ferry. OT 5 Place Saint-Pierre (tel 05 62 28 00 80).

Typical Gascon town situated on a spur between the rivers Gèle and Baïse, centre of the Armagnac industry. Cathedral of Saint-Pierre, churches of Saint-Barthélemey de Pradeau, Saint-Jacques and Saint-Michel. Musée de l'Armagnac, cloisters (now the *mairie*).

Turn L immediately after crossing bridge *(the building on L at end, now a theatre, was formerly a Carmelite convent)* along upper (RH) of two FPs alongside river, the **Chemin de la Digue**. This passes behind the **Eglise Saint-Jacques**, *which originally had a hospital attached to it.*

The statue above the blocked-up doorway on the street side is not St James but St Joseph – a dedication made in recognition of the latter's help in alleviating the sufferings of plague victims in that quarter of the town, La Bouguerie.

KSO past the **church of Saint-Jacques** then veer R *(Gîte Gabarre 100 metres to L)* to the D931, cross it, continue on banked-up lane and then turn first L down a minor road at the fork with the D15 *(the **Chemin des Capots de Teste**, the area in which there was a second Hôpital Saint-Jacques, as well as two other non-St James hospitals plus leprosaria)*. The minor road takes you through a residential area. Turn R at end by roundabout and then turn L 100 metres later on minor road to the hamlet of **Ciprionis**.

At top of hill KSO at first junction and KSO(L) at second. KSO, passing **L'Inquiétitude** (a farm). *The linguistically minded walker/pilgrim will already have noticed the place names 'Montravail' and 'Monrepos' elsewhere, with 'Monplaisir' still to come…*

Continue, passing other farms, for 2km, ignoring turns, and much more up than down. At sharp RH bend in road KSO(R) at fork near top of (present) hill; KSO(L) ahead along green lane, uphill to plateau. Unsurfaced road joins from R. KSO *(view of Larresingle to R ahead)* and 200 metres later reach road in a *lieu-dit* known as…

5km Le Carbon 179m (499.5/242.5)

To visit **Larresingle**, *a tiny fortified, walled medieval town, the fortress of the Bishops of Condom in the Middle Ages and well worth the 15min detour (in each direction), turn R along road at Le Carbon. You need not retrace your steps afterwards but, via a minor road to the SW, you can pick up the GR65 where it crosses the D278, just before the Pont d'Artigues, turning R to cross it. Hôtel-Restaurant de Larresingle, (7/7 Apr–Oct). Gîte d'étape/CH La Halte de Larresingle (tel 06 62 77 29 72, 5pl, K, 7/7 after 2.30pm all year but Oct–Mar by arrangement only). Gîte-Accueil à la Ferme Tollet (tel 05 62 28 02 45 & 06 87 36 04 34, K, all year).*

(For both these gîtes turn R 400 metres after the crossing at Le Carbon.) Point-Info May–Sept *(tel 05 62 68 22 49)*, ♣ by cemetery.

If you prefer not to visit Larresingle, KSO ahead down green lane, downhill for 1km. At crossing with another track veer L and then R to skirt small pond and veer L down FP through woods (in effect continuing in a straight line from where you broke off). KSO to reach a road (D278), cross it and 200 metres later cross the…

3km Pont d'Artigues (502.5/239.5)

Originally a Roman bridge over the Osse, with five arches. In the Middle Ages there was a pilgrim hospital belonging, successively, to the Diocese of Santiago, the Knights of the Order of Santiago and then the Order of Saint Jacques de-la-Foi-et-de-la-Paix, but there is no trace left of it today. There was also a church of Notre-Dame by the pilgrim bridge but nothing remains of this today either.

KSO to crossroads and turn R for 600 metres then turn L by HT pylon up grassy lane alongside trees (to your R) uphill into the woods. Cross minor road and KSO on gravel road which > a grassy track. Around 1km later reach a minor road and turn R and then L at T-junction 500 metres later (at RH turn to hamlet of Routges).

Pont d'Artigues

Eglise de Routges, Cagot door

2.5km Eglise de Routges (505/237)

About 100 metres ahead of you, off road, is the oldest church in the region (♣). Note the small door on the side of the church; this was the entrance used by the Cagots, an outcast population of uncertain ethnic origin. They were found mainly in this part of France and lived segregated lives until the end of the 19th century. Like many other pariah communities they were believed to be leprous, syphilitic, unclean and bearers of all types of evil. As a result they were only allowed to enter churches by a special side door reserved for their use and were not permitted to be buried in the cemeteries used by the rest of the population.

KSO ahead along ridge at staggered crossroads (D254) and KSO for 1km more, 300 metres after passing hamlet of **Laserre-le-Haut** *(gîte/CH, tel 05 62 29 57 98, 10+12pl, K)*. KSO(L) at fork to **Le Glesia** *(former Gallo-Roman site)* and 200 metres later KSO(L) down green lane. About 1km later, at **Pages**, track > tarred, and 200 metres later at bend *(fountain)* KSO ahead up green lane under trees, veering L. Just 1km later pass **Château de Lassalle-Baqué** and KSO(R) along D113. Turn L at junction with wayside cross (D15) then immediately R along D113 again (now **Rue Aurensan**) into…

6.5KM MONTRÉAL-DU-GERS 135M (511.5/230.5)

Gîte Compostela at 10 Rue du 14 Juillet, near town centre (tel 05 62 28 67 36 & 06 44 31 82 82, 14pl, 10 Mar–15 Oct). Gîte La Halte du Rempart, 11 Place Hôtel de Ville (tel 05 81 68 10 55 & 06 15 15 34 38, 10pl, K, Apr–Oct). Gîte Napoléon, Boulevard des Pyrénées (tel 05 65 29 44 81 & 06 37 55 48 24, 10–12pl, K, all year). CH Carpe Diem, Bitalis (at entry to village, tel 05 62 28 37 32 & 06 88 49 57 19, Mar–Nov, 2.30pm). CH La Pose du Mont Royal, Route de Gondrin (tel 06 74 80 07 48 & 06 89 35 01 68, all year, first house after town entrance board). CH/Camping à la Ferme, Le Couloumé (tel 05 62 29 44 78 & 06 85 35 51 26, K, all year, on D29 800 metres towards Eauze). Shop, bakery, café, several restaurants, OT Place de l'Hôtel del Ville (tel 05 62 29 42 85), ♣ by fountain.

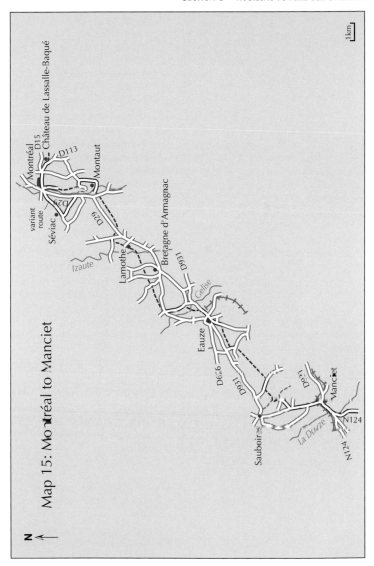

N ←

Map 15: Montréal to Manciet

1km

Montréal
D15
Château de Lassalle-Baqué
D113
Montaut
D29
variant route
Séviac
Izaute
Lamothe
Bretagne d'Armagnac
D931
Gélise
Eauze
D626
D931
D931
Sauboires
La Douze
D21
Manciet
N124
N124

Small town (population 1200) with 13th-century bastide, arcaded market place, 13th-century church, several interesting old houses, museum, ramparts. Galloroman villa at **Séviac** (2km, on variant route, worth visiting) also has CH (tel 05 62 29 44 12) near site and Halte de la Ferme du Soleil (gîte/CH, tel 05 62 29 45 77 & 06 14 44 60 64). CH Lou Prat de la Ressego, Chemin de Séviac (tel 05 62 29 49 55 & 06 72 94 81 38, at start of variant route via Séviac, Apr–Oct).

Enter town down **Rue Aurensan**, turn L into square. Go down RH side of church (under arch) and then turn R along **Boulevard des Remparts**, veering R *(shady seats)* and then turn hard L downhill, hard R immediately to the D15 and hard L onto a shady minor road. Road gradually > an unsurfaced track. KSO. At turning (L) to **Sallepissan** KSO(R) ahead. About 1km later reach minor road at bend and turn L along it, uphill KSO(R) and KSO, ignoring turns, for 800 metres to a road. Turn L along it then, at farm (**Ribère de Bas**), fork R down track (marked 'Barrière de Ribère'). KSO(L) for 1km along the bed of an old railway line *(shady)*, cross metal bridge (**Château de Montaut** *to L)* over a track and then ahead L 30 metres later and L again under bridge (in order to do a 'right turn'). KSO along track for a few hundred metres, then veer L uphill to road. Turn L and 100 metres later turn R up track leading between vines, continuously along line of trees to L. Veer L to gravel lane coming from L, KSO along it and 100 metres later turn L through more vines. Continue on road after 200 metres by farm and 150 metres later KSO ahead along grassy track following line of telegraph poles alongside vines (to R).

Pass farm (L) at road coming from R, KSO ahead along a track, then veer R alongside woods (L) at minor junction. KSO for 600 metres to road (D29). Cross over, continue alongside vines (L) for 200 metres, cross road leading to farm (**Bédat**) and continue alongside more vines to the D31.

Cross the D31 and KSO ahead (slightly staggered to L) on minor tarred road. About 400 metres later turn L alongside vines, continue on FP and then on green lane *(tower visible ahead)* to cemetery ♣ in village of…

9km Lamothe 167m (520.5/217.5)
Gîte d'Etape La Casa d'Elena (tel 06 50 62 13 46, camping possible, Mar–Oct X 26 Jul–5 Aug). Also has shop/café, drinks, snacks, light meals midday, 7/7 Mar–Oct. ♣ in cemetery. 13th-century guard tower.

From Lamothe to Nogaro the walking is fairly flat and easy, if not all that inter-esting. From here to Eauze the GR follows the former railway line.

Turn L and then hard R downhill past church *(shady porch)* to valley bottom and turn L along former railway line (tracks removed). KSO for 7km, mainly shaded, very slightly uphill all the time.

Pass turning (on R) to Restaurant Moulin du Pouy, 1km before entrance to town. Continue until you reach the D931 at the entrance to **Eauze** *(huge factory to R)*, turning R into the town by a large superstore. KSO into the **Place d'Armagnac** and church in the centre of...

7KM EAUZE 142M (527.5/214.5)

Population 3877. All facilities. Shops, cafés, several restaurants. OT 2 Rue Félix Soules (tel 05 62 09 85 62). Accueil Pèlerins Béthanie, 34 Avenue de Sauboires (600 metres after church, tel 07 87 72 07 82, but no reservations X evening before, 8pl, all year – phone ahead in winter, K, evening prayers, donation). Gîte d'Etape communal, 2 Rue Félix Soules, opposite OT (tel 05 62 09 85 62, 23pl, all year, K). Gîte Chez Nadine, 43 Avenue de Sauboires (tel 05 62 08 18 37 & 06 68 94 82 46, 10pl, K, all year with res). Gîte La Borde de Bidou, 27 Avenue de la Ténarèze (tel 05 62 09 70 44 & 05 62 09 92 88 & 06 27 33 59 98, all year (at entrance to town opp gendarmerie)). Gîte La Grange, 4 Avenue de la Ténarèze, (tel 05 62 09 99 09 & 06 61 24 48 04, 12pl, Apr–Oct, K, on GR at entry to town). Gîte Rabelais, Impasse Rabelais (tel 05 62 09 75 22 & 06 73 53 42 43, 6pl, K, all year). Gîte/CH Lou Parpalhou, 13 Rue du Lac (tel 05 62 09 72 84, 10pl, K, Apr–Oct). Hôtel-Restaurant Le Triana (tel 05 62 09 99 21), Hôtel-Restaurant Henri IV (tel 05 62 08 45 40).

Former Gallo-Roman capital (*Elusa*) and Roman colony. Benedictine priory founded in 10th century and attached to Order of Cluny. Church of Sant-Luperc (a local saint) built by the Benedictines, finished 1521, using rubble and stone from Roman sites mixed with local brick. Contains two 17th-century confessionals and, in side chapel, statue of St Roch pilgrim. Icons on long centre panel behind altar are modern (1977), by Nicholaï Greschny (Tarn artist). Numerous old houses, including Maison de Jeanne d'Albret, museum (with treasury of 28,000 Roman coins) and Andalusian style bullring (Arènes Nimeño II).

To leave, with church on your R turn L into **Rue Robert Daury** (pedestrianised) and go ahead down **Avenue des Pyrénées** (D931) for 500 metres then turn R down minor road by house no 58. Turn L at end and then continue up grassy track. Reach major road 500 metres later, cross over and continue on other side, past vines, cross minor road and KSO ahead. At junction of similar tracks turn R. Reach a minor road and turn L. About 300 metres later, at junction, KSO(R) ahead (marked 'Pennebert'). At RH bend in road by farm KSO ahead down gravel lane, KSO(R) at fork by goose farm and continue downhill. Turn R and then L alongside edge of large field, turn R at bottom corner along edge of two more fields *(stream below to R in trees)*, veering R at end and then turn L to cross FB over the **Bergou** (stream).

KSO ahead up RH side of next field, passing to other (RH) side of hedge halfway up and continue up old sunken tree-lined lane. Cross track, cross minor tarred road 1km later, KSO ahead along grassy lane, veer R up side of field and at T-junction of tracks turn L in front of vines to road 100 metres later.

Turn R *(first view of the Pyrenees on a clear day)*, pass farm (**Riguet**) and 400 metres later turn L (opposite end of a line of woods // to road on other side) between vines. Veer R downhill (hedge to L), cross stream (seasonal) and veer L and R then continue on sunken green lane to junction at top of hill.

7km Ferme de Peyret 160m (534.5/207.5)

For gîte d'étape associatif in old school in **Sauboires***, 800 metres further on (tel 06 30 94 19 53, 10pl, all year, K), turn R here and also for CH at La Hargue (tel 05 62 08 50 05 & 06 65 54 55 89, 8pl, K, all year). The next morning you can continue on D122 for 1.8km and rejoin GR65 2km before Manciet. Between Peyret and La Hargue there is also Le Chalet du Bonheur (tel 06 29 75 72 84, 8pl, K, all year but phone ahead out of season, donation basis).*

Otherwise, to continue, KSO along green lane. KSO(R) on track coming from back L and go downhill between vines. Pass several lakes *(a fish farm)* to L and turn L onto the D122 past **Au Moulin du Puoy** (L) and KSO for 2km to…

4km Manciet (538.5/203.5)

Gîte Chez Matthieu, Rue Centrale (tel 06 68 87 78 34 & 06 73 32 50 79, 12pl, K, all year). Hôtel-restaurant des Sports Chez Monique, Rue Principale (tel 05 62 08 56 40, 7/7). Hôtel-restaurant La Bonne Auberge (tel 05 62 08 50 04, all year), shop.

Rural bullring for *courses landaises* (cattle races, held on second Sunday in Sept every year along with the village *fêtes*) on L at entry to village. La Bonne Auberge is on site of former commandery (with Hôpital Saint-Jacques and chapel) set up by the Spanish Order of the Knights of Santiago. Church of Notre-Dame de la Pitié has 'viewing kiosk' and prayer desk accessible from the street when church is closed.

After the level crossing the GR65 waymarks lead you R *(picnic area)* to continue on the **Rue des Ecoles** then turn L over FB to cross the D931 to the church on the

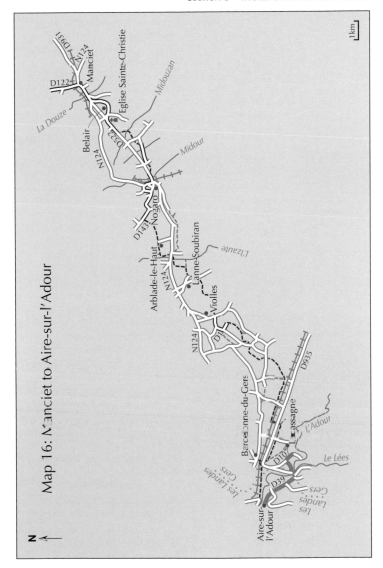

Map 16: Nanciet to Aire-sur-l'Adour

N

1km

D931
N124
Manciet
D122
Eglise Sainte-Christie
Midouzan
La Douze
Belair
N124
D522
Midour
D143I
Nogaro
Arblade-le-Haut
Lanne-Soubiran
l'Izaute
N124
Violles
N124
D1
Barcelonne-du-Gers
Cassagne
l'Adour
D935
Les Landes
Gers
Le Lées
D107
D39
Les Landes
Gers
Aire-sur-l'Adour

other side. Turn R here, down the **Rue Centrale** *(shops)* and rejoin the D931 300 metres later at a 'stop' sign, continuing ahead (L) along it.

After 1km *(opposite former Manciet railway station, now a used car dealership)* turn L along D153 (to 'Cravencères'). About 700 metres later (just before bend) turn R up unsurfaced road for 1km, passing farm **Bel Air** and then turn R 150 metres later onto tarred road. Turn L 200 metres later *(signposted also for the gîte d'étape/CH Le Relais du Haget, tel 05 62 08 54 02 & 06 11 66 13 98, 10pl, 15 Mar–31 Oct, K)* by pond marked 'Tucon' and then R, marked 'Eglise Chapelle de l'Hospitalet'…

4km Eglise-hôpital Sainte-Christie (542.5/194.5)

This is the church of Saint-Jean-Baptiste de la Commanderie de Saint-Christie de l'Armagnac, formerly belonging to the Order of the Knights of Malta. The key to the church is normally available to allow visitors to make an inside visit but the building may be kept locked at present as it has been in a dangerous condition.

To continue, KSO ahead past cemetery and 50 metres later turn R (by an 18th-century milestone with a Maltese Cross), following FP uphill and then into woods. At end KSO(R) along top side of field, with hedge to R and vines to L, veering L down towards road. Do **not** turn R here but KSO ahead, downhill on grassy track, // to the road. At junction turn second L, passing to RH side of farm, and KSO ahead on gravel road, downhill to stream (**Saint-Aubin**).

Cross over (small FB) then turn R on other side, veering L, then alongside stream. Turn L uphill, forking R near to modern bungalow on minor road. Turn L, veering L, then 150 metres later turn R at earth track through fields, veering L. KSO down short lane, downhill to bend in minor road. Turn R downhill and 1km later reach crossing with discoidal cross. KSO ahead. Go down grassy bank after last house then down shady lane *(seats)*. Reach (tree-lined) D522 and 400 metres later enter…

5km Nogaro 98m (547.5/194.5)

Population 2000. All facilities. Gîte d'étape Communal et Associatif, Avenue des Sports (on GR leaving town, tel 05 62 69 06 15, 26pl, 15 Apr–15 Oct, K). Seven CH, two hotels, OT (77 Rue Nationale, tel 05 62 09 13 30).

Small town taking its name from *Nogarium* (a 'place planted with walnuts') and established in the 11th century. Romanesque church with former Hôpital Saint-Jacques nearby. Bullring.

Enter the town on the D522 (**Avenue de Midour**), go over level crossing then either turn R onto the D931 (**Avenue de Daniate**) for gîte d'étape or KSO ahead to continue.

At junction KSO ahead on **Rue Nationale** to church. At junction, fork R (D143) on **Rue Broque**, which then > **Avenue du Cassou de Herre**. KSO, continue uphill, past *château d'eau* (water tower) and KSO. Around 200 metres later the D143 veers R. Continue ahead here but at second water tower you have a choice:

a) Main GR65: fork R onto a stony track which > earth track and KSO for 2km, downhill through woods, cross the **Jurone** (stream) and road > a track. Continue to **Claverie** (farm) on road. Turn R then veer L downhill for 1km and L along stream, until you reach the D931 again. Turn R and cross the **Pont sur l'Izaute**...

b) *Variante* (slightly shorter): KSO(L) ahead on road *(not normally a lot of traffic)*, passing pond (L) and wayside cross, marked 'Arblade-le-Haut' and KSO. KSO(R) at fork 80 metres later then KSO for 3km *(passing Gîte/CH 'L'Arbladoise' on L 1.5km later, tel 05 62 09 14 11 & 06 81 88 24 22, 9pl, 15 Mar–30 Oct)*. Reach junction with D931 by the...

5km Pont sur l'Izaute (552.5/189.5)

In the section between Nogaro and Aire-sur-l'Adour there is a lot of road walking, but with very little traffic apart from tractors.

KSO on D931 for 600 metres then turn L down tree-lined lane. KSO for 2km to farm. *(Note buildings with* colombages, *Tudor-style woodwork typical of the Landes region and already encountered elsewhere.)* Pass between buildings *(Gîte/ CH 'Maison Labarbe' to L, tel 09 61 33 93 91 & 06 66 29 44 55, 10–12pl, Apr–Oct, after 3pm, K)* and continue *(now a road)* for 500 metres to D152 in the hamlet of...

3km Lanne-Soubiran (555.5/186.5)

Church on R has large porch - good place for shady rest. Gîte d'étape Le Presbytère, Place de l'Eglise (tel 05 62 09 70 24 & 06 43 34 99 45, 12pl, K, camping possible, all year after 3pm X 2–3 months Nov–Mar: phone ahead then).

Turn R for 500 metres along D152 and then turn L 250 metres later down minor road at small crossroads by village place-name boards, veering R. About 500 metres later KSO(L) along minor road coming from back R. Pass lake, veer R alongside woods and at sharp LH bend turn R along earth track through fields, veering L into woods, downhill. At T-junction of similar tracks at bottom turn L towards field but then, just before the edge of the wood, turn hard R along grassy lane. KSO, then KSO(R) at fork. Veer R and then L along edge of wood and continue through fields to road (1.5km). Turn L and then R 100 metres later up (more) minor road. Pass one farm and, just before a second, turn L downhill on minor road and then L 500 metres later. Turn L again at crossroads. This is **Ferme Castin** (seat).

Veer R at fork 100 metres later and then 20 metres after that turn R down grassy track, veering L and then R slightly downhill and through fields. KSO. At crossing of tracks (Ferme Dubarry over to L has gîte: tel 05 62 69 64 82 & 06 27 35 84 13 & 06 15 72 45 72, 12pl, 1 Apr–15 Nov, reserve ahead rest of year, K) KSO(R) ahead R alongside vines (to R).

Pass alongside RH side of woods (vines to RH side now) and then turn L to enter woods. About 100 metres later reach minor road, turn R and 400 metres later reach minor road by church in village of…

7.5km Lelin Lapujolle (563/179)
Café/shop (15 Apr–15 Oct, 8.30am–1.30pm).

Veer L by mairie (shelter, picnic tables, WC, ♣) and reach D169 opposite a wayside cross and turn R. Around 150 metres later turn L up minor road, uphill, then L again 250 metres after that. At next crossing by houses, 750 metres later, turn R and then 1.2km later turn L up more minor road.

KSO for 1km then, 200 metres before you reach the D935, turn R on grassy track beside railway line and KSO. After 1.5km cross minor road and KSO again. About 800 metres later, by house, turn L over level crossing, veering R and then L and 300 metres later reach the D931. Cross over carefully (there is a lot of very fast, heavy traffic). Continue ahead on other side. Road > gravel track, and then 200 metres later turn R between fields and KSO for 2km, // to main road over to your R. Track > tarmac then fork R. Cross another road (large superstore and supermarket to R) and KSO ahead on other side in…

17km Barcelonne-du-Gers (580/162)
Gîte d'étape L'Hospitalet-du-Cosset/CH, 11 Place de la Garlande (next to pharmacy, tel 06 33 80 50 95, 12pl, K). Shops, bakeries. Two CH: a) 7 Lotissement Lacrouts (tel 06 88 67 93 43, May–Oct); b) 1 Lotissement du Moulia (tel 05 62 09 47 88 & 06 73 89 04 77, all year).

At junction with very large restored lavoir KSO ahead. At crossing KSO ahead between houses on **Rue de l'Abattoir**, turn R at end into **Rue de Casamont** and then turn L into **Rue de l'Hôpital**. Join minor road coming from back R then turn L into **Chemin de Berret** then turn first R (**Chemin des Moncaux**) into **Chemin de Saligats**. Turn R at end then turn L by petrol station and large superstore (with *cafeteria)* onto the D931. KSO (pavement) and 800 metres later reach the D834. Turn L, cross the bridge over the river **Adour** and enter…

3KM AIRE-SUR-L'ADOUR 81M (583/159)

Population 6092, all facilities. SNCF (buses). Accueil Spirituel Paroisse Sainte-Quitterie, Cathédrale St-Jean-Baptiste & Presbytère every afternoon 3–6pm, Apr–Oct X Sun & public holidays. Mass & pilgrim blessing 6pm Mon–Fri (no sleeping accommodation). La Maison des Pèlerins, 4 Rue Géneral Labat, run by former pilgrim, 50 metres from GR by car park near former Halle aux Grains (grain market: tel 07 80 04 11 40 & 05 58 71 68 07 & 07 80 39 36 58, 12–14pl, Mar–Oct, K). Gîte d'étape Hospitalet Saint-Jacques, 21 Rue Félix Despagnet, on GR near Eglise Sainte-Quitterie, also run by former pilgrims (tel 05 58 03 26 22, 14pl, K, walking pilgrims only: no back-up vehicles or baggage transfer service but phone if medical reasons). Gîte d'étape in Centre de Loisirs on way out of town towards the Pont sur l'Adour (tel 05 58 71 61 63, 23pl, all year X Fri & Sat nights, public holidays and previous evening, K, meals available). Chapelle des Ursulines, gîte in former chapel, opp church (tel 05 58 52 09 01 & 06 08 37 18 26, meals avail X Sun pm, 12pl, Apr–Oct after 3pm). Gîte au Gré de l'Adour, 24 Route de Duhort (tel 05 58 52 39 79 & 06 32 96 58 96, 5pl, K). Gîte Le Relai de Twickenham, 31 Rue Paul Duthil (opp Lidl, tel 06 82 02 12 02, 10pl, all year). Hôtel de la Paix-Gîte, 7 Rue Carnot (tel 05 58 71 60 70 & 06 81 39 50 02, has a special (cheap) pilgrim price including breakfast and gîte, 8pl, all year, K). CH Le Mas, 17 Rue du Château (tel 05 58 71 91 26 & 06 03 92 51 63). CH Relais Sainte-Quitterie, 32 Rue Félix Despagnet (tel 06 29 85 97 83, Apr–Oct, 50 metres before church). Three other hotels. Campsite by river near bridge (Les Ombrages de l'Adour, tel 05 58 71 75 10, 15 Apr–15 Oct, also rents caravans per person per night). Six restaurants, OT (Place du 19 Mars 1962, tel 05 58 71 64 70).

Ancient town in two parts: the lower section by the river with the cathedral of Saint-Jean Baptiste (12th century but altered several times; AP 3–6pm daily, pilgrim mass normally at 1pm), *mairie*, and 19th-century Halle aux Grains; and the 'Mas d'Aire' or higher town with the brick-built Eglise de Sainte Quitterie built on site of Benedictine monastery.

SECTION 4
Aire-sur-l'Adour to the Pyrenees

From here until Arzacq-Arraziguet (after which you enter the département of the Pyrénées-Atlantiques) the route is waymarked with blue-and-yellow shell stickers, as well as with the familiar red-and-white balises.

After crossing the bridge KSO(R) ahead along (pedestrianised) **Rue Carnot** *(turn L partway up for the cathedral and AP)*. At end turn R into **Rue Henri Labeyre** *(note brick building on RH side of street, former religious courts of justice and the 19th-century octagonal Halle aux Grains to R)* and then, at beginning of **Avenue des Pyrénées**, fork L up **Rue Félix Despagnet** *(passing gîte at no 21)* and the **Rue du Mas**, to the **Eglise de Sainte Quitterie**.

Continue to the end of the **Rue du Mas**, KSO ahead (**Avenue des Pyrénées**) then, opposite petrol station *(bar)* cross to RH side and KSO to end. At large roundabout turn R onto D2 (**Rue Nelson Mandela**) for 150 metres then turn L into **Rue Georges Fraisse** and L again along **Rue du Jardinet**. Turn R at end onto minor road leading down to a large reservoir, the **Retenue de Brousseau**.

Here you would normally continue ahead along the LH side of the reservoir but when this edition was being prepared large-scale repair works had been undertaken on this bank, necessitating a (well waymarked) detour, described here. (However, If this is no longer the case when you use this guide follow the waymarks in place at the time and you will pick up the normal GR65 further on at *).

Turn hard R when you reach the reservoir along a grassy path, go down some steps and turn L onto an embankment, alongside lake. At end turn R onto minor road then 150 metres later reach a busy road and turn L uphill. Go under bridge under motorway and at top, 600 metres later, turn L by large factory building and then R (marked 'Lourine'). KSO. KSO at two crossroads, KSO ahead at LH turn, and at staggered crossing KSO(R) and then L ahead to hamlet of **Bégorre**. KSO, veering L, and 500 metres after hamlet turn R onto gravel track between fields.*

There are very few distinguishing features in this region, which is flat, with large-scale agriculture. Due to remembrement – the regrouping of small, uneconomic portions of land into larger, more viable units – this whole area now consists of geometrically laid-out fields with irrigation channels and few hedge boundaries.

About 200 metres later turn L onto similar track and KSO for 2km to D62. Turn R here then L almost immediately onto another similar track. Turn L after 1km then immediately R. Some 600 metres later turn L again, watch out for RH fork R and then turn L by modern wayside cross to the D62 in…

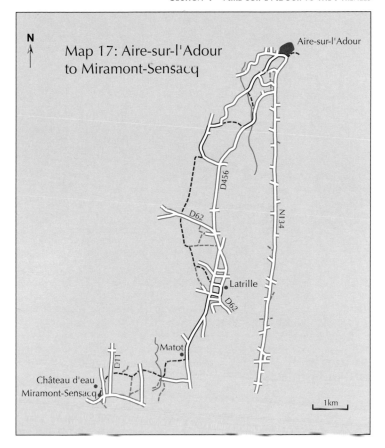

13.5km Latrille (596.5/145.5)

⚓ in churchyard, phone box, picnic area by church.

Continue past church onto D62 (**Route de Saint-Agnet**) then R on D375 (**Rue des Sorbets**) and first L onto a minor road (**Chemin de Saint-Pé**). KSO for 2km, passing **Matot** (farm, to R) then turn R at T-junction 100 metres later, which > grassy track. Follow it round for 1.5km then at another T-junction turn R onto grassy lane alongside a small river (the **Bahus**) to your L. Cross concrete FB and KSO uphill,

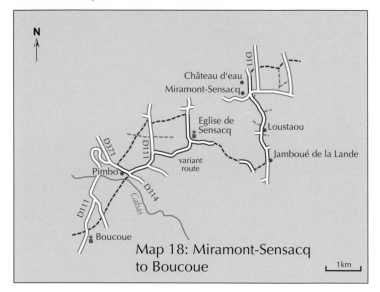

Map 18: Miramont-Sensacq to Boucoue

reaching minor road by farm. KSO ahead and 300 metres later, at crossing with another minor road, KSO ahead on gravel track through fields for 1km to the D11. Cross over, go up minor road on other side and turn L at junction *(seat)* into village. *(Turn R here for CH at La Maison du Bos, tel 05 58 79 93 18 & 06 42 79 84 26)*. Fork R 100 metres later towards château and church (on R) and go downhill into centre of…

6km Miramont-Sensacq (602.5/139.5)

Gîte d'étape communal, run by volunteers from the Association Landaise des Amis de Saint-Jacques (tel 05 58 79 94 06, all year after 3pm but reserve Oct–Apr, tel 05 58 79 91 23, K). CH La Prade 1294 route de Turson, 450 metres off GR before town (turn R at crossing with D11, tel 05 47 31 01 88 & 06 07 75 74 30, all year). Hotel-restaurant La Maison d'Hélène (tel 05 58 79 90 65, closed weekends). Two bakeries/limited groceries, ♣ opposite church.

Turn L along side of **Foyer Rural**, cross small square and turn R past *mairie (gîte d'étape next door)* to junction with D314 (marked 'Lauret, Pimbo') and turn L along it. KSO for 2km and turn R opposite farm (**Jamboué-de-la-Lande**) onto minor road.

Eglise de Sensacq, total immersion font for infant baptisms

Turn R, turn R at T-junction, pass two farms, and road > green lane, descending gradually to valley bottom. Veer L to cross stream by FB, enter woods and 200 metres later KSO ahead along track coming from back L. About 150 metres later KSO ahead along unsurfaced track coming from L. KSO when another minor road joins from back L. Cross bridge and 150 metres later at road turn R to the…

4.5km Eglise de Sensacq 149m (607/135)
11th-century church formerly dedicated to St James. Contains total immersion font (for infant baptisms) in north-west corner. Completely enclosed porch, vestibule style, with some benches (useful for rest).

After visiting church the GR65 continues R ahead up minor road. About 700 metres later turn L up stony track to continue on GR, which leads you to the D111 1km later *(or KSO for 300 metres if you want to go to the* accueil à la ferme *with* gîte at the Ferme de Marsan, Quartier Bestit, tel 05 58 79 94 93, 10pl, all year, K). Turn R and then almost immediately L downhill through woods and then up, after 1.5km, into the centre of **Pimbo**.

However, a more direct, shorter option is the old GR65 (no longer waymarked but very easy to follow). Return to junction (L) after visiting Eglise de Sensacq and KSO there, following road round uphill to D111 (1.5km). Turn L, passing hamlet of **Pibot**, *and KSO for 1km more to…*

Map 19: Boucoue to Arthez-de-Béarn

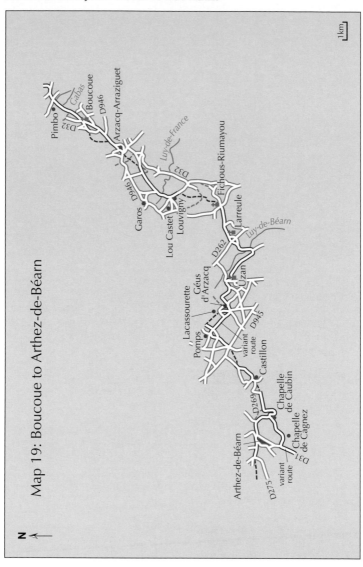

N ←

4km Pimbo 190m (611/131)
Gîte d'étape communal next to church (tel 05 58 44 46 57, 15 Apr–15 Nov, 17pl, but phone mairie Nov–Apr, tel 05 58 44 49 18). Two CH, both on GR: a) tel 05 58 44 49 59 & 06 84 98 21 64, Apr–Nov; b) tel 05 58 44 46 92 & 06 52 82 95 92, all year.

One of the oldest Bastide villages in the Landes, founded c1268, with collegiate church of Saint-Barthélmy on site of monastery founded by Charlemagne. ♣

If you took the main GR route, turn L through village and then fork R down road by wayside cross. If you took the *variante*, turn R to visit and then retrace your steps. Otherwise, turn hard L down road at entrance to village *(by wayside cross L, view of Arzacq Arraziguet ahead on skyline)*.

Turn hard R 200 metres later *(seat to L with splendid views)* down track leading to valley bottom and KSO. Cross the river **Gabas** *(ivy-covered house on L has ♣ with drinking water outside)*. KSO at crossroads and after 2km reach crossing with D32 in **Boucoue**.

Here the GR65 turns hard R then immediately L up track leading to a farm (**Miquéou**) after 700 metres. Turn L here, veering R to a junction with another track and turn L to return to the D32. Turn R along it to the junction with the D946 (coming from back L). Alternatively, however, you can turn L along the road in **Boucoue** *(note style of chapel, L)* for 1.5km to junction.

In either case KSO ahead at junction along D946 for 1km *(FP to RH side to start with)*. Turn R uphill up **Côte de Camot** at entrance to town then L at top and follow road round, passing petrol station and supermarket into main square in…

7KM ARZACQ-ARRAZIGUET 231M (618/124)

Shops, two bakeries, cafés, bank (+ATM). Gîte d'étape communal and campsite at Centre d'Accueil, 20 Place du Marcadieu (tel 05 59 04 41 41, meals possible, 35pl, all year X 8–10 Jul, K, reservations recommended as used by a lot of groups). CH 25 Place du Marcadieu (tel 05 59 04 16 12 & 07 85 32 01 26, all year). CH Restaurant La Maison d'Antan, 1 Place de la Républiique (tel 05 59 04 51 01, all year). Hôtel-Restaurant al Vieille Auberge, Place du Marcadieu (tel 05 59 04 51 31 & 06 08 54 66 44, 7/7 all year). OT Place de la République (tel 05 59 04 59 24).

Bastide town with two main squares, side by side, founded by 'les Anglais' in 13th–14th centuries, Arzacq was in France at that time, not in the Béarn (a separate country); note names of rivers in the area: Luy-de-Béarn and Luy-de-France. Arzacq used to mark the boundary between France and the (then independent) Béarn country. Parish church of Saint-Pierre has stained-glass window of St James.

You have now left the département of Les Landes and entered the Pyrénées-Atlantiques. From here on churches along the route are very often closed, unlike those in the Haute Loire, Lozère, Aveyron, Lot, Tarn et Garonne, Gers and Landes, which are normally open all day long from Easter to November.

To continue, KSO ahead (one square to L, other to R) along small street (**Chemin de Saint-Jacques**) to R of bank. Turn L 100 metres later down walled lane, veering R, then turn L alongside large artificial lake. Just before the end (and before a deserted house) fork R onto grassy track leading around end of lake and along other side of it, turning L 300 metres later uphill into woods. Continue to road (400 metres) and turn R. *Note 'arbre du pèlerin' to R when you pass signboard for 'Vignes'. Good views over to the Pyrenees on a clear day.*

KSO for 2.5km (road > track), descending all the time to bridge over the **Luy-de-France**. Turn L by watermill (**Chemin du Moulin**) and 400 metres later turn second L (**Chemin de Fichous**) to church in…

4km Louvigny (622/120)
Modern church of St Martin replaces original church belonging to château formerly above the village in hamlet of Lou Castet; the remains of castle (dungeons) and church were demolished during the 20th century. One stained-glass window in new church contains a *coquille* and a pilgrim staff and gourd.

Continue on road to R of church then turn R uphill (**Chemin de Lassoulade**) 200 metres later up steep grassy lane to hamlet of **Lou Castet** *(site of former château; turn R here for 650 metres to CH at Ferme de la Houn de Lacoste, 1 Route d'Orthez, tel 05 59 04 42 73 & 06 80 42 68 94, all year, camping possible)*. Turn L at T-junction and then fork L 400 metres later at junction (**Moundy**) up **Chemin de Pédebignes**, veering R very steeply uphill by new houses and continue ahead on ridge. *Splendid views on a clear day.*

KSO. KSO when stony track joins from back L, undulating at times, and ignoring turns, for 2.5km. At T-junction at end turn R and then KSO(R) ahead at junction 100 metres later, veering R downhill to valley bottom. Zigzag up on other side to emerge by Romanesque church in…

5km Fichous-Riumayou (627/115) ⚲

Turn L by war memorial onto D279 (**Route de Fichous**) and 150 metres later turn R onto D278 (**Route de Larreule**). KSO downhill for 2km to…

2.5km Larreule (629.5/112.5)

Gîte L'Escale-restauration rapide, 1 Route de Mazerolles (tel 05 59 81 49 24 & 06 32 02 25 48, 12pl, K, all year, camping). Site of a Benedictine monastery about AD995 which was an important pilgrim stage in the Middle Ages, with church of Saint-Pierre, partly Romanesque. (The name *Larreule* means '*La Règle*' in Gascon – ie monastic rule – and is also found elsewhere, near Maubouget on the Arles route and in La Réole on the Vézélay route.)

Turn L for 100 metres to visit church (**Chemin de l'Eglise**; *adjoining garden is a nice place for a rest*) then retrace your steps to continue.

Cross the D262 in centre of village and KSO ahead on **Route de Mazerolles**, veering R when **Chemin de l'Eglise** joins from back L. Cross the **Luy-de-Béarn** (again), KSO(L) on other side and fork R at top of hill onto **Route de Uzan**. Turn R at T-junction after farm and continue on this road for 2.5km more to junction by church in…

4km Uzan (633.5/108.5)

Gîte d'étape on GR in village, 65 Chemin du Bourg (tel 05 59 81 65 76 & 06 82 97 47 29, 8pl, Apr–Oct, K). Church of Sainte-Quitterie, Fontaine Sainte-Quitterie (a saint very revered in the area) on other side of road.

Turn R on D49 for 100 metres, turn R again and 100 metres later turn L onto minor road (*gîte at first house on l*) marked 'Géus', veering R. Turn L at large wayside cross, veering L, and 100 metres later turn R. Turn L at end by barn (*seat*) and KSO. Cross bridge over river **Ayguelongue** (*seat*) and continue to end of **Cami de la Lebe** in…

1.5km Géus d'Arzacq (635/107)

Gîte Ayguelongue, 11 Route de l'Eglise (tel 05 89 51 41 90 & 07 81 77 90 17, 15 Apr–15 Oct, reserve ahead, 4pl).

a) Main GR65: turn R to **Chapelle de Géus** then turn L alongside *mairie (large, shady grassed area with seats beside it)* on **Cami de Compostelle** (*large shady grassed area with seats by* mairie). About 500 metres later at farm (**Lacassourette**) road > track and 200 metres later KSO(L) ahead, at bend, on grassy lane. KSO for 1km until you reach a road and turn R along it into **Pomps**.

b) *Variante* (useful in bad weather or if you are in a hurry): KSO here to junction 300 metres later then turn *second* R (**Route de Pomps**). KSO for 2km to...

2.5km Pomps (637.5/104.5)

Gîte d'étape communal (tel 06 84 91 94 00 & 05 59 81 60 61, 22pl, 15 Mar–15 Nov, K). 17th-century church of Saint-Jacques (with statue of the saint), château with octagonal tower.

At wayside cross turn R for bar/restaurant and church but KSO ahead for shop and gîte. To continue, turn L on **Rue de Caneigut** then R on **Route de Géus** and 150 metres later, after bridge, turn L on minor road, **Route de Brana**, veering R. Turn R at junction onto another minor road (**Route du Pèbe**) leading to D945 (1.5km from centre of Pomps).

Cross over, marked 'C2, Doazon,' and 150 metres later, after houses, fork R down track which disintegrates to FP (often overgrown but easy enough to follow as it goes in a straight line all the time). Turn R at end, after 1km, to D269 by bridge over the **Lech**. Turn L and follow road round to L after second bridge and then up to the village of **Castillon**, visible 2km away in front of you on top of the hill.

4.5km Castillon 198m (642/100)

Hospital for pilgrims and travellers in 11th century, church of Saint-Pierre. ♣ in cemetery.

Turn L at church and then, at junction with large wayside cross, KSO ahead down minor road which > a green lane after farm (**Lacoume**). Rejoin road (D269) again after 800 metres and KSO(L) ahead for 1km. Turn L (**Chemin de Benicet**) and KSO for nearly 1km to the D276. Turn R and 250 metres ahead of you on the LH side is the...

3km Chapelle de Caubin (645/97)

Restored Romanesque chapel on the site of the remains of a former Commandery of the Knights of St John. Garden opposite (picnic tables) contains a sculpture recalling the passage of pilgrims en route to Santiago.

Continue on road, uphill, and 100 metres later you have a choice: a) KSO ahead into **Arthez-de-Béarn**, or b) turn L for the 10km *variante* route (not waymarked but easy to follow) which goes via the **Chapelle de Cagnez** and the **Cami Salié** (old salt route) and rejoins the main GR65 after the church in Argagnon, 1.5km before Maslacq. *For a description of this option see* page 155.

Corn cobs drying in the Landes

2km Arthez-de-Béarn 211m (647/95)
Popuation 1663. Shop (X Sun), cafés, two restaurants (no hotel). Gîte d'étape communal La Maison des Pèlerins, La Carrère (tel 05 59 67 70 52, 20pl, all year, K, camping possible), right at end of village, past church. Gîte-boulangerie Broussé (tel 05 59 67 74 46, 8pl, all year, X Sun pm & Mon, meals for pilgrims if restaurant closed, K). Three CH.

A very long town along a ridge (nearly 2km from one end to the other), originally developed around the Augustinian commandery whose monastery was destroyed in the Wars of Religion. Several interesting old houses, ramparts. Note transition towards Basque-style architecture.

Enter the town along the **Route de Caubin** and continue along the **Rue de Begoue**. Pass mairie (on R) and KSO. When D946 turns R (to Orthez) KSO(L) ahead (**Rue du Bourdalet**) marked 'Gendarmerie', on ridge. At fork 500 metres later, with large wayside cross, fork R along **Chemin du Bosc**, along a ridge all the time, with superb views on a clear day *(the Pyrenees are over to your L in the distance)*.

KSO. Road > gravel track after a while. Continue for 3.5km then, 400 metres after passing under HT cables, 4.5km from church in Arthez, reach bend in small tarmac road (this is the **Route Impériale**) by house ahead (**Lasserre**) and fork L on it, downhill (**Route de l'Eglise**). Follow road down for 2.5km, passing various farms. Turn R at crossroads by house no 1857. KSO at next crossing 1km later *(bar/tabac signposted to R)* and reach bend in N117 by the...

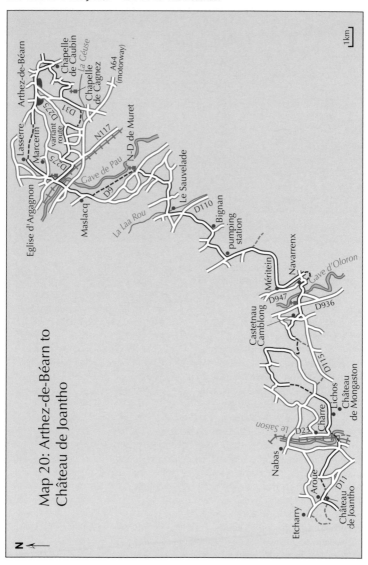

Map 20: Arthez-de-Béarn to Château de Joantho

7km Eglise d'Argagnon (654/88)

Eglise d'Argagnon

Restaurant La Bulle, all year lunchtime + Sat eve. Bakery (X Sun pm).

If you happen to arrive here at noon you will hear the Angelus *being rung, as you may have done already in several other places along the route, at 7am and 7pm. The name comes from the first word of the Latin text of a devotional office commemorating the Incarnation, and was said morning, noon and night, the bell being rung to announce it. Nowadays this is all that remains of the practice.*

Turn L along small FP to LH side of D117 to avoid a *lot* of very fast traffic, and just past the turn (R) to **Maslacq** cross over to other side of road then turn R to return to junction and then turn L onto the D275 ('Maslacq 2'). *(This is the* lieu-dit **Maysonnave**, *where the* variante *rejoins the main route from the L.)* Cross the railway line, the **Gave de Pau** (river) and the A64 motorway and KSO to village of **Maslacq**.

Cami Salié variante

About 100 metres after the **Chapelle de Caubin** turn L off D233 onto very minor road leading through woods to the **Chapelle de Cagnez**. *Built in the 11th–12th centuries, this was formerly a parish church, important at a time when the pilgrim route led south to ford the Gave de Pau at a crossing place just below the Sanctuaire de Muret.* After visiting the church retrace your steps for 100 metres and then turn L on a track leading to D31 after 1km. Turn L along it for 1km and after wood (to L) and gas post on R turn R onto gravel track. About 1km later reach T junction with tarred road, turn R for 500 metres then L onto the **Cami Salié** *(route used in former times for transporting salt, produced further west in Saliés-de-Béarn).* Continue on it for 2km, along the side of the hill, until you reach the D275. Turn R here for 400 metres then, at a small junction, turn L onto a track. KSO for 1km and rejoin the main GR65 at the *lieu-dit* **Maysonnave** on the N117, just before its junction with the D275.

2km Maslacq (656/86)

Gîte d'étape Chambres La Halte, 35 Rue Carrère (tel 06 45 63 68 23, 5pl, K, 15 Apr–15 Oct). CH Les Tilleuls (tel 05 59 38 21 65 & 06 19 42 76 20, all year after 3pm). CH la Ferme de Bicatou, 8 Rue de l'Ecole (tel 05 59 67 62

17 & 06 22 77 57 38 & 06 63 74 02 56, camping possible). Hôtel/restaurant Maugouber (tel 05 59 38 78 90, reservation needed). Bar/shop.

Turn L (C9, Lagor) to continue on **Rue du Fronton**, passing *fronton. (Turn R for shop, hotel and gîte.)* Turn L again opposite château onto the D9. About 300 metres later cross bridge over the **Géü** *(shady picnic area)* and turn L onto a minor road by a bus shelter. Fork L 300 metres later onto gravel track through fields and 300 metres after that, after bend, turn R onto similar track. Cross minor road and KSO towards woods ahead, more or less // to river (**Gave de Pau** on your L). Continue uphill through woods (**Chemin de Girault Naule**), emerging at a crossing near the...

4km Sanctuaire de Notre-Dame de Muret (660/82)
Neo-Byzantine oratory, 1936, on site of 11th-century sanctuary. To visit, turn hard L for 300 metres.

To continue, KSO to D9 (200–300 metres). *The 'monster' in the valley below L is the Usine de Lacq, one of France's biggest natural gas works, resembling lighted candles on a giant industrial birthday cake...*

Cross over, turn L behind house (**Chemin Bernadet**) and then L 100 metres later down minor road (**Chemin Bernadet**) then turn R 100 metres after that on **Chemin Saubade** to valley bottom. KSO over bridge at fork. KSO(R) at next fork, KSO(L) ahead at next (**Chemin de la Coume**) and continue to farm (**Haut-de-la-Coume**). Pass between buildings and continue on grassy track at edge of wood (field to R). Follow edge of woods round to L, enter woods, cross stream over FB. Go through (electric) fence and turn R, following it uphill, veering L alongside a line of trees to reach gravel lane to R of farm at **Larqué**. Turn R along it and 150 metres later at crossing ♣ *(seat)* turn R along road, leading down and then steeply uphill. At top (a ridge) cross another road and go straight downhill on other side for 1km, veering R and then L to...

4km La Sauvelade (664/78)
Gîte-Auberge-Café-Epicerie-Multiservices Le P'tit Laa, 64 Camin Gaston Crotzat (tel 05 59 67 33 69, 18pl, 1 Apr–1 Nov). CH Les Campanhas, 280 Camin de la Crotz de Loupin (tel 05 59 67 60 57, all year).

The church is all that remains of the monastery, originally Benedictine (and later Cistercian), founded by Gaston IV of Béarn in 1128. It was sacked by the Huguenots in 1569, restored after 1630 and then sold at the time of the French Revolution. The church was built between 1215 and 1250, originally dedicated to St Mary, but later changed to St James the Great in recognition of all the pilgrims who rested in the abbey. Statue of St James inside.

(Ecogîte-Bistrot-Epicerie Blo La Maison du Grillon-Oustou Grigt Café, 1559 Route Deu Lavarth, just opposite shortcut via Roman bridge, tel 05 59 09 44 30, 06 76 27 36 38 & 06 84 38 14 21, 10pl, K, 7/7 Apr–Oct.)

Turn L along D110 (**Route de Larvath**) for 1km, passing *mairie*, then fork R uphill *(Camin de Compostela, D110 continues L)* and KSO for 3km. At the very top (**Hameu de Bignon**, *seat*), opposite a large restored house, turn R along a road coming from the L (**Camin de Berduguen**). Continue on ridge for 600 metres then fork L (still the **Camin de Berduguen**) and 300 metres later turn L, downhill at junction marked 'ancienne école' to cross the river **Saleys** *(gîte d'étape privé Le Grand Saule, tel 05 59 67 33 39, K, 1 Apr–20 Nov X Aug)*. Continue uphill for 1.5km to a T-junction with a road running at right angles along a ridge *(former school to R, small water tower in front)*.

Turn L along the ridge, KSO for 1.5km then turn second R down a minor road. *(Splendid views over to the Pyrenees in clear weather.)* KSO for 3.5km, downhill through woods and then along the level. KSO(L) (**Camin dous Barrets**, > **Camin Clavarette**) at fork in residential area then turn L after crossing small bridge and continue to church in.

11km Méritein (675/67)

About 500 metres later, at church (R), turn L for 50 metres then L again down a minor road, **Chemin de la Biasse**, with fields to either side, for 1.5km. Cross another road via a tunnel underneath it then KSO to junction with the D111. Turn R, cross bridge over river, continue and cross **Avenue de Mourenx** and KSO on other side (**Rue de la Batteuse**) between former petrol station (L) and ramparts (R). Turn R *(PTT now on your L)* and continue down **Rue Saint-Germain**, turning L into **Place Carrérot** to the **Eglise Saint-Germain** in...

2KM NAVARRENX 125M (677/65)

Population 1500. Shops, cafés, several restaurants. AP (6pm, in church, 6.30pm *verre d'amitié* in presbytery (no sleeping accommodation), 11 Apr–Oct). Gîtes d'étape communaux l'Arsenal & Le Foirail & Avenue de France (tel 05 59 66 10 22; 12, 16 & 26pl, all year, K. Keys from Bar Le Dahu, 23 Rue Saint-German until 6pm, tel 05 59 66 02 67). CH-Gîte Le Relais du Jacquet, 42 Rue Saint-Germain (tel 05 59 66 57 25, Mar–Oct). L'Alchimiste-accueil bénevole des pèlerins,

Maison Philosophale, 10 Rue de l'Abreuvoir (tel 09 67 03 26 84 & 06 32 78 13 76, 11pl, all year but reserve Nov–Mar, camping possible, donation). Gîte d'étape-CH le Cri de la Girafe, 12 Rue du Faubourg (tel 05 59 66 24 22 & 07 60 75 19 14, 8pl, all year). Gîte d'étape Charbel, Cami du Mouli near entrance to town (tel 05 59 66 07 25 & 06 08 93 56 41, 21pl, Apr–Sept). CH 4 Place d'Armes (tel 05 59 66 27 59 & 07 80 00 50 16, Easter–1 Nov). Hôtel-restaurant du Commerce (tel 05 59 66 50 16, all year). Camping-snack Beau Rivage, Allée des Marronniers by river (end Mar–mid Oct). OT 2 Place des Casernes (tel 05 59 38 32 85). **Note**: there are no ATMs (*distributeurs de billets de banque*) after this until you reach Saint-Jean-Pied-de-Port.

First town in France to be fortified with Italian-style ramparts (16th century); ask at OT for town plan with walking tour. Church of Saint-Germain, finished 1562, but rapidly converted into a Protestant *temple* under the orders of Jeanne d'Albret, remaining so until 1620 when it was reconverted to a Catholic church (note pilgrim boss in ceiling near side chapel to RH side, with head with leather hat and *coquille*). In former times Navarrenx also had a significant *Cagot* (outcast) population (see page 134), many of whom became prominent public figures in the early 20th century.

To continue, with your back to the church and **Place Darralde,** KSO(L) ahead down **Rue Saint-Antoine** into the **Place Caserne** and then turn L to go through the **Porte Saint-Antoine** and continue down to cross the bridge over the **Gave d'Oloron** (river).

Cross bridge, turn R onto D115 on other side (**Avenue de la Gare**). Cross roundabout, continue ahead on other side (**Route de la Chapelle**) and 500 metres later turn R, marked 'Centre Bourg', into the lower part of…

2.5km Castetnau-Camblong (679.5/62.5)
CH Domaine Lespoune (tel 05 59 66 24 14). Supermarket at 9 Route de Bayonne. Castetnau is '*villeneuve*' in Béarnais; Camblong is '*le champ long*'. 17th-century church, note Béarn-style houses.

Turn R at T-junction, pass church (on your R) and 100 metres later turn L down minor road (**Rue de Débantets**) to T-junction (approx 600 metres) with wayside cross. Turn L onto unsurfaced road through forest, descending to cross the **Pont de Camblong** over the **Lausset** (1km).

About 100 metres later turn R at crossing of tracks and KSO, through woods uphill (800 metres). At junction turn R over stream then 100 metres later turn hard

R on better track *(back downhill again, a manoeuvre necessitated by not being able to go through private land)*. Track joins from back R. KSO and cross wooden bridge over the **Harcelanne**. About 150 metres later reach minor road. Turn L for 1.2km then turn R up grassy track, forking L 50 metres later and veering R and then L uphill.

Continue ahead uphill, through fields, veering R again and > track and reach T-junction (1.5km). Turn L, descend to cross the **Cassol du Boué** (small river), pass to R of large shed and then veer L uphill on stony track to a cross-roads with the D115 (1km after stream). *On the other side of the road the Jean Haget pâté manufacturer has erected a covered rest area with picnic tables for pilgrims and walkers, with some of their products for sale. Opposite is the Eco-Accueil Le Jardin des Rêves (tel 05 24 37 42 07, 10pl, K, 1 May–31 Oct, donation basis)*. Turn R then immediately L (the **Route de Saint-Jacques**, marked 'Château de Mongaston') onto minor road (D343) and go downhill for 2km to bridge over the **Apaure** *(picnic tables)*. KSO ahead. Just 400 metres later pass entrance road (L) to…

9.5km Château de Mongaston (689/53)

Castle built in the 13th century by Gaston IV of Béarn, destroyed by fire 1929 and now restored by its present owner. Visits 1 May–30 Oct X Tues, 2.30–6pm.

Continue on road and 500 metres later turn R (**Route du Saison**) in hamlet of **Cherbeys**. About 300 metres later turn L by entrance boards for **Charre** then 600 metres after that cross the D23. Go over cattle grid and turn L onto track // to road, with fields to R. Around 300 metres later return to D23 (L) and on FP alongside it reach road bridge over the river **Saison**. Turn R over it immediately and then fork R on other side down a slope onto minor road veering R to village of…

2km Lichos (691/51)

Six CH: a) Maison Carrère, by church (tel 05 59 28 83 28 & 06 11 11 17 55, all year, on GR); b) 23 Route Départmentale (tel 05 59 28 29 45, 15 Apr–15 Oct); c) CH/*cabane à sandwiches/boissons* (tel 05 59 28 82 48 & 06 79 27 42 10, 15 Apr–15 Nov); d) Lotissement Les Monts (tel 05 59 28 85 39 & 06 86 28 47 33, all year, on GR on leaving Lichos); e) CH Torttua, Chemin d'Héguilus (tel 05 59 28 93 45 & 06 34 16 43 99, 15 Apr–15 Oct, on GR after Lichos); f) Maison Etchegoyenborda, *lieu-dit* Etchemborde (tel 05 59 28 91 42 & 06 24 28 54 55, all year, between Lichos and Aroue).

Birthplace of Saint-Grat, Bishop of Oloron.

Turn L at junction, then R at wayside cross, veer L and then R to cross bridge over river **Borlaas** *(seats)*. KSO, cross a road and KSO ahead on minor road for 1.8km, uphill.

Just after farm to R (**Bouhaben**) and before LH bend, KSO(R) at fork and continue ahead up grassy lane. KSO(L) at fork, go through gate into meadow and continue alongside hedge to L then turn R down towards house. *This is the **Maison Bellerive** (Belabua), with the gîte d'étape familial (tel 05 59 65 70 19 & 06 16 48 73 65, 14pl, all year, K, 2km after Lichos, camping possible, groceries and bread for sale).* Go through large metal gate, go past house and then down tarred lane to D11 (500 metres, accueil à la ferme *opposite at Ferme Behoteguya, tel 05 59 65 85 69, gîte for pilgrims only, 6pl, meals, snacks, Mar–Nov*). KSO(R) along it for 600 metres to the…

6km Château de Joantho (695/47)

18th-century manor house, privately owned. However, to continue into **Aroue** KSO ahead for 500 metres. Small gîte d'étape communal 150 metres before church on L (tel 05 59 65 95 54, 12pl, Apr–Nov, K, camping possible). Romanesque church of St Etienne has 12th-century bas-reliefs with Santiago Matamoros ('the Moor-slayer') in lintel in sacristy doors.

To continue you have a choice of two waymarked routes:

a) main GR65: *This is a high-level route, with splendid views on a clear day, but it does not pass the Eglise d'Olhaïby directly.* Turn L down a minor road alongside **Château de Joantho** and KSO for 2km. Then, at a junction just before a RH

Eglise d'Olhaiby

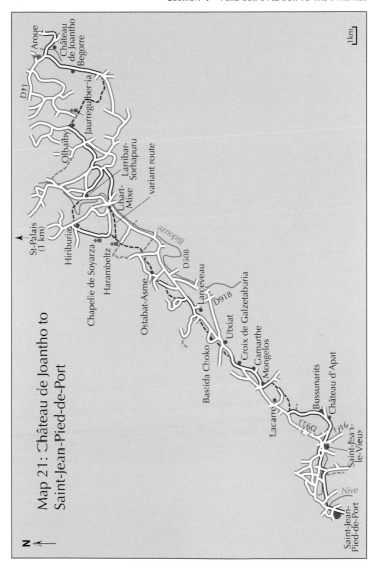

Map 21: Château de Joantho to Saint-Jean-Pied-de-Port

N ←

1 km

Aroue

Château de Joantho Begorre

D11

Jaurreguberria

Olhaiby

Larribar-Sorhapuru

variant route

Chart-Mixe

St-Palais (1 km)

Bidouze

Hiriburia

D508

Chapelle de Soyarza

Harambeltz

Larceveau

Ostabat-Asme

D918

Utxiat

Bastida Choko

Croix de Galzetaburia

Gamarthe Mongelos

Bussunarits

Château d'Apat

D933

D118

Lacarre

Saint-Jean-le-Vieux

Nive

Saint-Jean-Pied-de-Port

161

bend and LH fork, turn R up a gravel lane, steeply uphill. KSO then continue on ridge, up and down, 'on the roof of the world' style. Around 2km later, by isolated stone barn, do **no**t turn L on route waymarked in yellow but KSO ahead. About 600 metres later reach large house by minor road and turn hard L downhill. Some 800 metres later reach minor road by another isolated stone barn and turn R; 500 metres later either turn L straightaway to continue or KSO ahead to the **Eglise d'Olhaïby** and then retrace your steps to the junction.

b) The variant route (waymarked) continues on the D11 through **Aroue** and takes you directly to the church in **Olhaïby**.

5km Eglise d'Olhaïby (700/42)

Simple Romanesque church of Saint-Just (not always open but large, covered porch is a good place for rest/shelter).

Retrace your steps to junction then KSO(R) ahead on minor road for 1km, ignoring turns (road > track after 1km). KSO, turn R on road by farm (**Etcheberria**) and then veer L to another farm (**Jaurriberria**). Turn hard L onto wide gravel lane and pass to L of it and continue uphill on wide lane onto plateau (**Archelako**) and KSO, ignoring turnings, on ridge. About 2.5km later (after Jaurriberria) turn R at T-junction with 'balcony' view of landscape ahead to the…

4km Ferme de Benta (704/38)

If you want to go to **Saint-Palais** (7km, *Donapaleu* in Basque), the capital of the Basque province of Basse-Navarre *(to continue in Spain along the* Camino del Norte*, for example, or to find somewhere to sleep – see Appendix B)*, KSO ahead 100 metres later at farm on minor road to **Quinquilenia**, continuing through **Uruxondoa** and **Béhasque-Lapiste** *(Gîte Errekaldia, 8pl, all year, K)*, turning L onto the D11 to Saint-Palais at **Quintalena**.

Saint-Palais, population 2000, all facilities. Gîte d'étape in Maison Franciscaine, 1 Avenue de Gibraltar, on way out of town leading back to GR65 (tel 05 59 65 90 77, 39pl, Easter–1 Nov, K, run by volunteers from the Association des Amis de Saint-Jacques des Pyrénées Atlantiques). Gîte Soretena, 2 Avenue Frédéric de Saint Jayme (tel 06 10 10 73 97 & 09 73 67 88 27, 4pl, all year). OT (14 Place Charles de Gaulle), two hotels, eight restaurants. Musée de la Basse Navarre et des Chemins de Saint Jacques de Compostelle, next to mairie.

You can pick up the GR65 again at **Hiriburia** by taking the D302 south and either continuing on the road or taking the turning L onto the Vézelay route. However, a new waymarked variant is reported to be in preparation, leading from Saint-Palais to the Stèle de Gibraltar in Hiriburia.

Otherwise, to continue on main route from **Ferme de Benta**, turn L (farm to L) 100 metres later down minor road, steeply downhill. KSO, KSO(L) at fork and KSO, ignoring turns, for 1km then turn R along D242 for 400 metres. *Here you have two options: the 2km longer, main GR via Larribar-Sorhapuru to Harambeltz or the shortcut route via Uhart-Mixe but which misses out both the Chapelle de Soyarza and Hiriburia, where the routes from Paris/Tours, Vézelay and Le Puy all meet up at the Stèle de Gibraltar to form a single Chemin de Saint-Jacques into Spain.*

a) Main GR65: continue ahead on the D242 for 600 metres more then turn L along C2 ('Larribar 1,2') for 1km then veer L at *fronton*, L to church, cross bridge over D933 and then KSO down minor road in…

4km Larribar-Sorhapuru 89m (708/34)

Veer R between two farms and continue downhill to cross four-arched bridge over the **Bidouze**. *(Note shrine to R with small statue of St James behind glass in a 'stèle' and also watercolour of church under glass.)*

At a T-junction turn L onto grassy track, enter woods and track > FP with rocky 'steps', becoming narrower as you climb. When it levels out, veer L and path > wider. Go through 'gate', continue along narrow FP between hedges, gradually widening out, and reach road at farm.

2km Hiriburia 151m (710/32)

A few metres to the R, where the routes from Paris, Vézelay and Le Puy are thought to have met, the Société des Amis de Saint Jacques has erected a

Meeting point of three French routes, Hiriburia

small monument. (You can also go to Saint-Palais from here: KSO(R) for 3km.) If you look at the monument's 'feet' and follow the direction pointed by those marked 'Ostabat' you will also see where you are going next: up the clear track uphill in front of you, the 'Chemin de Procession' leading to the chapel.

To continue, KSO ahead for 100 metres then cross the D302 and turn L up the **Chemin de Procession** leading up to the **Chapelle de Soyarza** *(300 metres – a modern building replacing a much older oratory dedicated to Notre-Dame. Adjoining the chapel is a covered rest area with pilgrim book. Superb views all round from the top on a clear day).*

Continue downhill on the other side on a wide track, veering L alongside woods. About 800 metres later, 100 metres past modern shrine (L), turn R down clear grassy track, veering L to join track coming from back L. Veer R then L downhill to village of **Harambeltz**.

b) Shortcut via Uhart-Mixe: turn L at next junction (ie after 400 metres on the D242) and then immediately R *(here you will see the first 'snail' waymark)* very steeply uphill, which > a gravel road after farm buildings. KSO, undulating between fields, and 400 metres later cross minor road. KSO ahead, downhill. Pass farm, veering R and then L and KSO, ignoring turnings. Reach the D302, turn R over two road bridges over the river **Bidouze** and reach junction with the D933 by the church in...

4km Uhart-Mixe (Uhartehiri) (714/28)
Gîte d'étape l'Escargot-Bar-Camping Chez Stef (tel 05 59 65 60 00 & 06 16 33 72 13, 15 Mar–15 Oct, 14pl, Easter–1 Nov, 7/7).

Cross D933 and continue on other side by *mairie* (L), steeply uphill *(waymarked in this section with red arrows)*. Turn (not fork) L at top by wayside cross and KSO. KSO(L) at fork and KSO. Pass another wayside cross (L) by junction and KSO ahead, uphill. At the top, at a four-way junction, the main GR65 joins from above R (forking down), marked (pointing uphill) 'Chapelle de Soyarza'. KSO ahead here, though, marked 'Harambeltz, Ostabat'. KSO downhill and 600 metres later turn R into the village of...

3km Harambeltz (717/25)
Maison d'Hôte Echetoa (opp chapel, tel 06 17 90 45 59, three rooms, all year). Site of former Benedictine priory-hospital of Saint-Nicholas. The 1000-year-old chapel remains and has an 18th-century altarpiece and statue of St James, but belongs to the families in the village and is not a parish

church. It has now been restored but is difficult to visit, although the *grille* (but not the door) is sometimes open, enabling you to see inside. Note interesting old houses in the village.

KSO(R) down main street, pass to L of church, KSO ahead under trees at LH bend, veering R and then L downhill immediately on FP veering R at bottom to cross stream. On other side track is wider; KSO up it, ignoring turns until you emerge from the woods at a T-junction with a track (1.5km). Turn L and go downhill, veer L at bottom then R and follow road round ignoring turns. Pass **Lagunatona** *(group of houses)* and at crossroads KSO. About 200 metres later fork L down grassy track *(sculpture at start)* which > walled lane into village of…

4km Ostabat-Asme (Izura) 124m (721/21)

Gîte d'Etape Maison Ospitalia in lower part of town (tel 05 59 37 83 17 – at meal times & 06 10 04 65 75, 10pl, 1 Apr–31 Oct, K). Gîte d'étape Aïr-ona (tel 05 59 37 88 75 & 06 33 65 77 15, 12pl, 15 Apr–15 Oct X Sun in Jul– Aug). Gîte d'étape Burguzaharia (tel 05 59 65 46 69 & 06 72 68 13 24, 6pl, Apr–Oct). CH Auberge Ametzanea (tel 05 59 37 85 03 & 05 59 37 81 56). Bar-multiservices.

Ostabat is a small village today, but in the past it was an important gathering point for pilgrims coming along different routes. In the Middle Ages its hospitals and inns could accommodate up to 5000 pilgrims, but only the Maison Ospitalia remains and is now a gîte d'étape. There are no big pilgrim monuments in the French Basque country, but there were formerly many small hospitals and chapels (in Harambeltz and Itziat, for example).

Pass gîte d'étape, turn R uphill to village centre (*mairie*, church) then veer L on road out of village. KSO at crossing and KSO on tarred lane leading uphill. *(Gîte d'étape-CH Meals (four rooms) and Gîte d'Etape Izarrak (33pl) both at Ferme Gaineko-Etxea on GR 800 metres after leaving Ostabat: tel 05 59 37 81 10 & 06 72 73 78 56, Apr–Oct, after 3pm.)* KSO(L) ahead at bend by farm on shady lane. Around 1km later KSO at crossing with large concrete wayside cross and KSO ahead. Pass farm, track > tarmac road and at junction with another road coming from back R KSO(L) ahead. Turn L at crossing by farm and reach the D933. Turn R along it for 300 metres (FP on LH side) then turn R up tarmac lane, veering L to T-junction *(bakery/shop 60 metres to L)* on the edge of…

3.5km Larceveau (Lartzabale) 160m (724.5/17.5)

Gîte Bichta Eder, quartier Chaharra (tel 05 59 37 49 24 & 06 86 67 77 91, on GR at top of village, 5pl, Apr–Oct after 3.30pm, X Wed & Thurs). Hotel-restaurant

Espellet (tel 05 59 37 81 91, 7/7 X Jan, on main road). Restaurant, snack bar, bakery am Tues–Sun, *superette* X Sun pm and all day Mon.

From here to Saint-Jean-Pied-de-Port you are following the D933 along the valley all the time, mainly on old lanes, on one side of the main road or the other.

Turn R up minor road, veering L to continue // to D933 below. Just before the hamlet of **Chahara** (main road now 100 metres to L). KSO at crossroads with electricity substation and go through hamlet, passing to R of large house and continue ahead on lane between fences. Turn L at minor road and 50 metres later turn R onto green lane. *(Gîte Paradis on GR at Mendiondoua, 2km after Larceveau, tel 05 59 37 82 67 & 06 81 43 12 47, 6pl, K, Apr–Sept.)*

Join minor road coming from L and KSO(R) ahead, veering L past farm in hamlet of **Bastida-Choko**. About 300 metres later, just after houses, continue ahead on grassy track to cross stream and then turn L alongside it, returning to D933 again. Turn R along FP alongside but above road and in hamlet of **Utxiat** *(there was a hospital for pilgrims here in the 12th century and you pass the former mill attached to it)*. KSO ahead along minor road in front. Veer R and almost immediately turn L through gateway, to continue alongside hedge to your R. (You are now // to road again.) Follow the hedge, pass inside the edge of a wood and then above vines before returning to the D933 again (1km). KSO along road for 300 metres to a roadside cross (R), the…

5.5km Croix de Galzetaburia 262m (730/12)

This cross (1714; the name means '*tête du chemin*') was placed at this crossing of Roman roads where pilgrims from secondary routes joined the *Via Podensis*. It has Christ on one face, the Virgin and Child on the other, and two inscriptions on its base: a Latin hymn and a Basque text indicating that you are halfway between the Soule and the Labourd, two of the three Basque provinces in France.

Turn L down a minor road (D522) leading to the village of **Gamarthe**. *(Some 500 metres after the Croix de Galzetaburia the Famille Berhocoirigoin*

Croix de Galzetaburia

at the Ferme Uhartia runs a pause-café from Apr–Oct, 7.30am–2pm, and where they also serve breakfast. CH Maison Larralde Borda, tel 06 17 79 40 92, five rooms, all year.)

Turn hard L then hard R and continue through village, past church, veering R, and (pink) *fronton*. Continue ahead on minor road out of village leading back to the D933 at **Mongelos**. *(CH Domaine de Schiltenea, Route de l'Eglise, tel 05 59 37 22 56, two rooms, K, open from 15 Mar.)* Turn L along it for 100 metres then turn L down minor road. About 750 metres later turn R along another minor road. KSO at staggered junction then at the next junction turn L uphill. Cross *passage canadien* (cattle grid) and KSO, ignoring turns. Just before a second cattle grid, and 250 metres from the D933, turn hard L uphill, veering R. KSO, ignoring turns. Road > a wide track for a while and then a minor road again; follow it downhill in a large 'C'-shaped loop all the time, ignoring turnings. Pass through the village of **Bussunarits** *(CH at Ferme Etxekonia, on GR65, tel 05 59 37 00 40, all year)*. Join larger road coming from L at junction with very large, red wayside cross, just before the 11th-century **Château d'Apat**, cross bridge, veer R to crossroads and KSO ahead on smaller road. Veer R near end and emerge on the D18, turning R to church and main square in…

8km Saint-Jean-le-Vieux (Donazaharre) 212m (738/4)

Shop, cafés, restaurant. Hôtel-restaurant Mendy, Route d'Iraty (tel 05 59 37 11 81, 15 rooms, Apr–Nov). Campsite on D 933, between Saint-Jean-le-Vieux and Saint-Jean-Pied-de-Port (see below).

Pilgrims originally went straight from Saint-Jean-le-Vieux to Saint-Michel (the route described in Aymery Picard's 12th-century guidebook). The deviation via Saint-Jean-Pied-de-Port developed from the 13th century onwards.

Church of Saint Pierre, an example of a typically Basque church, with galleries on two levels around three sides of the nave. Until the 14th century it was affiliated to the Augustinian Canons in Roncesvalles. Musée archéologique.

With your back to the church and facing the *fronton*, turn L at LH far corner of square onto a minor road. Veer L at bend, go under the D933 and turn L on other side. Turn L at crossroads (marked 'Magdaleine') and 250 metres later turn L to D933. Turn R along it for 100 metres then turn L down tree-lined lane (marked 'La Magdaleine'). Some 150 metres later turn R down minor road between fields, leading through the **Quartier de la Madeleine** *(Camping Au Naturel-Aire Naturelle de Camping to R, 15 Apr–30 Sept, plus mobile homes, K)*.

Pass *fronton* (L) and turn L down side of the **Eglise Sainte-Marie-Madeleine** *(the present building in pink stone replaces an earlier one)*. Cross the river

Laurhibar and KSO, uphill to crossing with D401 (**Route de Caro**). Cross over, KSO up **Chemin Saint-Jacques**, go through the **Porte Saint-Jacques** and down the **Rue de la Citadelle** to the church (L) in…

4KM SAINT-JEAN-PIED-DE-PORT (DONIBANE GARAZI) 180M (742/0)

Bridge over the river Nive, Saint-Jean-Pied-de-Port (Photo: Marigold Fox)

Population 1553. All facilities and numerous bars and restaurants. OT (14 Place De Gaulle, tel 05 59 37 03 57). Four hotels, nine CH. SNCF (Bayonne). Direction Compostelle-Boutique du Pèlerin (bookshop/walking gear), 1 Place Floquet & 32 Rue de la Citadelle. Daily bus service Pamplona–Saint-Jean-Pied-de-Port from Mar to 1 Nov run by Compagnie La Conda (ask in OT or tel +34 9 48 31 42 24, +34 9 48 22 10 26 or +34 9 02 42 22 42 for information, preferably in French or Spanish).

AP, information service run by volunteers (mainly former pilgrims) from the Association des Amis de Saint-Jacques des Pyrénées Atlantiques (ASJPA), 39 Rue de la Citadelle (tel 05 59 37 05 09 all year, early morning to late evening in summer, although they operate shorter hours out of season). *Crédentiale* (pilgrim passport) available (€2), help with accommodation and info on the route in Spain. Check here to see if the (higher-level) *Route Napoléon* option is open out of season and check too, at all times of the year, to see whether or not this is safe to take (eg gale-force winds, storms) and if it is not recommended, *be sure to heed their advice* and take the lower-level (*Valcarlos*) route instead. It is suggested you call in at the *accueil* as soon as you arrive in Saint-Jean-Pied-de-Port.

Accueil Paroissial Kaserna, 43 Rue d'Espagne (tel 05 59 37 65 17 after 3pm, 14pl, 4 Apr–30 Oct, foot pilgrims only, carrying their own rucksacks (no back-up vehicles or baggage transfer services accepted except for medical reasons – proof needed – and reservations only taken the previous evening), *crédentiales* available for pilgrims staying in gîte). Refuge municipal, 55 Rue de la Citadelle (run by the Association des Amis de la Vieille Navarre, 32pl, no reservations, all year after 2pm, K, foot pilgrims only, carrying their own rucksacks (no back-up vehicles or baggage transfer services accepted except for medical reasons – proof needed)).

Gîte Beilari (formerly 'L'Esprit du Chemin'), 40 Rue de la Citadelle (tel 05 59 37 24 68, 18pl, Mar–Oct). Gîte d'étape Ultreïa, 8 Rue de la Citadelle (tel 06 80 88 46 22, 15pl, K, 11 Mar–15 Oct). Gîte Compostella, 6 Route d'Arneguy (tel 05 59 37 02 36, 15pl, K, 15 Mar–30 Oct). Gîte Izaxulo, 2 Avenue Renaud (tel 05 24 34 19 00 & 06 84 33 12 05, 22pl, K, Mar–Oct). Gîte-Bar-Brasserie Zuharpeta, 5 Rue Zuharpeta (tel 05 59 37 35 88 & 06 21 30 03 05, 14pl, all year). Camping municipal Plaza Berri, Avenue du Fronton (Easter–30 Oct).

This is 'Saint John-at-the-Foot-of-the-Pass', a small border town on the river Nive, capital of the Basque province of Basse Navarre with an ancient cobbled '*haute ville*'. Several places of interest: Citadelle overlooking the town, built by Vauban, with its system of ramparts, accessed either from the top end of the Rue de la Citadelle or by staircase ('*escalier de la poterne*') leading up from the footpath along the river by the side of the church – worth the climb on a clear day; Prison des Evêques; Musée de la Pelote; 14th-century Eglise Notre-Dame-du-Bout-du-Pont ('Our Lady at the end of the bridge', part of the former priory hospital); Pont Romain and the different *portes* (Saint-Jacques, d'Espagne, for example). Note architecture of Basque-style houses with often ornate wooden overhangs at roof level and balconies. If you have time to spare the OT has a booklet of waymarked walks in the area.

Traditionally pilgrims entered the town by the Porte Saint Jacques at the top of the Rue de la Citadelle, and those who have followed the GR65 will have done the same. After that there were two routes to Roncesvalles. The older one, following the course of the river Valcarlos, is now the modern road (D933 in France, N135 in Spain). This route is also waymarked. It is about the same length, but even though the pilgrim path short-cuts many of the road's hairpin bends, it is far from flat – but it is not as high and if, as indicated above, the weather is very bad or visibility poor, you should take this.

The other, the high-level *Route Napoléon*, was the one the Emperor took to cross into Spain, following existing tracks used by shepherds and pilgrims for several centuries. It leads over the Pyrenees via the Col de Bentarte and the Porte de Cize, continuing along the path of the old Roman road from Bordeaux to Astorga, and is normally accessible without any trouble (such as too much snow) from May to October. It is 26km long and a spectacular route on a clear day, but do not attempt it if it is already very windy down below in Saint-Jean-Pied-de-Port; higher up you can experience force 9 gales and appalling weather conditions, even in the height of summer.

The *Route Napoléon* was also the one favoured by pilgrims in centuries gone by. Although it was much more strenuous, it was also exposed for most of the way, and pilgrims were thus less likely to be ambushed by bandits than on the densely wooded route through Valcarlos. If you are a fairly fit walker allow at least seven hours' actual walking (excluding stops); if not, allow much longer – especially if it is windy (when it will almost always be against you).

If you do decide to take the high-level route you also have the option, to shorten the stage to Roncesvalles, of continuing (very steeply) uphill for 5km after reaching Saint-Jean-Pied-de-Port to **Hounto** (540m), where there is a CH and gîte d'étape, or for 8km to the **Refuge-Auberge d'Orisson** (790m, see Appendix A; given the isolated locations of both these places, however, it is recommened that you reserve ahead if you want to sleep there). This should present no problems in summer but remember that the weather can be very bad (snow, thick fog, high winds) in the spring and autumn and that once you have committed yourself to this route you will either have to stick with it or retrace your steps back down to Saint-Jean-Pied-de-Port, spend the night there and then continue via Valcarlos the following day.

Whichever route you take, though, and especially if you sleep in Saint-Jean-Pied-de-Port, start early in the day (6.30am in summer, or as soon as it is light), not only to avoid the heat but also to avoid being high up later in the day when the light is fading and you are tired. If you do choose the *Route Napoléon*, be sure to **take enough food and water** with you, including (both routes) the following morning's breakfast and, if you do not want to eat in one of the restaurants in Roncesvalles, something for an evening meal as well. Descriptions of both alternatives are given in Appendix A.

APPENDIX A
Saint-Jean-Pied-de-Port to Roncesvalles

A. Valcarlos route

From the **Rue de la Citadelle** go through the **Porte d'Espagne** (passing the church on your L ♣), cross the bridge over the river **Nive**, go up the **Rue d'Espagne** but then turn R into the **Rue d'Uhart**. Continue along **Place Floquet** (under the *jardin public*), through the rampart gateway and then, after 20 metres, bear L when you see a signpost for the D933, marked 'Arnéguy 8'. Follow the road round for 1.5km then look out for a RH fork taking you down off the road towards a farm and then veering R to cross the bridge over the river **Nive**. Around 500 metres later reach a T-junction with a road coming from your R (from **Lasse**) and turn L here. KSO(L) ahead at fork 1km later and KSO(L) again at the next fork. Then KSO on this road, an old tarred lane in parts, that follows the **Nive** (to your L below), often at some considerable distance above it, up and down along the side of the hill. Continue ahead all the time (the route is very easy to follow) until you pass a hotel and come out on the Spanish side of the road bridge in the border town of...

8km Arnéguy 267m
Bar. A lot of *ventas* (originally country inns but nowadays duty-free-type shops).

KSO(R) on the D933 but watch out for way-marks that may take you off the road *(the walkers' route to Roncesvalles is very clearly marked off-road once you are in Spain)* to its LH side on a section of the D128 as far as Ondarolle, when you turn R to...

3km Valcarlos (Luzaïde) 365m
Border town on the Spanish side, with shops, OT, two banks (one with ATM), restaurants. Albergue municipal turístico (+34 9 48 79 01 17, 22pl, K, all year), Hotel-Rte, Hostal-Rte, all three in Calle Elizaldea. Three CH. Church of Santiago contains a life-size representation of Santiago Matamoros, plus statue of Santiago Peregrino.

Roldán (Roland) monument, Puerto de Ibañeta

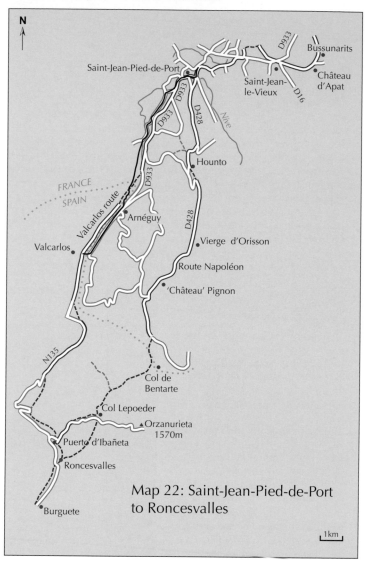

Map 22: Saint-Jean-Pied-de-Port to Roncesvalles

Continue on the main road *(waymarked from time to time, both with yellow arrows and red-and-white* balises*)*. There is a short, off-road section to the L before the hamlet of **Gañecolata** and then, just before the road KM 57 post, you fork L down a gravel track downhill, crossing an old stone bridge over a small river at the bottom. Shortly after going through a gate watch out carefully, as you then leave the track (which continues to a farm at the end) and fork R uphill on a FP. This undulates along the side of the hill, with splendid views on a clear day. When track goes uphill again fork hard R (by a *camino* bollard) then hard L up grassy lane, leading uphill.

When the line of electric pylons turns R, KSO(L) on forest track, veering R through beech woods, winding its way up to a junction of similar tracks (marked with another *camino* bollard). Turn L, veering R then L uphill to emerge on the main road again at a bend by a small farm. Turn L and 50 metres later turn L down shady level lane through woods, rising gently at first and then more steeply as grassy track winds along the side of the hill, following the line of the electric pylons. This section is very easy to follow and brings you out on a minor road to L of the main road, just before the chapel and orientation table at the...

13KM PUERTO D'IBAÑETA 1057M

As related in the 10th-century narrative poem *Chanson de Roland*, the hero of this name, Count of Brittany and Charlemagne's nephew, attempted to resist the rear guard of the Saracen army at a famous battle in the Pyrenees in 778, single-handed and with only his faithful sword Durendal to defend himself. Too proud to blow his horn (the *olifant*) to summon assistance as instructed, he only did so after he had been mortally wounded. The Puerto d'Ibañeta is where Charlemagne and his retreating army had got to when they heard the sound of Roland's horn – too late to go back to help him.

A bell used to toll at the original chapel to guide pilgrims in bad weather. The modern *ermita* (chapel) of San Salvador was built in 1965 to replace the earlier ruined chapel of Charlemagne, with a sign in French, Spanish, Basque and Latin inviting pilgrims to pray to Notre-Dame de Roncevaux. It is usually locked, but you can see inside through the apertures in the door; the interior is very plain but has some nice stained-glass windows, best seen with the sunlight behind them. Outside altar for outdoor masses. There is also a modern monument nearby to Roland (Roldán in Spanish).

* Cross road and go up mound ahead to chapel. From here you walk through the woods for the last 1.5km to Roncesvalles. With your back to the chapel, go down FP to LH side of road and the RH side of a small white building and follow

it gently downhill all the time. Shortly before you get to the abbey you are joined by a track coming from back L, after which you enter the rear of the monastery. Turn R and then L under arch, go through a courtyard and pass in front of the church in…

3km Roncesvalles (Orreaga) (see page 177)

B. Route Napoléon

The Route Napoléon *is the continuation of the GR65 over the Pyrenees. It is now tarmacked as the D428 until just before the Col de Bentarte, but this road is normally very quiet, with little traffic except at weekends when the hunting season opens in October. It is clearly waymarked with yellow flashes and/or arrows (these 'flechas amarillas' will continue all through Spain too), with scallop shells as well as with the familiar red-and-white balises, and is easy to follow as you continue up the D428 all the time, ignoring turns, apart from a few occasions when you short-cut some of its many hairpin bends.*

Go down the **Rue de la Citadelle** in Saint-Jean-Pied-de-Port, past the church of **Notre-Dame-du-Bout-du-Pont** (♣), through the **Porte d'Espagne**, cross the bridge over the river **Nive** and KSO on up the **Rue d'Espagne**. Continue ahead up the **Route Saint-Michel** for approx 100 metres, bear L at a fork and after 20 metres you will come to a junction with the **Route Maréchal Harrispe**. *(Gîte d'Etape Zazpiak-Bat, 13 bis Route Maréchal Harispe, is on the GR65 itself, 900 metres from the town centre (tel 05 59 49 10 17 & 06 75 78 36 23, 18pl, all year after 3pm), as is CH-Gîte Portalburu (13 Route Maréchal Harispe, tel 05 59 49 10 74 & 06 43 04 62 04, K, all year).)* Take this (bear R off the **Route Saint-Michel**, which bends round to the L ♣. KSO and after approximately 500 metres there is a small junction and the road name changes to **Route Napoléon** *(and where you will find the Gîte la Coquille Napoléon, tel 06 62 25 99 40, 10pl, all year).*

Follow the road as it winds (mostly) up and (sometimes) down, past small roadside farms. At fork bear L. KSO following road all the time *(but keep turning round from time to time to admire the view – after this there is nothing as steep until you climb up to O Cebreiro and enter Galicia. At this level there are still trees to provide some shade).*

Pass a T-junction (**Maison Etchébestia**, 302m), and KSO. About 100 metres further on, road forks at massive tree *(good place for a rest)*; keep R here *(fork to L goes down to village of Saint-Michel)* and KSO to…

5km Hounto   540m

CH (13pl) and gîte d'étape (17pl, K), K and light meals at the Ferme Ithuriburia (tel 05 59 37 14 73, 21pl, all year X 15 Nov–20 Dec).

About 150 metres after passing Hounto the road veers R, but the GR65 bears L up a grassy track (the old road), leaving the modern road for a while (to rejoin it later) making a shortcut via the old, steep route that zigzags between walls/banks at first and then on open ground. The path joins the (modern) road again (at 710m), after eight of nine hairpins, by two small houses I and R of the road. ♣ *to RH side and orientation table opposite. Gîte Kayola, run by the owners of the Refuge-Auberge d'Orisson 800 metres further on (uphill – see below for contact details) is located here, a 15-place gîte d'étape for pilgrims who want only a place to sleep (but no meals), with K, shower and WC. Its name derives from* kaiolar, *a shepherd's bothy.*

From here you can see over the mountains to the east towards the Col de Somport, Mont d'Aspe, and beyond, snow-covered (peaks) for much of the year.

KSO on road and pass the...

3km Refuge-Auberge Orisson 790m
26pl in dormitory accommodation, meals available (café-restaurant open all day), Apr–Oct, tel 05 59 49 13 03.

KSO on road again, ignoring tracks to either L or R. When you see a farm building off to the L, where a stream crosses under the road, the road veers round to the R and shortly afterwards, after three or four more hairpins, the road flattens out and you reach the...

5km Vierge de Biakorri 1095m
A small statue of the Virgin Mary in a prominent position at the side of a road junction and in a level area, brought there from Lourdes by shepherds. Panoramic views and a good place for a rest (although not for too long...). At the Vierge de Biakorri you are halfway in time (but not in distance) between Saint-Jean-Pied-de-Port and Roncesvalles. It is still 5km to the border and the route still climbs, albeit less steeply now, up to the Col de Bentarte, after which it is either fairly level or nearly all downhill. The temperature may be cooler as you climb higher, but the sun will still be just as strong.

Be careful to take the R fork here *(the LH option, with wide parking area, leads you back down again!)* and continue on road (having taken R fork) and KSO at road junction (with the D128, R, to Arnéguy). At 1177m pass the 'remains' of **Château Pignon** (L). Ignore a turn to L after 300 metres and also a fork to R after 300 metres (to a farm 100 metres off road).

Continue on road until it begins to veer round to L, at which point the *camino* leaves the road to the R (at 1240m) up a clearly marked grassy track by a cairn and then the **Croix Thibaut**, *a modern wayside cross erected in 1990 on the RH side of* *the road with an inscription in Basque ('I am the way...'). However, although the point at which you leave the road is indicated clearly enough, this section is not well waymarked at present until after the cattle-grid at the Spanish border. There are some red-and-white balises on the ground but you will mainly have to follow the track that is clearly marked by heavy use, particularly in poor visibility.*

The D428 continues for another 3km to the border at the **Col d'Arnostéguy**, more or less on the level, before it comes to a dead end. However, if you get caught unexpectedly in foggy weather you can continue along this road and then backtrack along the border fence until you reach marker no 199 and where the terrain is slightly shaded. When you see the border fence, to your R, go down towards it, after which the track become very clear, and reach the Spanish border at the...

5km Col de Bentarte 1337m

Once over the border pass a fountain (L) and the yellow arrows start – very large and extremely clearly *(some people may consider them 'overkill' but they are needed for safety)*. KSO on a wide, clearly marked track for 4km until, 150 metres after a cattle grid, you reach a minor road, the...

4km Col Lepoeder 1440m

From here you have the first, plunging view of the rooftops of the abbey at Roncesvalles down in the valley below, the village of Burguete and, on a clear day, right across into the province of Navarra. You may find remains of snow here, even in early June.

Cross the road, go down a stony FP and 60 metres later reach a junction. Here you have a choice as there are, in fact, two routes down to Roncesvalles, both of them well waymarked and both described here.

a) Turn L for the 'short, sharp' option. This goes via a **Calzada Romana** (an old Roman road) and is very steep, describing a 'J'-shaped loop straight down to the abbey in Roncesvalles. It passes to the L of the hill known as Don Simon and drops over 500m in only 3.5km. When you reach the bottom turn R to enter the abbey from the west (the back). Cross diagonally through a courtyard and pass in front of the church in **Roncesvalles (Orreaga)**.

b) Turn R for the slightly longer (4.2km), less steep option. This takes you via the **Puerta de Ibañeta** (1057m). Go down a grassy track and then a stony FP to a small road coming from back L. KSO(R) along it. After 1km look out for (way-marked) shortcuts to its hairpins. After several of these fork L downhill to side of road, continue through woods and rejoin road 500 metres later at U-bend and KSO(L) downhill.

Around 300 metres later fork L off road again and when you return to it the waymark indicates that you should cross over for a steep 'shortcut'. However, it is just as easy to turn L on the road here, veering R, and pick up the waymarks again 300–400 metres later. After this you will see the chapel at **Ibañeta** below you and the path down to it clearly indicated.

Continue as described at * on pages173 and 174.

3KM RONCESVALLES (ORREAGA) 925M

Population 30. Shop with guidebooks and so on, two hotel-restaurants (for evening meal at both book and pay at bar before Mass), monastery-run *posada* (hotel, with ATM inside), Hotel Roncesvalles. Albergue de la Colegiata Real-Oficina del Peregrino (all year) has 183 beds in high season, fewer in winter, and is run by volunteer wardens from Easter–Nov (walker pilgrims have preference over cyclists). Mass every evening in the church (check times), followed by pilgrim blessing.

Augustinian monastery and hospital founded early in the 12th century. Set in the 'valley of thorns' in the foothills of the Pyrenees, it has a long tradition of looking after pilgrims (feeding 25,000 a year during the 17th century). Collegiate church chapel of Santiago, 14th-century royal pantheon containing the 13th-century tombs of Sancho the Strong and his wife Doña Clemencia of Toulouse. Museum (entrance free for pilgrims over 65 with *credencial* – pilgrim passport – reduced rate for others) with religious paintings and sculpture, treasury.

The whole section from Roncesvalles to shortly before the outskirts of Pamplona is shady in the main and so can be walked comfortably even in July/August unless you are unusually affected by the heat. There are *refugios* as well as other accommodation en route in Zubiri (22km), Larrasoaña (6km) and Trinidad de Arre (12km, 4km from the centre of Pamplona) and bars, restaurants and other accommodation in intervening places along the way.

The description of the Spanish section of the pilgrim road to Santiago is given in the sequel to this guide by the same author: *Way of St James: Pyrenees–Santiago–Finisterre*, also published by Cicerone Press.

APPENDIX B
Saint-Palais to Irún

This three- to four-day route enables you to connect up with the start of the *Camino del Norte* in Irún, the route along the north coast of Spain, which will be a great deal less crowded than the vastly-oversaturated *Camino Francés*, particularly in the summer months. If you take this you then have the option of 'turning left' later onto the *Camino Primitivo*, joining the *Camino Francés* in Palas do Rei, or continuing further on to turn south after Ribadeo and join the *Camino Francés* two days before Santiago in Arzúa. There are plans to waymark the route from Saint-Palais to Irún. (A Cicerone guide by Laura Perazzioli and Dave Whitson describes both these options: *The Northern Caminos: Norte, Primitivo and Inglés Routes*.)

You will need IGN maps 14450 (Saint-Palais), 1345OT (Cambo-les-Bains) and 1245OT (Hendaye), all at a scale of 1:25,000.

Saint-Palais *All facilities*

9.5km Harribeltzaguéko

5.5km Armendarits

8km Hélette *Hotel-Restaurante Aguerria (tel 05 59 37 62 90)*

4km Ospitalia

3km Zahiola

10km Itxassou *Hotel-Restaurante du Frontón (tel 05 59 29 75 10)*

4.5km Haranéa

2.5km Espelette *OT, shops, restaurants, Hotel-Restaurante Euzkadi (tel 05 59 93 91 88) and two others*

3.5km Col de Pinodieta 176m

7km Pont d'Amotz

7km Sare *Shops*

3km Col de Saint-Ignace

3.5km Ascain

5km Bridge over the A63

2.5km Saint-Jean-de-Luz *All facilities*

10km Hendaye *All facilities*

1km Irún *All facilities*

APPENDIX C

GR651 – Variant along the Vallée du Céle

This is not the historic route but a pleasant 54km variant along the river Célé until this runs into the Lot in Bouziès and where it joins the GR36. From here you can continue (west) for 21km along the common course of the GR36 and GR46 to rejoin the main GR65 in Les Bories-Basses. The routes are waymarked throughout with the usual red-and-white *balises*.

Note: there are no cash dispensers along this route.

Béduer *Bar/resto, bread, 7/7. Two CH on Chemin du Chateau: a) La Coquille (tel 05 65 11 40 18 & 06 60 03 71 93 & 06 88 16 66 15, K, all year; and b) La Mythié (tel 05 65 34 22 25 & 06 42 47 92 93, K, Mar–Oct). CH also at Le Mas de la Croix, at junction of GR65 and GR651 (tel 05 65 11 40 86 & 06 38 94 10 47, restaurant nearby, all year). Camping Pech Ibert (tel 05 65 40 05 85, gîte d'étape in marquee in summer, caravans, 25 Mar–20 Oct, K).*

4km Boussac ♣, *WC*

2km Corn

4km Sainte-Eulalie *CH (tel 05 65 50 26 57, Apr–end Oct, meals X Tues – but reserve ahead)*

3km Espagnac *Gîte d'étape communal (tel 05 65 11 42 66, 21pl, Apr–Oct, K). AP opp mairie tel (tel 05 65 40 05 24, 4pl, Jun–Sept, donation).*

4km Brengues *Gîte la Brenguoise (tel 09 63 26 31 46, 2–8pl, all year). Camping municipal near bridge over Célé (tel 05 81 48 06 99 & 05 65 40 05 71, light meals in summer, 15 Jun–30 Sept). Hôtel-Restaurant-Bar de la Vallée (tel 05 65 10 07 53, all year). Bakery/limited groceries Tues–Sun.*

4km Saint-Sulpice *Camping Le Célé (tel 05 65 40 87 55 & 06 29 46 48 22, May–Sept, snacks avail, also tents & heated caravan)*

5km Cazals *CH at Ferme de Cazals, Route de Pailhès (tel 05 65 50 07 89, all year, meals available – reserve ahead)*

2km Marcilhac-sur-Célé *Two shops, hotel, three restaurants, bar, OT (in season only, tel 05 65 40 68 44). Gîte Accueil Saint-Pierre (tel 05 81 24 06 30 & 06 34 36 54 60, Apr–Oct, 14pl, K). Gîte d'étape de Galance, on GR (tel 05 65 34 23 97 & 08 15 94 91 97, 20pl, 1 Apr–1 Nov). CH Route de Pailhès (tel 05 65 11 63 68, to R of mairie, Mar–Oct). Camping du Pré de Monsieur (tel 05 65 40 77 88,*

2 Apr–30 Sept, also caravans). CH at Mas de Picarel on leaving town (tel 05 65 34 47 13, Apr–Sept).

9km Sauliac-sur-Célé *Gîte aux Lodges du Mas de Nadal (tel 05 61 31 20 51, 60pl in 24 'lodges', 15 May–15 Oct, on R before entering Sauliac). CH L`Autre Chemin (tel 05 65 31 91 64 & 06 87 14 96 28, Apr–Oct). CH de Geniès, Château de Geniès (tel 05 65 30 37 39, mid Apr–end Jul, reserve ahead). Snack-Bar Poivré-Célé (7/7 Jul–Aug).*

3.5km Château de Cuzals *Gîte de la Flèche Bleue, Le Liauzu, Les Granges, off route to L on D41 by river Célé (tel 05 65 23 36 72, 32pl, 15 Apr–31 Oct, K, limited groceries)*

6.5km Cabrerets *OT next to* mairie *(tel 05 65 31 31 31, May–Sept, w/ends only but extended hours Jul & Aug). Gîte du Barry (tel 05 65 22 91 79, 15pl, K, all year). Refuge du Célé (tel 09 66 88 20 15, 13pl, K, Apr–Oct). Camping familial Cantal (May–Oct). Two hotel-restaurants, three restaurants, small supermarket (X Sun pm), bank but no ATM.*

5.5km Conduché *Gîte d'étape des Deux Vallées, Gare de Conduché (tel 05 65 24 58 92, 8–10pl, K, Mar–Nov)*

5km Saint-Cirq-Lapopie *OT, seven restaurants, shop, gîte d'étape communal La Fourdonne (tel 05 65 31 21 51, 23pl, Easter–15 Nov, K). Two CH: a) tel 05 65 31 49 10 & 06 12 29 76 55; b) tel 06 35 37 43 39. Two hotels. Camping de la Plage (all year, bar Easter–Oct). Camping La Truffière, lieu-dit Pradine, La Causse (700 metres from GR, tel 05 65 30 20 22, 9 Apr–30 Sept, small shop, eve meals Jun–Aug, also chalets).*

From here you can continue on the GR36–46 to rejoin the GR65 in Les Bories-Basses.

10km Concots

7km Les Bories-Basses *CH à la Ferme (tel 05 65 31 26 02 & 06 88 04 13 24, all year.*

Here you rejoin the GR65 (see page 100).

APPENDIX D

St James's and other pilgrim references

Le Puy-en-Velay
- Statue of St James by pillar to RH side of cathedral (facing altar)
- Tiny modern statue of pilgrim in niche above Hôtellerie du Fauçon, Rue des Farges
- Statue of St James in niche above chemist's shop on corner of Rue Saint-Jacques and Place du Plô
- Musée Crozatier contains:
  - two paintings with St James pilgrim in background
  - a woodcut of St James pilgrim
  - a statue of Saint-Roch
  - a small collection of *coquilles* and statues originally housed in the former pilgrim hospital
- Ceramic roundel (modern) of St James and headless pilgrim on stone calvary along Rue Saint-Jacques on leaving Le Puy
- Large wooden statue of St James as pilgrim on I at the top of the Rue des Capucins on leaving Le Puy

Montbonnet
- Chapelle Saint-Roch, early 13th-century Romanesque chapel, the first of many along the way dedicated to the patron saint of pilgrims. It was originally dedicated to St James, then Saint-Bonnet (a local saint) and then, in the 17th century, to Saint-Roch. (Many chapels originally dedicated to St James changed their dedication due to Saint-Roch's success in curing plague victims.)
- Chapel contains two engravings and one statue of Saint-Roch pilgrim

Saint-Christophe-sur-Dolaison
- Church contains freestanding statue of Saint Roch with pilgrim staff and scallop shells on shoulders

Rochegude
- Tiny chapel dedicated to St James, perched on top of rocky belvedere with wooden statue of St James inside

Monistrol-d'Allier
- Headless bas-relief of pilgrim on cross in churchyard of Saint-Marcellin

Saugues

- Town was meeting point of pilgrims coming from the Auvergne via secondary routes and had 12th-century pilgrim hospital (now an old people's home near the Chapelle des Pénitents) dedicated to St James. Large wooden polychrome statue of St James inside (visits possible).

- Stained-glass Saint-Roch in church of Saint-Médard and niche statue high up above west portal

- Niche statue of Saint-Roch in nearby street

- 'Tree' sculpture of pilgrims leaving Saugues by river

Fontaine Saint-Roch (after Domaine du Sauvage, 200 metres before chapel)

- Site of a 13th-century oratory and pilgrim hospital

Chapelle Saint-Roch (3km after Domaine du Sauvage)

- Also known as Chapelle de l'Hospitalet du Sauvage, this was a hospital for pilgrims and travellers founded at this col in 1198, originally dedicated to St James (chapel was next to present fountain). The chapel was rededicated to Saint-Roch after the Wars of Religion (1562–98) but then fell into ruin. The new chapel, built at the end of the 19th century, was destroyed by a cyclone in 1897 and the present one rebuilt in 1901.

- Statue of Saint-Roch as a pilgrim, with stick, calebasse and scallop shells on hat and clothing, above the altar (visible through the grille in the door)

Les Estrets

- Church contains statue of Saint-Roch inside; lectern has carvings of scallop shell, scrip and pilgrim staff

- Village formerly had a pilgrim hospital

Aumont-Aubrac

- Niche of south wall of church of Saint-Etienne has shaft of cross with tiny pilgrim carved on it

La Chaze-du-Peyre

- Church with (former?) St James's chapel; statue of pilgrim-looking figure with *coquille*, blessing another figure

Nasbinals

- 11th-century Romanesque church with statue of Saint-Roch and (modern wood) Saint-Jacques inside

Saint-Chély d'Aubrac

- 15th-century church:
    - stained-glass window of Saint-Roch as pilgrim to L of apse
    - gold statue of Saint-Roch pilgrim to LH side of wall behind altar, with a lot of scallop shells on his lapel
    - statue of Saint-Jacques (among other apostles)
- Old bridge over the river Boralde has 16th-century cross, with pilgrim sculpted in its base, with his stick and rosary

Saint-Côme-d'Olt

- Pilgrim hospital dedicated to St James adjoining Chapelle des Pénitents
- *Ouradou* (pilgrim oratory)

Espalion

- Pilgrim bridge over the Lot
- Stained glass St Alexis dressed as a pilgrim with staff and *coquilles* in parish church

Estaing

- 15th-century church of Sainte-Fleuret has stone cross outside depicting tiny pilgrim and gilded statue of St James inside

Golinhac

- Church of Saint-Martin has statue of Saint-Roch (with *coquilles*) inside
- Cross at entry to village has tiny pilgrim and staff on its base

Espeyrac

- Church of Saint-Pierre has statue of Saint-Roch pilgrim inside

Sénergues

- Church of Saint-Martin has statue of Saint-Roch pilgrim inside

Fontromieu

- A farm whose name indicates the site of a former 'pilgrim fountain'

Saint-Marcel

- Stained-glass windows above door of church of Saint-Marcel has three scallop shells
- Leprosarium here in 17th and 18th centuries and a Chapelle Saint-Roch built in 1629 at the height of the plague

- In 1997 a statue of Saint-Roch was to be found inside the church (with hat, scallops, stick and gourd – as a pilgrim), but it is no longer there – any information welcome.

Conques
- Chapelle Saint-Roch, perched on top of hill in lower town
- Modern wood Saint-Jacques in abbey church
- Painting and statue of Saint-Roch in front of abbey church in museum

Chapelle Sainte-Foy (partway uphill leaving Conques)
- Modern stained-glass window inside depicting St James the pilgrim

Chapelle Saint-Roch (near Noailhac)
- Statue of Saint-Roch as pilgrim outside on tympanum
- Another statue of the saint (not as a pilgrim) is inside, above the altar

Chapelle Saint-Roch (2km after Decazeville)
- A parish church, rather than the usual chapel/hermitage dedicated to Saint-Roch
- Two statues of the saint inside, one above the main altar in full pilgrim gear
- Two other statues of the saint in the side chapel, one as a pilgrim (minus hat), the other a small alabaster figure as non-pilgrim, to side of altar
- There is also a modern drawing of Saint-Roch the pilgrim on the move, walking with his dog but his cloak is down, covering his sore.

Saint-Félix
- Romanesque church of Sainte-Radegonde has later stained-glass window of St James

Saint-Jean Mirabel
- Framed painting of a very sturdy looking Saint-Roch inside church on R
- Modern stained-glass pilgrim window above altar in church with rucksack, stick and gourd

Cajarc
- Pilgrim bridge over the Lot built in 1320
- Pilgrim hospital existed in 1269

Cahors
- 15th-century cloister in cathedral of Saint-Etienne has sculpture of small pilgrim apparently disagreeing violently with another non-identified figure

- Cahors formerly had four hospitals (one dedicated to St James) and a Chapelle de Saint-Jacques des Pénitents

Lascabanes
- Pilgrim hospital in the 15th century

Moissac
- Ruins of Hôpital Saint-Jacques
- Former church of St James is now used as Musée Saint Jacques
- Bas-relief of Saint-Jacques (apostle) on corner pillar of abbey cloister

Auvillar
- Rue Saint-Jacques

Lauzerte
- Modern statue of St James pilgrim inside church of Saint-Barthélmy

Miradoux
- Church has modern statue of St James pilgrim

Lectoure
- Cathedral of SS Gervais and Protais has stained glass window of St James
- Town formerly had a Hôpital Saint-Jacques

Marsolan
- Remains of Hôpital Saint-Jacques at entrance to village

Chapelle d'Abrin
- Former pilgrim hospital (now a private house) at meeting of two routes (the other came from Rocamadour and Moissac via Agen)

La Romieu
- Village taking its name from the *romieux* (pilgrims) who passed through on their way to Santiago
- Gilded bust of Saint-Jacques in Collégiale

Condom
- Eglise Saint-Jacques on leaving town (statue over blocked up doorway is St Joseph, not St James), originally with a hospital behind it. There was also a second Hôpital Saint-Jacques nearby.

Pont d'Artigues

- Pilgrim hospital by the bridge over the Osse, run by the Order of the Knights of Santiago in the Middle Ages
- Statue of Saint-Roch pilgrim in a side chapel in church of Saint-Luperc
- Stained-glass Saint-Jacques in apse and stained-glass Saint-Roch on south wall

Manciet

- La Bonne Auberge (restaurant) is on the site of the former commandery (with Hôpital Saint-Jacques and chapel) set up by the Order of the Knights of Santiago
- Modern statue of Saint-Jacques above church portal and statue of Saint-Roch inside

Nogaro

- Romanesque church with former Hôpital Saint-Jacques nearby
- Medieval paintings of pilgrims inside church of Saint-Nicolas

Lanne-Soubiran

- Wooden polychrome statue of St James the pilgrim in church of Saint-Pierre

Eglise de Sensacq

- 11th-century church formerly dedicated to St James

Arzacq-Arraziguet

- Stained-glass window of St James in parish church of Saint-Pierre

Louvigny

- Modern church of Saint-Martin has stained-glass window with *coquille* and pilgrim staff and gourd

Pomps

- Eglise Saint-Jacques (with statue of the saint)

Castillon

- Hospital for pilgrims and travellers in 11th century

Chapelle de Caubin

- Garden of restored Romanesque chapel contains sculpture recalling the passage of pilgrims en route to Santiago

La Sauvelade

- Church of St James (originally dedicated to St Mary) is all that is left of monastery, with statue of St James inside

Navarrenx
- Church of Saint-Germain has pilgrim boss at base of ceiling vaulting near side chapel to RH side, with head with leather hat and scallop shell; three other heads believed to be of modern pilgrims

Aroue
- Romanesque church of Saint-Etienne has 12th-century bas-reliefs of Santiago Matamoros in lintel on sacristy doors

Saint-Palais
- Musée de la Basse Navarre et des Chemins de Saint-Jacques de Compostelle contains statue of St James the pilgrim and much other historic pilgrim material from the region, including a copy of the bas-relief of Santiago Matamoros from Aroue church (which is often closed)

Larribar-Sorhapuru
- Shrine to R of four-arched bridge over the Bidouze with small statue of St James behind glass in a *stèle*
- Monument erected by the Société des Amis de Saint-Jacques to mark the place where the routes from Paris, Vézelay and Le Puy are thought to have met

Harambeltz
- Statue of St James inside chapel

Ostabat-Asme
- Important pilgrim gathering point in past for those coming from or along different routes and its inns and hospitals could accommodate up to 5000 pilgrims; today only the Maison Ospitalia remains, as the present gîte d'étape

Saint-Jean-Pied-de-Port
- Porte Saint-Jacques, through which pilgrims entered the town
- Formerly there was also a Chapelle St Jacques

APPENDIX E
Suggestions for further reading

General

Atwood, Donald and John, CR, *Penguin Dictionary of Saints* (3rd edn, Harmondsworth: Penguin, 1995)

Coleman, Simon and Elsner, John, *Pilgrimage Past and Present in the World's Religions* (London: British Museum Press, 1995)

Davies, JG, *Pilgrimage Yesterday and Today: why? where? how?* (London: SCM Press, 1988)
Studies the nature of pilgrimages and motives behind them, from patristic times to the Middle Ages, Protestant condemnation of pilgrimages and the 19th-century revival of pilgrimages amongst Protestants, ending with a review of the devotional aspects of modern pilgrimages.

Frey, Nancy Louise, *Pilgrim Stories* (Berkley & Los Angeles: University of California Press, 1998)
This refers specifically to the experiences of modern pilgrims along the road to Santiago de Compostela, before, during and after after making their pilgrimage, but the questions raised confront any modern pilgrim on a route where the journey itself, rather than the destination, is the real issue at stake.

Robinson, Martin, *Sacred Places, Pilgrim Paths: an anthology of pilgrimage* (London: Fount, 1997)
An anthology reflecting the experiences of pilgrims through the ages, dealing with places of pilgrimage, preparation for the journey, the journey itself, the inner journey, worship on the way and on arrival and the questions raised once the pilgrimage is over.

Sumption, Jonathan, *Pilgrimage* (London: Faber and Faber, 1975)
A study of the traditions of pilgrimage prevalent in Europe from the beginnings of Christianity to the end of the 15th century, examining all its aspects: major destinations, motivations, the cult of the saints and their relics, medicine and the quest for cures, penitential pilgrimage, the practicalities of the journey and the pilgrims themselves.

Eade, John and Sallnow, Michael J (eds), *Contesting the Sacred: the anthropology of Christian pilgrimage* (London: Routledge, 1991)
Contributors examine particular Christian shrines (in France, Italy, Israel, Sri Lanka and Peru), analysing the dynamics of religious expression and belief but also the political and economic processes at local and global levels, emphasising that pilgrimage is primarily an arena for competing religious and secular discourses.

French, RM (trans), *The Way of a Pilgrim* (London: Triangle, 1995)
   First published in English in 1930, this book was written by an unknown Russian pilgrim
   in the 19th century, telling the story of his wanderings from one holy place to another in
   Russia and Siberia in search of the way of prayer.

Way of St James

Barret, Pierre and Gurgand, Jean-Noël, *Priez pour nous à Compostelle* (Paris: Hachette,
1978)
   An account of the authors' journey from Vézelay to Santiago on foot, interspersed
   with parallel accounts of pilgrims from previous centuries. Contains a very extensive
   bibliography.

Bourdarias, Jean and Wasielewski, Michel, *Guide Européen des Chemins de Compostelle*
(Paris: Fayard, 1997)
   Guide to all the European routes to Santiago (from Holland, Denmark, Poland, Hungary,
   Brenner, Croatia, Italy and Portugal), as well as the currently more well-known routes
   through France and Spain. Contains maps, distances, over 800 photographs, history and
   descriptions of places, lives of saints and relevant biblical extracts.

Mullins, Edward, *The Pilgrimage to Santiago* (London: Secker & Warburg, 1974, and
London: Sigma Books, 2001)
   An account of the art, architecture, history and geography of the pilgrim route from Paris
   to Santiago.

Neillands, Rob, *The Road to Compostela* (Ashbourne: Moorland Publishing Co, 1985)
   An account of the author's journey from Le Puy to Santiago by bicycle.

Shaver-Crandell, Annie and Gerson, Paula, *The Pilgrim's Guide to Santiago de Compostela:
a Gazeteer* (London/Langhorne: Harvey Miller, 1995)
   Contains 730 entries and 575 illustrations describing all the relics of saints, important
   monuments, towns and buildings encountered by the 12th-century pilgrim along the
   four main routes through France and then in Spain. Includes a new translation of the
   Latin text of the *Codex Calixtinus* plus discussion of the pilgrimage phenomenon in the
   Middle Ages as well as the tradition of travel literature.

Tate, Brian and Marcus, *The Pilgrim Route to Santiago* (Oxford: Phaidon, 1987)
   Explains the pilgrim phenomenon and the history of the shrine as well as discussing the
   different routes. Contains 137 photographic illustrations by Pablo Keller, 50 of them in
   colour.

Vielliard, Jeanne, *Guide du Pèlerin de Saint Jacques de Compostelle* (Paris: Klincksieck, 4th
edition 1989)
   A French translation, on facing pages, of what is probably the first known guidebook:
   Aymery Picaud's 12th-century description of the pilgrim routes to Santiago.

The Pilgrim's Guide: a 12th-century Guide for the Pilgrim to St James of Compostela, translated from the Latin by James Hogarth (Confraternity of St James, 1992)

Specialist

Guide Spirituel du Pèlerin (distributed jointly by Hospitalité Saint-Jacques, Rue du College, 12190 Estaing (tel 05 65 44 19 00, www.hospitalite-saint-jacques.fr) and the Abbayé Sainte-Foy, 12320 Conques (tel 05 65 69 85 12, www.abbaye-conques.org)
Pocket-size (A6) booklet intended as a spiritual aid, containing themes for personal meditation, prayers and hymns and notes on the many saints whose churches, chapels and sanctuaries line the route.

Clouteau, Lauriane and Jacques, *Miam Miam Dodo, Le Chemin de Saint Jacques de Compostelle: La Voie du Puy* (Les Sables d'Olonne: Les Editions du Vieux Crayon)
An extremely detailed guide to where to sleep and eat along the way, updated annually. As well as being available from the Confraternity of St James's online bookshop, from the cathedral and other bookshops in Le Puy and in other places along the route as well as in some gîtes d'étape, it can also be obtained direct from the publishers: see Appendix F.

Higginson, John, *The Way of Saint James' Cyclist Guide: A Cyclists' Guide from Le Puy-en-Velay to Santiago de Compostela* (Milnthorpe: Cicerone, 2nd edition 2015)

Perazzoli, Laura and Whitson, Dave, *The Northern Caminos* (Milnthorpe: Cicerone, 2nd edition 2015)
A walker's guide book to the *Camino del Norte*, *Camino Primitivo* and *Camino Inglés* routes for those pilgrims who prefer an alternative to the 'classic' *Camino Francés* when they continue on from the Pyrenees to Santiago de Compostela.

APPENDIX F

Useful addresses and websites

Confraternity of Saint James
27 Blackfriars Road
London SE1 8NY
tel 020 7928 9988
www.csj.org.uk
online bookshop: www.csj.org.uk/
bookshop
email: office@csj.org.uk

The Confraternity also has a picture gallery on its website, including an extensive collection from the Le Puy route.

Stanfords (travel bookshop)
12–14 Long Acre
Covent Garden
London WC2E 9LP
tel 020 7836 1321

and

29 Corn Street
Bristol BS1 1HT
tel 0117 929 9966

www.stanfords.co.uk

The Map Shop
15 High Street
Upton-upon-Severn
Worcestershire WR8 0HJ
tel 01684 593146
www.themapshop.co.uk

Editions du Vieux Crayon (publishers of the *Miam Miam Dodo* guide)
119 Route de l'Aubraie
85100 Les Sables d'Olonne
France
tel +33 2 51 90 84 97
www.levieuxcrayon.com
email info@levieuxcrayon.com

APPENDIX G
Glossary

balise	waymark
barry	suburb (Occitan)
bastide	walled hilltop town
borie	farm (Occitan)
buron	shepherd's bothy
calade	paved road or path (Occitan)
carrier	street (Occitan)
caselle	small round hut of drystone construction
chasse guardée	private ground/hunting
cause	limestone plateau in south-west France with
scrubby	vegetation
château d'eau	water tower
cledo	flexible gate made of wire and palings
col	mountain pass
commanderie	commandery (of military order)
couderc	enclosed field/village green (Gascon)
draille	drove road
écluse	(canal) lock
fronton	pelota court (Basque country)
gave	mountain stream/river in the Pyrenees
gaviote	stone hut, similar to caselle
halle	(covered) market place
hameau	hamlet
jacquet	pilgrim going to Santiago
lavoir	outdoor washing-place, (public) wash-house
lieu-dit	locality, place known as
luy	river (Gascon)
mairie	town hall, town council
mas	house/farm in south of France (Occitan)
mirador	watchtower, mirador
montjoie	cairn
montredon	rounded hill (Occitan)
palombière	hide in forest used by pigeon-hunters
passage canadien	cattle grid
passerelle	footbridge
patte d'oie	junction

pech	hill, mountain (Occitan)
pèlerin	pilgrim
pigeonnier	dovecote
puy	hill, mountain
réserve de chasse	hunting preserve
romieu	pilgrim who has been to Rome
sauvetat/sauveté/sauveterre	town or area serving as safe haven
tampon	(rubber) stamp
temple	Protestant church

For those pilgrims who like to attend Mass and would like to be able to participate at least once during the service, the French text of the Lord's Prayer is given here:

Notre Père qui es aux cieux,
que ton nom soit sanctifié,
que ton règne vienne,
que ta volonté soit faite
sur la terre comme au ciel.
Donne-nous aujourd'hui
notre pain de ce jour.
Pardonne-nous nos offenses,
comme nous pardonnons aussi
à ceux qui nous ont offensés.
Et ne nous soumets pas à la tentation,
mais délivre-nous du Mal

APPENDIX H

Index of principal place names

APPENDIX I
Index of maps

APPENDIX J
Summary of route

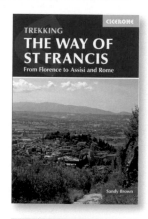
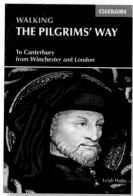
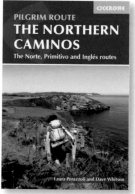

LISTING OF CICERONE GUIDES

Walking on the Gower
Welsh Winter Climbs

DERBYSHIRE, PEAK DISTRICT AND MIDLANDS

Cycling in the Peak District
Dark Peak Walks
Scrambles in the Dark Peak
Walking in Derbyshire
White Peak Walks:
  The Northern Dales
White Peak Walks:
  The Southern Dales

SOUTHERN ENGLAND

20 Classic Sportive Rides
  in South East England
20 Classic Sportive Rides
  in South West England
Cycling in the Cotswolds
Mountain Biking on the
  North Downs
Mountain Biking on the
  South Downs
North Downs Way Map Booklet
South West Coast Path Map
  Booklet – Minehead to St Ives
South West Coast Path Map
  Booklet – Plymouth to Poole
South West Coast Path Map
  Booklet – St Ives to Plymouth
Suffolk Coast and Heath Walks
The Cotswold Way
The Cotswold Way Map Booklet
The Great Stones Way
The Kennet and Avon Canal
The Lea Valley Walk
The North Downs Way
The Peddars Way and Norfolk
  Coast Path
The Pilgrims' Way
The Ridgeway Map Booklet
The Ridgeway National Trail
The South Downs Way
The South Downs Way
  Map Booklet
The South West Coast Path
The Thames Path
The Thames Path Map Booklet
The Two Moors Way
Walking in Cornwall
Walking in Essex
Walking in Kent
Walking in London
Walking in Norfolk
Walking in Sussex
Walking in the Chilterns
Walking in the Cotswolds
Walking in the Isles of Scilly
Walking in the New Forest

Walking in the North
  Wessex Downs
Walking in the Thames Valley
Walking on Dartmoor
Walking on Guernsey
Walking on Jersey
Walking on the Isle of Wight
Walking the Jurassic Coast
Walks in the South Downs
  National Park

BRITISH ISLES CHALLENGES, COLLECTIONS AND ACTIVITIES

The Book of the Bivvy
The Book of the Bothy
The C2C Cycle Route
The End to End Cycle Route
The End to End Trail
The Mountains of England and
  Wales: Vol 1 Wales
The Mountains of England and
  Wales: Vol 2 England
The National Trails
The UK's County Tops
Three Peaks, Ten Tors

ALPS CROSS-BORDER ROUTES

100 Hut Walks in the Alps
Across the Eastern Alps: E5
Alpine Ski Mountaineering
  Vol 1 – Western Alps
Alpine Ski Mountaineering Vol 2
  – Central and Eastern Alps
Chamonix to Zermatt
The Tour of the Bernina
Tour of Mont Blanc
Tour of Monte Rosa
Tour of the Matterhorn
Trail Running – Chamonix and
  the Mont Blanc region
Trekking in the Alps
Trekking in the Silvretta and
  Rätikon Alps
Trekking Munich to Venice
Walking in the Alps

PYRENEES AND FRANCE/SPAIN CROSS-BORDER ROUTES

The GR10 Trail
The GR11 Trail – La Senda
The Pyrenean Haute Route
The Pyrenees
The Way of St James – France
The Way of St James – Spain
Walks and Climbs in the Pyrenees

AUSTRIA

The Adlerweg
Trekking in Austria's Hohe Tauern
Trekking in the Stubai Alps

Trekking in the Zillertal Alps
Walking in Austria

SWITZERLAND

Cycle Touring in Switzerland
The Swiss Alpine Pass Route –
  Via Alpina Route 1
The Swiss Alps
Tour of the Jungfrau Region
Walking in the Bernese Oberland
Walking in the Valais
Walks in the Engadine –
  Switzerland

FRANCE

Chamonix Mountain Adventures
Cycle Touring in France
Cycling the Canal du Midi
Écrins National Park
Mont Blanc Walks
Mountain Adventures in
  the Maurienne
The Cathar Way
The GR20 Corsica
The GR5 Trail
The GR5 Trail – Vosges and Jura
The Grand Traverse of the
  Massif Central
The Loire Cycle Route
The Moselle Cycle Route
The River Rhone Cycle Route
The Robert Louis Stevenson Trail
The Way of St James –
  Le Puy to the Pyrenees
Tour of the Oisans: The GR54
Tour of the Queyras
Tour of the Vanoise
Vanoise Ski Touring
Via Ferratas of the French Alps
Walking in Corsica
Walking in Provence – East
Walking in Provence – West
Walking in the Auvergne
Walking in the Cevennes
Walking in the Dordogne
Walking in the Haute Savoie:
  North
Walking in the Haute Savoie:
  South
Walks in the Cathar Region
Walking in the Ardennes

GERMANY

Hiking and Biking in the
  Black Forest
The Danube Cycleway Volume 1
The Rhine Cycle Route
The Westweg

For full information on all our
guides, books and eBooks,
visit our website:
www.cicerone.co.uk

Walking – Trekking – Mountaineering – Climbing – Cycling

Over 40 years, Cicerone have built up an outstanding collection of over 300 guides, inspiring all sorts of amazing adventures.

Every guide comes from extensive exploration and research by our expert authors, all with a passion for their subjects. They are frequently praised, endorsed and used by clubs, instructors and outdoor organisations.

All our titles can now be bought as **e-books**, **ePubs** and **Kindle** files and we also have an online magazine – **Cicerone Extra** – with features to help cyclists, climbers, walkers and trekkers choose their next adventure, at home or abroad.

Our website shows any **new information** we've had in since a book was published. Please do let us know if you find anything has changed, so that we can publish the latest details. On our **website** you'll also find great ideas and lots of detailed information about what's inside every guide and you can buy **individual routes** from many of them online.

It's easy to keep in touch with what's going on at Cicerone by getting our monthly **free e-newsletter**, which is full of offers, competitions, up-to-date information and topical articles. You can subscribe on our home page and also follow us on **Facebook** and **Twitter** or dip into our **blog**.

Cicerone – the very best guides for exploring the world.

CICERONE

Juniper House, Murley Moss, Oxenholme Road, Kendal, Cumbria LA9 7RL
Tel: 015395 62069 info@cicerone.co.uk
www.cicerone.co.uk and **www.cicerone-extra.com**